# READINGS

By the same editor

*Directions in the Teaching of English*
George Sampson: *English for the English*
*Discrimination and Popular Culture*

# READINGS

CHOSEN AND EDITED BY

## DENYS THOMPSON

CAMBRIDGE UNIVERSITY PRESS

Published by the Syndics of the Cambridge University Press
Bentley House, 200 Euston Road, London NW1 2DB

This collection © Cambridge University Press 1974

ISBN: 0 521 20311 2

First published 1974

Composition by Linocomp Ltd., Marcham, Oxfordshire

Printed in Great Britain
at the University Printing House, Cambridge
(Brooke Crutchley, University Printer)

# CONTENTS

PART III: RESPONSE

**Love**  127

**Love 2**  135

## PART IV: THE CHRISTIAN YEAR

# CONTENTS

# INTRODUCTION

The purpose of this book is didactic. It is intended both for those who themselves welcome assistance in answering the question 'How to live?' and for those whose profession it is to guide others.

The assumptions that lay behind the 1944 requirement that the school day should begin with collective worship no longer hold good; and the type of school assembly normal a generation ago is now anomalous. But there is no general feeling that assemblies should be dropped, and there are constructive critics who wish to reshape the nature of 'worship' in school. One of them, Mr A. R. Bielby, believes that 'the atomization of society engendered by urbanization and industrialization needs to be countered in education by strengthening constructive group experience'. It is thought that in these circumstances the school assembly can help to build up a feeling of belonging and create the community which makes belonging possible. Another headmaster, Mr Kenneth Barnes, has observed that the tendency today is to encourage people to sheer away from the impact of events. 'It hurts too much and there is no material profit to be gained. So they race from one trivial experience to another.' When even courage is superficialised, he feels, a 'large part of our readings (in assembly) must illustrate what it means to take the full impact of experience. They must show people going through critical situations'.

Considerations such as these may seem to take too instrumental a view of religion, retained not for its essence but as therapy for the ills of civilisation, applied from outside. And there have been plenty of warnings against the 'using' of religion, ever since Constantine defeated Maxentius in the belief that he was backed by the God of the courageous Christians. We still hear of Christianity as a 'bulwark against Communism' after half a century of seeing the results of this useful doctrine in operation. The two writers just quoted take some of the further steps that are required. Mr Bielby bases the demand for religious observance in school on the feeling of need for something transcendental in life, some absolute

in values. And Mr Barnes writes: 'I think of worship as the discovery, revelation, and expression of what is of supreme worth, of
the fulfilment that man has struggled towards throughout his
history, of what we seek for in the depth of our relationship
through the changes and crises of life.'

The feeling of need for something that will sanction the standards we live by and reinforce the best human aspirations is a part
of all true religions. Moreover, when it seems to spring from man's
experience and wisdom it is recognised by humanists as valid for
them:

> Human beings in the midst of these possibilities . . . need con-
> fidence . . . if this does not come from religious faith, it can come
> only from the available natural and human resources. Such
> resources are not themselves a vision that can create confidence,
> but they are resources which have inspired such visions in the
> past, and they have power to do so now. For the human being is
> more than himself and he has more than the present which he
> grasps. He may become deeply aware of the interpretation of
> phases in his own life and in that of mankind. There is no present
> moment that is not charged with the past and pledged to the
> future . . . Humanism is an aspiration to breed this confidence
> rooted in available resources and thus to reduce the pointlessness
> of individual lives.
> H. J. Blackham, in *Objections to Humanism*

> What, then, is religion? It is a way of life. It is a way of life which
> follows necessarily from a man holding certain things in reverence,
> from his feeling and believing them to be sacred. And those things
> which are held sacred by religion primarily concern human destiny
> and the forces with which it comes into contact.
> Julian Huxley, *Religion Without Revelation*

To the layman the gap between the writers just quoted and
modern Christian apologists seems narrow. The first of the latter
to be quoted says that belief in a personal God came to him
through discovering in a community 'the creative and "numinous"
power' inherent in ordinary personal relationships:

> It is indeed one of my strongest convictions . . . that experience of
> this type is common to all human beings . . . Prayer and mystical
> vision are real and important, but they cannot be the primary basis
> for religious conviction; this must come from *common* experience,
> and special experiences like prayer are only meaningful, in my
> view, in so far as they refer back to common experience. But it is

one thing to say that religious propositions can be referred to the common experience of personal relationships: it would be quite another to say that people commonly recognize their experience of personal relationship for what it is – an encounter with the Transcendent.
John Wren-Lewis, quoted by J. A. T. Robinson

The presence of Christ with his people is tied to a right receiving of the common, to a right relationship with one's neighbour . . .
    The test of worship is how far it makes us *more sensitive* . . . to the Christ in the hungry, the naked, the homeless and the prisoner.
J. A. T. Robinson, *Honest to God*

Our new consciousness of space no longer admits the traditional religious imagery by which we represent to ourselves our encounter with God. At the same time, we must also recognise that this traditional imagery *was never essential to Christianity*. We must recover the New Testament awareness that our God does not need a temple (Acts 7: 47-53) or even a cathedral. The New Testament teaches in fact that God has one indestructible temple: which is man himself (I Cor. 3:17). To understand that God is present in the world *in man* is in fact no new or radical idea. It is, on the contrary, one of the most elementary teachings of the New Testament.
Thomas Merton

Further to illustrate the way in which beliefs, religious and non-religious, shade into each other, one might quote other writings on religion, and cite the pure and original form of Buddhism, which had no God, and the Jainas, who do not accept God as the supreme spirit and believe that any soul can be a supreme spirit. If we see a gap, it is not between science and religion, those called believers and unbelievers, or other categories, but between those on the one hand who believe that the individual must look outward from himself for guidance and encouragement to a God and/or to the best hopes and achievements of mankind; and those on the other hand to whom man is no more than an animal.

In any case a concern for full education requires not merely religious education, the imparting of knowledge about a subject, but also the opportunity to learn and sense what religious experience is. The point for us is that there is ample common ground among teachers to support religious assemblies as part of education. Some readers may agree with Sir Alister Hardy that the roots of religion go 'much deeper down into biological history than is generally conceded', and all probably will accept the view that the needs are not only intellectual, moral and social, but also spiritual and emotional. It is this latter element of the human being that has been and still is badly neglected in education. If this is clear in various modes, to the specialist teacher of science quite as much to those concerned with music, art and literature, it is possible to enlist the support of both staff and pupils for a religious meeting on educational grounds.

The form and content of assembly have been widely discussed, and there are some excellent contributions in the volumes listed at the end of this book. Many of the teachers concerned agree on some of the points that follow. The whole of a school should not meet at once, except on special occasions – there should be division by age or house; variety is desirable; a good choice of music is an asset; dance, mime and art have their place; active participation by pupils is essential – there is consensus on this over a wide range of schools; the general character should be Christian, but not in a dogmatic sense, because Christianity is the nominal background of most of those attending, because it underlies some of the better attitudes and values of our society – it thus provides something to build on – and because the view that the right way to a relationship with God is in and through the persons of the world so readily commends itself. Other faiths will be drawn on and presented at their best, and the common elements of the great religions will thus emerge. It is necessary to 'start where the children are' by providing for their conscious concerns and interests. But not to stay there; children must grow, and teachers like gardeners will wish to see their charges develop fully according to their nature. They will not be content to cater solely for juvenile tastes in so far as these are stimulated and moulded by the mass media. Teachers will know, for example, how far to encourage the introduction of pop words and music; there is not much pop in these pages because it does not wear well. Experimentation is good, but as Richard Jones observes, 'to insert a Beaumont tune (already hackneyed), a folk song, or a pop group item into an otherwise conventional service does no justice to worship or to youth'.

The passages that follow are arranged in four parts. The first deals with common experience: the created and still evolving world and the life upon it; the natural human response of praise and reverence for its beauty; the family and the fate of all human beings. The second presents some of the situations and difficulties that men encounter on their way through life; the third shows how they have faced and sometimes triumphed over their problems; and the fourth tries to promote understanding of the Christian year among both believers and non-believers. Of course, there are wide overlaps between many of the sections into which the readings are grouped. The order of the sections is not meant to be a sequence for reading through. The themes can be linked with events and concerns in school or district or nation, or with the seasons, or with the important days of the Christian year. It may be best to start with a topic of immediate interest.

Some of the important passages from the Bible are included, with references to others. The New English Bible is drawn on for the New Testament, as it so often provides an explanation; and users of the book may care to read the same passage twice in a few days, first in the New English Bible and then in the Authorised Version. The latter by itself through its soothing power and familiarity can lull rather than awaken the hearer. For the Old Testament the Authorised Version is used in most cases. The common elements of the great religions are brought out by quoting what they have to say about things that matter. Poems are often chosen, because a poem can say more than prose in a short space, and make its impact more quickly and more permanently. Some of the passages are difficult as they stand, and intended for small groups, though they can often be paraphrased.

Ideas on the form that assembly can take are given in some of the books listed; other relevant titles can be found as they are published in the libraries of institutes of education. The user is advised to be cavalier in his treatment of the readings, selecting, cutting and altering as circumstances require. The old advice, 'Tell them what you're going to tell them; tell it to them; then tell them what you've told them', is very much to the point. The reader's own introduction and summary can be most helpful; and in many cases a second reading after an interval is helpful. When pupils read, the most careful rehearsal is vital; as well as a general convincing grasp, timing, pace, volume, tone and feeling must be attended to. Forms and groups can present readings on themes of their choice, adding material from books and periodicals, and introducing music and pictures and mime. It is hoped that the recommendations for further reading will be helpful here. It is an advantage, too, if the art department and some good calligraphers can regularly write out in bold, and perhaps illuminate for notice boards, extracts from some of the readings, especially the verse. Such 'publication' is a useful form of the reiteration that brings the point home.

*September 1973*                                    DENYS THOMPSON

# ACKNOWLEDGEMENTS

The editor wishes to thank the readers and staff of the Cambridge University Press for their help at many points.

Thanks are also due to the following authors or their representatives, and publishers, for permission to quote copyright material (the order of listing follows that of the contents except where authors have several sources acknowledged to the same copyright owner, when all details are listed under the first appearance):

Juan Mascaró and Associated Book Publishers Ltd for the translated extract of The Rig Veda from *Lamps of Fire*;

Fred Hoyle and Basil Blackwell and Mott Ltd for the extract from *The Nature of the Universe*;

passages from the New English Bible, second edition © 1970 by permission of Oxford and Cambridge University Presses;

Gopal Singh and Asia Publishing House Ltd for the extracts from *Religion of the Sikhs*;

William Heinemann Ltd for 'In the beginning' by Dorothy Wellesley from *Poems of Ten Years*;

James Weldon Johnson and George Allen and Unwin Ltd for 'The creation' from *God's Trombones*;

the Headmaster of Sevenoaks School for 'Is God your name?' by C. T. Whall, and for 'Birth' by F. M. Turner, both from *Numbers* (1959);

F. W. Harvey and Sidgwick and Jackson Ltd for 'God must have smiled' ('Ducks') from *Gloucestershire: A Selection from the poems of F. W. Harvey*;

Farley Mowat and Hughes Massie Ltd for the extract from *People of the Deer*;

C. G. Jung and Collins for the extract from *Memories, Dreams, Reflections*;

Edwin Muir and Faber and Faber Ltd for 'The animals' from *Collected Poems 1921–1958*;

Jacquetta Hawkes and Leonard Woolley and George Allen and Unwin Ltd for the extract from *Prehistory and the Beginnings of Civilization*;

extracts reprinted by permission of Schocken Books Inc. from *Tales of the Hasidim: Early Masters* by Martin Buber, Copyright © 1947 by Schocken Books Inc.;

Collins for the extract by Phyllis McGinley from *Saint-Watching*;

Constable for the extract by Helen Waddell from *Beasts and Saints*;

George Allen and Unwin Ltd for the extract by Albert Schweitzer from *Civilization and Ethics*;

Heinemann Educational Books Ltd for 'Battery hens' by Sally Grant, and 'Old age and youth' by Sara Burt, both from *Children as Poets*;

Collins for the extracts by Simone Weil from *Waiting on God*;

W. H. Murray and J. M. Dent and Sons Ltd for the extract from *The Scottish Himalayan Expedition*;

Dennis Brutus and Heinemann Educational Books Ltd for 'To find the stars' and 'Talking to God' from *Letters to Martha*;

Laurence Pollinger Ltd and the Estate of the late Mrs Frieda Lawrence, and William Heinemann Ltd, for the following by D. H. Lawrence: the extract from 'Nottingham and the Mining Countryside' in *Phoenix*, 'Beautiful old age' and 'Poverty' from *The Complete Poems*, extracts from *The Rainbow*, and an extract from 'The Risen Lord' in *Phoenix II*;

the Chief Education Officer and Cambridgeshire and Isle of Ely C.C. for 'The field' by Adrian Brunt, and 'Don't go' by Patricia Buck, both from *At the Rainbow's Foot*;

Faber and Faber Ltd for 'Prayer before birth' and 'A week to Christmas' by Louis MacNeice from *Collected Poems*;

Karen Gershon and Victor Gollancz Ltd for 'Birth' from *Selected Poems*;

Penny Blackie and the East Suffolk Association for the Teaching of English for 'Authority' by S. Freestone;

S.W. Lancashire Branch of the National Association for the Teaching of English for 'Night scene' by S. Farnall from *Poetry: Eleven to Eighteen*;

George Barker and Faber and Faber Ltd for 'To my mother' from *Collected Poems 1930–1955*;

Doris Odlum for the extracts from *Journey through Adolescence*;

Gavin Ewart and London Magazine Editions for 'Daddyo' from *The Deceptive Grin of the Gravel Porters*;

Constable for 'Blaming sons', 'The big rug', 'The little cart', and 'A protest in the sixth year of Ch'ien Fu', translated by Arthur Waley, from *170 Chinese Poems*;

Weissberger and Frosch and Mrs Ellen Masters for 'Washington McNeely' by Edgar Lee Masters from *Spoon River Anthology*;

Kahlil Gibran and William Heinemann Ltd for 'The madman' and 'Builders of bridges' from *The Wanderer*;

Shakuntala Masani and Blackie and Son (India) Ltd for the extracts from *Gautama, the Story of Lord Buddha*;

George Allen and Unwin Ltd for the translated extracts by Arthur Waley from *The Way and Its Power*;

H. Polano and Frederick Warne and Co. Ltd for the translated extract from *The Talmud, Selections and Brief Sketches*;

Arthur Barker Ltd for the extract by Peter Freuchen from *The Book of the Eskimos*;

Danilo Dolci and MacGibbon and Kee for the extracts from *The Outlaws of Partinico* and *For the Young*;

C. M. Bowra and George Weidenfeld and Nicolson for 'Song to the rainbow' from *Primitive Song*;

Victor Gollancz Ltd for 'For birds' from *God of a Hundred Names*;

Thomas Merton, New Directions Publishing Corporation and Anthony Clarke Books (formerly Burns, Oates) for the extracts from *Conjectures of a Guilty Bystander*;

Myra Kendrick for 'Psalm for vigour' from *The Circle and Other Poems*;

Victor Gollancz Ltd for the extracts by Dorothy L. Sayers from *Unpopular Opinions*;

Idries Shah and Jonathan Cape Ltd for 'The King and the beans' from *The Way of the Sufi*;

Gladys Williams and Macmillan, London and Basingstoke, for the extract from *Barnardo: the Extraordinary Doctor*;

John Grieve and others and the Scottish Academic Press Ltd for the extract from *Homelessness in London*;

W. Rahula and Gordon Fraser Ltd for the extracts from *What the Buddha Taught*;

Henry McKeating and S.C.M. Press Ltd for the extract from *Living with Guilt*;

Hodder and Stoughton Ltd for the extract by Martin Luther King from *Chaos or Community?*;

James Kirkup and J. M. Dent and Sons Ltd for 'Black shadows' from *White Shadows, Black Shadows*;

Trevor Huddleston and Collins for the extract from *Naught for Your Comfort*;

Alan Rodgers and John Charlesworth for 'The number eight';

J. H. Thomas for 'Colour' from *Doves for the Seventies*;

Colin McGlashan and *Christian Action Journal* for extracts from an article, 'The Roots of Violence';

Artyomy Mikhailov, Keith Bosley and the Longman Group Ltd for 'If you've never been in a concentration camp' from *Russia's Other Poets*;

Quintin Hogg and Hodder and Stoughton Ltd for 'Molecular biology' from *The Devil's own Song*;

Erich Fromm and Routledge and Kegan Paul Ltd for the extract from *The Fear of Freedom*;

Colin Welland and the Editor of *The Observer* for extracts from an article, 'How to Disarm the Football Hooligans';

Raymond Garlick for 'Thug' from *Doves for the Seventies*;

Carl Burke and Collins for the extracts from *God is for Real, Man*, and *God is Beautiful, Man*;

the Headmaster of Breckenbrough School for 'Where was God?' by D. Williamson from *Breckenbrough Poetry*;

John Morris and Barrie and Jenkins for the extract from *The Phoenix Cup*;

Victor Gollancz Ltd for the extracts by Victor Gollancz from *The New Year of Grace*;

Mary McCarthy and George Weidenfeld and Nicolson for the extracts from *Vietnam*;

Peter Appleton for 'The other time';

*The Catholic Worker* for the extract by Dorothy Day;

John Kent and B. T. Batsford Ltd for the extract from *Elizabeth Fry*;

G. and C. Carawan and TRO Essex Music Ltd for the extract from *We Shall Overcome*;

Ernest Gordon and Collins for the extract from *Through the Valley of the Kwai*;

Sydney Carter and Galliard Ltd for 'The rat race' © 1961 Galliard Ltd. From *Songs of Sydney Carter in the Present Tense*, Book 2;

Brian Frost and Sheed and Ward Ltd for 'Out of prison' from *Citizen Incognito*;

Michael De-la-Noy and Pergamon Press Ltd for the extract from *Delinquency and Guilt*;

Vallentine, Mitchell and Co. Ltd for the extract by Joseph Ziemian from *The Cigarette Sellers of Three Crosses Square*;

Mary Hawkins and Save the Children Fund for the extract from an article in *The World's Children* (December 1972);

Peter Hazlehurst and the Editor of *The Times* for part of a report from the issue of 4 June 1971;

War on Want for an item from *Frontline*;

C. A. Watts Ltd, London, for the extract by Julian Huxley from *Religion Without Revelation*;

George Allen and Unwin Ltd for the extract by A. J. Arberry from *The Koran Interpreted*;

Rosalind B. Brooke and The Clarendon Press, Oxford, for the translated extract from *The Writings of Leo, Rufino and Angelo*;

Yevgeny Yevtushenko and Collins for the extract from *A Precocious Autobiography*;

G. A. Studdert Kennedy and Hodder and Stoughton Ltd for the extracts from *The New Man in Christ* and *The Best of Studdert Kennedy*;

Paul Ostreicher and the Editor of *The Times* for part of a reported sermon;

Eva Engholm for the extract from *Company of Birds*;

Miyazawa Kenji and Penguin Books Ltd for 'November third' from *The Penguin Book of Japanese Verse*, translated by Geoffrey Bownas and Anthony Thwaite, Copyright Geoffrey Bownas and Anthony Thwaite, 1964;

Fulton J. Sheen and Simon and Schuster Inc. for the extract from *Guide to Contentment*;

Victor Gollancz Ltd for the extract from *Left News*;

Alan Paton and Collins for the extract from *Instrument of Thy Peace*;

Christian Frontier Council for an extract from *Christian News Letter*;

Geoffrey Ainger and Notting Hill Group Ministry for 'The Jericho road' from *More Songs from Notting Hill*;

Geoffrey Gorer and Oxford University Press (U.S.A.) for the extract from an essay in *Man and Aggression*, edited by Ashley Montagu;

John Ferguson and the Fellowship of Reconciliation for an extract from the Alex Wood Memorial Lecture (1971);

Basil Liddell Hart and George Allen and Unwin Ltd for the extract from *Why Don't We Learn from History?*

G. H. C. MacGregor and the Fellowship of Reconciliation for the extracts from *The New Testament Basis of Pacifism*;

J. B. Levner and James Clarke and Co. Ltd for the extract from *The Legends of Israel*, translated by Joel Snowman;

Monica Furlong and Hodder and Stoughton Ltd for the extracts from *Travelling In*;

Douglas Hyde and William Heinemann Ltd for the extract from *I Believed*;

Alister Hardy and Collins for the extract from *The Living Stream*;

Teresa Hooley and Jonathan Cape Ltd for 'Tryst' from *Selected Poems*;

Laura Huxley and Chatto and Windus Ltd for the extracts by Aldous Huxley from *Ends and Means*;

Collins for the extract by C. S. Lewis from *The Problem of Pain*;

H. J. Blackham and Constable for the extract from *Objections to Humanism*;

Collins for the extract by Søren Kierkegaard from *The Last Years*, translated by Ronald Gregor Smith;

George H. Gorman and the Friends Home Service Committee for the extracts from *Introducing Quakers*;

Douglas Steere and the Friends Home Service Committee for the extract from the Swarthmore Lecture, 'Where Words Come From';

W. G. Lambert and The Clarendon Press, Oxford, for the translated extract from *Babylonian Wisdom Literature*;

Kenneth C. Barnes and George Allen and Unwin Ltd for the extract from *The Creative Imagination*;

Faber and Faber Ltd for the extract by Dag Hammarskjöld, from *Markings*;

The Bodley Head for the extract by Shannon Dickson from Margaret Mead's *Culture and Commitment*;

Jack Putterill for the extract from his pamphlet about John Ball;

Iris Murdoch and Constable for the extract from 'Existentialists and Mystics' in *Essays and Poems Presented . . .*;

Lord Oxford and Asquith, Sheed and Ward Ltd and Sheed and Ward Inc. for the extracts by Ronald Knox from *Lightning Meditations* and *The Creed in Slow Motion*;

Constance Reaveley and John Winnington and Chatto and Windus Ltd for the extract from *Democracy and Industry*;

Ann Elmo Agency Inc. for 'A worker reads history' by Bertolt Brecht, translated by H. R. Hays, from *Compact Poets: Brecht*;

Oxford University Press (by arrangement with The Society of Jesus) for the extract by Gerard Manley Hopkins from *The Letters of Gerard Manley Hopkins to Robert Bridges*, edited by Claude Colleer Abbott and for 'The Bethlehem star' ('Moonless darkness stands between') from *Poems of Gerard Manley Hopkins*;

Vivian J. Hall for 'Extol the unregarded men' by W. Stewart Rainbird;

Brian Patten and George Allen and Unwin Ltd for the title poem from *Notes to the Hurrying Man*;

Stephan Hopkinson and the British Broadcasting Corporation for the extract from *More from Ten to Eight on Radio Four*;

Malcolm Muggeridge and the British Broadcasting Corporation for the extract from *Muggeridge Through the Microphone*;

Keith Prowse Music Publishing Co. Ltd for 'The madman's will';

Des Wilson and the Editor of *The Observer* for an extract from a report on the Upper Volta;

James Gordon for 'Prayer for Michaelmas' by Viola Garvin;

William Heinemann Ltd for the extract by Laurence Whistler from *The English Festivals*;

Tom Earley for 'Instead of a carol';

J. M. Dent and Sons Ltd for the extract by Dylan Thomas from *Quite Early One Morning*;

Philip Howard and the Editor of *The Times* for an extract from an article 'Where Real Spirit of Good Will Survives'. Reproduced from *The Times* by permission;

W. H. Auden and Faber and Faber Ltd for 'Three old sinners' from *For the Time Being*, now in *Collected Longer Poems and Collected Shorter Poems 1927–1957*;

Mary Taylor and Mowbrays Publishing Division for the extract from *Stories and Prayers at Five to Ten*;

Clive Sansom and Methuen for 'The donkey's owner' from *The Witnesses*;

R. S. Thomas and Granada Publishing Co. Ltd for 'The Musician' from *Tares*;

Macmillan and Co. Ltd for 'Unkept Good Fridays' by Thomas Hardy from *Collected Poems*;

Collins for the extract by C. S. Lewis from *Miracles*;

Maurice Hussey and Heinemann Educational Books Ltd for the extract from *The Chester Mystery Plays*;

Collins for the extract by Rose Macaulay from *Letters to a Friend, 1950–52*;

Sister Mary Agnes and Workshop Press Ltd for 'Easter' from *Daffodils in Ice*;

Francis X. Weiser and Harcourt Brace Jovanovich Inc. for the extract from *The Holyday Book*;

Handley Stevens and the Notting Hill Group Ministry for 'The twelve disciples' from *Songs from Notting Hill*.

In one or two cases it has not been possible to reach holders of copyright. Publisher and editor will be glad to make any corrections of which they are informed.

# I

# Common ground

# Creation

Most of the world's religions have a myth about the creation of the universe. The myths fall into two main groups. In one we have creation from nothing; things come into existence as a supreme being thinks about them – an example is the Red Indian account below. In the second group creation is effected by division: a primordial being is dismembered, as in one or two of the passages included here; or the chaos that existed before creation is sorted, and a uniform undifferentiated substance is divided into separate materials. A Babylonian creation epic is an example of the type in which order is made out of chaos. Gods are produced first, and they quarrel; stability is attained with the victory of Marduk over Tiamat, a female deity of chaos and darkness. Marduk then split the body of Tiamat in two and formed heaven and earth from the two halves; later he created other gods and eventually men.

The myths are often good stories, but they are more than that. Even in the few examples included here we can see two trends. First, there is a shift from many gods to one God, and this represents progress, for polytheism is never without its rogues' gallery. The second is also a move in the direction of a moral position; order and light prevail over chaos and darkness, and the powers of evil, like the serpent in Genesis, retreat before advancing good.

On a yet higher level is the Creation Hymn from the Rig (or royal) Veda. Containing more than a thousand hymns, the Vedas were the earliest Indian scriptures, composed between 1500 and 1000 B.C. to record religious experiences, and learned by heart for transmission from generation to generation. This hymn, with 'its sense of depth, and mystery, and above all the unity of creation' (M. Eliade), tells us that before time, when even nothingness did not exist, there developed in the darkness hidden by darkness a warmth, in which arose love, or desire. This single being was the real creator, who existed before all other gods. In its mood of doubt and free speculation the hymn seems to look very far ahead.

By the time the New Testament was being written, the Genesis account was no longer taken literally, as we can see in the quotation from Philo, a Jew living at Alexandria. A. C. Bouquet in his *Sacred Books of the World* recommends this passage to Fred Hoyle, the astronomer who first explained the scientific theory of continuous creation to the layman. St Paul also believed (if we interpret him rightly) that the creation was not a single once-for-all act, but a continuous process. To him the coming of Christ was a further stage in evolution; for a time God became a man, and by his life and teaching and death released mankind from old and bad ways, opening up new and splendid possibilities for humanity. We can see something of St Paul's 'The whole created universe groans in all its parts' in C. C. Jung:

> The assumption that man in his whole glory was created on the sixth day of Creation, without any preliminary stages, is after all somewhat too simple and archaic to satisfy us nowadays . . . It is not probable that the extremely indirect methods of creation, which squander millions of years upon the development of countless species and creatures, are the outcome of purposeful intention. Natural history tells us of a haphazard and casual transformation of species over hundreds of millions of years of devouring and being devoured. The biological and political history of man is an elaborate repetition of the same thing.

The section continues with Sikh, Anglo-Saxon, Maori and modern poems, and some light-hearted verses to end with.

*Further reading*: Genesis 1 and 2; Psalms 136 (3-9) and 140 (1-6); Isaiah 40: 12, 13; Colossians 1: 16; A. C. Bouquet, *Sacred Books of the World*; Jennifer Westwood, *Gilgamesh and other Babylonian Tales*.

## Our father

What it was our father lay on when he came to consciousness we do not know. He moved his right arm and then his left arm, his right leg and then his left leg. He began to think of what he should do; and finally he began to cry and tears began to flow from his eyes and fall down below him. After a while, he looked down below him and saw something bright. The bright objects were his tears that had flowed below and formed the present waters . . . Earthmaker began to think again. He thought: 'It is thus; if I wish anything it will become just as I wish, just as my tears have become seas.' Thus he thought.

So he wished for light and it became light. Then he thought: 'It is as I supposed; the things that I have wished for have come into existence as I desired.' Then he thought again, and wished for the earth and the earth came into existence . . . Then he began to talk for the first time. He said, 'As things are just as I wish them I shall make one being like myself.' So he took a piece of earth and made it like himself.

Then he talked to what he had created, but it did not answer. He looked upon it and he saw that it had no mind or thought. So he made a mind for it. Again he talked to it, but it did not answer. So he looked upon it again and saw that it had no tongue. Then he made it a tongue. Then he talked to it again but it did not answer. So he looked upon it again and saw that it had no soul. So he made it a soul. He talked to it again and it very nearly said something. But it did not make itself understood. So Earthmaker breathed into its mouth and talked to it and it answered.

Red Indian myth, quoted in M. Eliade, *From Primitives to Zen*

### The song of creation

There was not then what is nor what is not. There was no sky, and no heaven beyond the sky. What power was there? Where? Who was that power? Was there an abyss of fathomless waters?

There was neither death nor immortality then. No signs were there of night or day. The ONE was breathing by its own power, in deep peace. Only the ONE was: there was nothing beyond.

Darkness was hidden in darkness. The all was fluid and formless. Therein, in the void, by the fire of fervour arose the ONE.

And in the ONE arose love. Love the first seed of soul. The truth of this the sages found in their hearts; seeking in their hearts with wisdom, the sages found that bond of union between being and non-being.

Who knows in truth? Who can tell us whence and how arose this universe? The gods are later than its beginning: who knows therefore whence comes this creation?

Only that god who sees in highest heaven: he only knows whence comes this universe, and whether it was made or uncreated. He only knows, or perhaps he knows not.

from The Rig Veda, translated from the Sanskrit by Juan Mascaró under the title *Lamps of Fire*

### The view of a Jewish philosopher

It is quite foolish to think that the world was created in six days, or in a space of time at all. Why? Because every period of time is a series of days and nights, and these can only be made by the movement of the sun as it goes over and under the earth: but the sun is a part of heaven, so that time is confessedly more recent than the world. It would therefore be correct to say that the world was not made in time, but that time was formed by means of the world, for it was heaven's movement that was the index of the nature of time . . . God never leaves off making, but even as it is the property of fire to burn and of snow to chill, so it is the property of God to make: nay more so by far, since he is to all the source of action . . . Whereas things produced by human arts when finished stand still and remain as they are, the products of divine skill, when completed, begin again to move.

Philo Judaeus (30 B.C. to A.D. 45)

### Continuous creation

Although I think there is no doubt that every galaxy we now observe to be receding from us will in about 10,000,000,000 years have passed entirely beyond the limit of vision of an observer in our galaxy, yet I think that such an observer would still be able to see about the same number of galaxies as we do now. By this I mean that new galaxies will have condensed out of the background material at just about the rate necessary to compensate for those that are being lost as a consequence of their passing beyond our observable universe. At first sight it might be thought that this could not go on indefinitely because the material forming the background would ultimately become exhausted. But again I do not believe that this is so, for it seems likely that new material is constantly being created so as to maintain a constant density in the background material. So we have a situation in which the loss of galaxies, through the expansion of the Universe, is compensated by the condensation of new galaxies, and this can continue indefinitely.

The idea that matter is created continuously . . . in itself is not new. I know of references to the continuous creation of matter that go back more than twenty years, and I have no doubt that a close enquiry would show that the idea, in its vaguest form, goes back very much further than that. . .

From time to time people ask where the created material comes from. Well, it does not come from anywhere. Material simply appears – it is created. At one time the various atoms composing the material do not exist and at a later time they do. This may seem a very strange idea and I agree that it is, but in science it does not matter how strange an idea may seem so long as it works – that is to say, so long as the idea can be expressed in a precise form and so long as its consequences are found to be in agreement with observation. In any case, the whole idea of creation in queer. In the older theories all the material in the Universe is supposed to have appeared at one instant of time, the whole creation process taking the form of one big bang. For myself I find this idea very much queerer than continuous creation.

Fred Hoyle, *The Nature of the Universe*

### Creation continues

For I reckon that the sufferings we now endure bear no comparison with the splendour, as yet unrevealed, which is in store for us. For the created universe waits with eager expectation for God's sons to be revealed. It was made the victim of frustration, not by its own choice, but because of him who made it so; yet always there was hope, because the universe itself is to be freed from the shackles of mortality and enter upon the liberty and splendour of the children of God. Up to the present, we know, the whole created universe groans in all its parts as if in the pangs of childbirth. Not only so, but even we, to whom the Spirit is given as first fruits of the harvest to come, are groaning inwardly while we wait for God to make us his sons and set our whole body free. For we have been saved, though only in hope. Now to see is no longer to hope: why should a man endure and wait for what he already sees? But if we hope for something we do not yet see, then, in waiting for it, we show our endurance.

St Paul, Romans 8 : 18-25

### Renewal, not creation

'Creation' is for the Buddhist only the renewal of an extinct world or system of worlds. The destructions of worlds are caused by forces of nature and catastrophes of various kinds, but they always remain confined to a small part of the universe at one time. Such destructions and renewals of heavenly bodies take place continually in immeasurable space. Modern European science stands in this respect exactly where the Buddhists have stood for the last 2,500 years.

Subhadra Bhikku, *The Message of Buddhism*

### Riddle

The riddle below (to which the answer is of course 'Creation') comes from the largest collection of Old English poetry in existence, the Exeter Book. Beautifully written on vellum, this volume was given to Exeter Cathedral Library before the Normans conquered England by Leofric, first Bishop of Devon and Cornwall. It is still there, and on view in the library.

I am greater than this world,
I am less than a worm,
Lighter than the moon,
Swifter than the sun.
All the floods of the sea,
The face of the earth, the green fields,
Are within my holding.
I reach to the depths;
I plunge beneath hell;
I mount above heaven, the abode of glory;
I range over the dwelling of the angels.
Far and wide I fill with myself the earth,
The whole world and the ocean streams.
Tell me my name.

### Creation

From the conception the increase,
From the increase the swelling,
From the swelling the thought,
From the thought the remembrance,
From the remembrance the consciousness, the desire.

The word became fruitful;
It dwelt with the feeble glimmering;
It brought forth night;

The great night, the long night,
The lowest night, the loftiest night,
The thick night, to be felt,
The night to be touched, the night unseen,
The night following on,
The night ending in death.

From the nothing the begetting,
From the nothing the increase,
From the nothing the abundance,
The power of increasing, the living breath;
It dwelt with the empty space,
It produced the atmosphere which is above us.

The atmosphere which floats above the earth,
The great firmament above us, the spread out space dwelt with the
    early dawn,
Then the moon sprung forth;
The atmosphere above dwelt with the glowing sky,
Forthwith was produced the sun,
They were thrown up above as the chief eyes of Heaven:
Then the Heavens became light,
The early dawn, the early day, the mid-day. The blaze of day from
    the sky.

The sky which floats above the earth. .

Maori poem

### Chaos before creation

Sikhism believes that God created the world to express his power
and his holiness, and that it is the destiny of man to realise this
power and holiness within himself. Before the creation there was
nothing but chaos in the world, only God within himself:

For aeons of years, there was chaos upon chaos.
Neither earth there was, nor the sky; only
God's infinite Will was.
Neither was there night nor day; neither the sun,
nor the moon; and God was seated
in His Absolute Trance.

Neither air there was, nor water; neither birth,
nor death; neither coming nor going; neither
divisions of the world, nor the underworld; neither
the seas, nor the rivulets; neither the sky, nor
the stars; neither time nor space; neither heaven
nor hell. Neither woman there was, nor man;
nor pain. Neither creeds were there, nor garbs;
nor the manifold ways. And there was no one
to utter: 'Lo, there is also another.'

Gopal Singh, *Religion of the Sikhs*


## In the beginning

Within Pacific beds a labouring earth,
With boom and roar,
Split, wrenched, and tore
Her vitals wide, and gave a moon its birth:
A future moon half free,
Loosened in uproar from a molten sea;
And through that din upgathering, shoal and wall
Of shelving mud arose; and spurting cones
Of fire shot up, and slung dry hissing stones
Down on the ocean-sludge; and in wild hanks,
Light lightning forking in impetuous changes,
Earth wrinkled into ranges;
And the sea grappled, clinging to the ball.

Dorothy Wellesley, *Poems of Ten Years*


## The creation

And God stepped out on space
And he looked around and said:
I'm lonely –
I'll make me a world.

And as far as the eye of God could see
Darkness covered everything,
Blacker than a hundred midnights
Down in a cypress swamp.

Then God smiled,
And the light broke,
And the darkness rolled up on one side,
And the light stood shining on the other,
And God said: That's good!

Then God reached out and took the light in his hands,
And God rolled the light around in his hands,
Until he made the sun;
And he set that sun a-blazing in the heavens.
And the light that was left from making the sun
God gathered it up in a shining ball
And flung it against the darkness,
Spangling the night with the moon and stars.
Then down between
The darkness and the light
He hurled the world;
And God said: That's good!

Then God himself stepped down –
And the sun was in his right hand,
And the moon was on his left;
And the stars were clustered about his head,
And the earth was under his feet.
And God walked, and where he trod
His footsteps hollowed the valleys out
And bulged the mountains up.

Then he stopped and looked and saw
That the earth was hot and barren.
So God stepped over to the edge of the world
And he spat out the seven seas –
He batted his eyes, and the lightnings flashed –
He clapped his hands, and the thunders rolled –
And the waters above the earth came down,
The cooling waters came down.

Then the green grass sprouted,
And the little red flowers blossomed,
The pine-tree pointed his finger to the sky,
And the oak spread out his arms,

The lakes cuddled down in the hollows of the ground,
And the rivers ran down to the sea;
And God smiled again,
And the rainbow appeared,
And curled itself around his shoulder.

Then God raised his arm and he waved his hand
Over the sea and over the land,
And he said: Bring forth! Bring forth!
And quicker than God could drop his hand,
Fishes and fowls
And beasts and birds
Swam the rivers and the seas,
Roamed the forests and the woods,
And split the air with their wings.
And God said: That's good!

Then God walked around
And God looked around
On all that he had made.
He looked at his sun,
And he looked at his moon,
And he looked at his little stars;
He looked on his world
With all its living things,
And God said: I'm lonely still.

Then God sat down –
On the side of a hill where he could think;
By a deep wide river he sat down;
With his head in his hands,
God thought and thought,
Till he thought: I'll make a man!

Up from the bed of the river
God scooped the clay;
And by the bank of the river
He kneeled him down;
And there the great God Almighty,
Who lit the sun and fixed it in the sky,
Who flung the stars to the most far corner of the night,

Who rounded the earth in the middle of his hand;
This Great God,
Like a mammy bending over her baby,
Kneeled down in the dust
Toiling over a lump of clay
Till he shaped it in his own image;

Then into it he blew the breath of life,
And man became a living soul.
Amen. Amen.

James Weldon Johnson, *God's Trombones*

### Is God your name?

Is God your name;
Or should I call you Jove?
Are you and Allah both the same;
Are you even there?
Are you the Sun, this bridge, a tree?
Are you the world? Or are you me?

I can prove that I exist. Can you?
Are we a figment of our imagination?
Didst thou, Almighty Lord, make me –
Or are you my creation?

C. T. Whall, 18

### 'God must have smiled'

When God had finished the stars and whirl of coloured suns
He turned His mind from big things to fashion little ones,
Beautiful tiny things (like daisies) He made, and then
He made the comical ones in case the minds of men
                    Should stiffen and become
                    Dull, humourless and glum:
And so forgetful of the Maker be
As to take even themselves – *quite seriously.*
Caterpillars and cats are likely and excellent puns;
All God's jokes are good, even the practical ones!
And as for the duck, I think God must have smiled a bit

Seeing those bright eyes blink on the day He fashioned it.
And He's probably laughing still at the sound that came
out of its bill!

F. W. Harvey, *Gloucestershire: A Selection from the Poems of
F. W. Harvey*

# Animals

Animal life seems always to have existed in abundance wherever
the earth would support it; the scale and vitality of this life
emerge vividly in the records of explorers. David Livingstone
writes of his travels in the middle of the last century not far from
the modern Lusaka, and a hundred years later Farley Mowat
describes the migration of the caribou to their fawning ground
about 150 miles west of Hudson Bay. Jung introduces the idea
that by being aware of it man completed the creation of the world,
and follows St Paul in the view that there was no single act of
creation and that instead creation in the form of evolution is continuous: 'Man had put the stamp of perfection on the world by
giving it objective existence . . . man is indispensable for the completion of creation . . . in fact, he himself is the second creator of
the world, who alone has given to the world its objective existence
– without which, unheard, unseen, silently eating, giving birth,
dying, heads nodding through hundreds of millions of years, it
would have gone on in the profoundest night of non-being down
to its unknown end. Human consciousness created objective experience and meaning, and man found his indispensable place in
the great process of being.'

Edwin Muir lights up another facet of the truth. He shows that,
without names and language, the animals have only a limited
consciousness; they live only in the present. One stage in the
continuing creation was the growth of stable relationships between
animals themselves and between animals and man. Mowat notes
that in Canada 'until the coming of the white man, wolves, men
and deer lived in mutual adjustment with each other for more
centuries than we can count'. The relationship was more than 'the
balance of nature', for the hunters respected the animals they
lived on. Now however civilisation has replaced the chase by the
fattening pen and the broiler house, and is exterminating wild
animals.

Many religions have insisted that men should respect other living things. Some forbid killing at all; Judaism required a rest day for animals as well as men; and Christianity enjoins reverence for everything created in the first of the two great commandments: 'Love the Lord your God with all your heart, with all your soul, with all your strength, and with all your mind.'

*Further reading*: Genesis 1:24, 25; Proverbs 30:24-31; Psalms 29, 50: (7-11) and 104; R. Kipling, 'Eddi's Service', in *Definitive Edition of Poems*; *The Little Flowers of St Francis*; 'Fougasse', *The Neighbours* (Universities Federation for Animal Welfare); C. S. Lewis, 'Animal Pain' in *The Problem of Pain*; R. Manning-Sanders, *Birds, Beasts and Fishes*; K. Lorenz, *King Solomon's Ring*; Helen Waddell, *Beasts and Saints*.

## Wild life abundant

When we came to the top of the outer range of the hills, we had a glorious view. At a short distance below us we saw the Kafue, wending away over a forest-clad plain . . . and on the other side of the Zambesi lay a long range of dark hills. The plain below us, at the left of the Kafue, had more large game on it than anywhere else I had seen in Africa. Hundreds of buffaloes and zebras grazed on the open spaces, and there stood lordly elephants feeding majestically, nothing moving apparently but the proboscis. I wished that I had been able to take a photograph of a scene so seldom beheld, and which is destined, as guns increase, to pass away from earth. When we descended we found all the animals remarkedly tame. The elephants stood beneath the trees, fanning themselves with their large ears, as if they did not see us, at 200 or 300 yards' distance. The number of animals was quite astonishing, and made me think that here I could realize an image of that time when Megatheria fed undisturbed in the primeval forests. We saw great numbers of red-coloured pigs, standing gazing at us in wonder. The people live on the hills, and having no guns seldom disturb the game.

David Livingstone, *Travels in South Africa*

## The caribou stream

From our vantage-point we waited for the coming of the deer. We had not long to wait. Franz caught my arm and pointed to the convoluted slopes of the distant southern hills, and I could just discern a line of motion. It seemed to me that the slopes were sliding gently downward to the bay, as if the innumerable boulders that protruded from the hills had suddenly been set adrift to roll, in slow motion, down upon the ice. I watched intently, not certain whether the sun's glare had begun to affect my eyes. Then the slow avalanches reached the far shore and debouched over the bay. I tried to count the little dots. Then, fifty, a hundred, three hundred – and I gave up. The deer streamed out on to the ice until they were moving north across a front of several miles . . .

The leaders reached our shore and began the ascent, but across the bay the avalanche continued and grew heavier. The surface of the bay, for six miles east and west, had become one undulating mass of animals, and still they came.

Without hurry, but without pause, unthinking, but directly driven, they filed down to the ice, and following the tracks of those who had crossed first, made for our shore . . . The herds were swelling past our lookout now. Ten paces from us, five, then we were forced to stand and wave our arms to avoid being trampled on. The does gazed briefly and incuriously at us, swung a few feet away and passed on to the north without altering their gait.

Hours passed like minutes. The flow continued at an unbroken level until the sun stood poised on the horizon's rim. And I became slowly conscious of a great apathy. Life, my life and that of Franz, of all things living I knew, seemed to have become meaningless. For here was life on such a scale that it was beyond all comprehension. It numbed my mind and left me feeling as if the inanimate world had been saturated with a reckless prodigality in that sacred and precious thing called life.

Farley Mowat, *People of the Deer*

**Man's awareness of the creation**

From Nairobi we used a small Ford to visit the Athai Plains, a great game preserve. From a low hill in this broad savannah a magnificent prospect opened out to us. To the very brink of the horizon we saw gigantic herds of animals: gazelle, antelope, gnu, zebra, warthog, and so on. Grazing, heads nodding, the herds moved forward like slow rivers. There was scarcely any sound save the melancholy cry of a bird of prey. This was the stillness of the eternal beginning, the world as it had always been, in the state of non-being; for until then no one had been present to know that it was this world. I walked away from my companions until I had put them out of sight, and savoured the feeling of being entirely alone. There I was now, the first human being to recognise that this was the world, but who did not know that in this moment he had first really created it.

C. G. Jung, *Memories, Dreams, Reflections*

### The animals

They do not live in the world,
Are not in time and space.
From birth to death hurled
No word do they have, not one
To plant a foot upon,
Were never in any place.

For with names the world was called
Out of the empty air,
With names was built and walled,
Line and circle and square,
Dust and emerald;
Snatched from deceiving death
By the articulate breath.

But these have never trod
Twice the familiar track,
Never never turned back
Into the memoried day.
All is new and near
In the unchanging Here
Of the fifth great day of God,
That shall remain the same,
Never shall pass away.

On the sixth day we came.

Edwin Muir, *Collected Poems 1921–1958*

### Cave paintings

It was those Magdalenian hunters, finding life easy with the abundant game of the open grassland and tundra of their day, who brought cave-painting, engraving and carving to a superb peak of achievement . . . In their art all the Upper Palaeolithic peoples give us the first opportunity in history to enter into communion, however imperfectly, with the mind, imagination and emotions of our forebears. Looking at these studies of the mighty mammoth and rhinoceros, the great oxen and reindeer and bison, the graceful herds of stag and wild horses, each of us can experience according to his imaginative powers something of what it was like to live as a hunter at that time twelve thousand years ago, when civilization was still hidden from knowledge far in the future, but when self-consciousness and the power to grasp all kinds of mental images was rapidly transforming the human psyche.

> Jacquetta Hawkes and Leonard Woolley, *Prehistory and the Beginnings of Civilization*

### Man and animals

[All creatures] know individually pleasure and displeasure, pain, terror, and sorrow. All are full of fears which come from all directions. And yet there exist people who would cause greater pain to them. . . . Some kill animals for sacrifice, some for their skin, flesh, blood, feathers, teeth, or tusks. He who harms animals has not understood or renounced deeds of sin.

In particular we must be careful not to injure insects with fire:

By careless or wicked acts one may harm other beings by means of fire. . . . For there are creatures living in earth, grass, leaves, wood, cowdung, or dustheaps, and jumping creatures which fall into a fire if they come near it. If touched by fire they shrivel up . . . lose their senses, and die.

> Jainist scripture

### Talk to them

When Rabbi Wolf drove out in a carriage, he never permitted the whip to be used on horses. 'You do not even have to shout at them,' he instructed the coachman. 'You just have to know how to talk to them.'

### Ransoming prisoners

Once Rabbi Zasya travelled cross-country collecting money to ransom prisoners. He came to an inn at a time when the innkeeper was not at home. He went through the rooms, according to custom and in one saw a large cage with all kinds of birds. And Zasya saw that the caged creatures wanted to fly through the spaces of the world and be free birds again. He burned with pity for them and he said to himself: 'Here you are, Zasya, walking your feet off to ransom prisoners. But what greater ransoming of prisoners can there be than to free these birds from their prison?' Then he opened the cage, and the birds flew out into freedom.

When the innkeeper returned and saw the empty cage, he was very angry, and asked the people in the house who had done this to him. They answered: 'A man is loitering about here and he looks like a fool. No one but he can have done this thing.' The innkeeper shouted at Zasya: 'You fool! How could you have the impudence to rob me of my birds and make worthless the good money that I paid for them?' Zasya replied: 'You have often read and repeated these words in the psalms: "His tender mercies are over all his works." ' Then the innkeeper beat him until his hand grew tired and finally threw him out of the house. And Zasya went on his way serenely.

Martin Buber (trans.), *Tales of the Hasidim*

### St Francis

He felt so strongly for the mistreated animals of his day, for the snared birds and beaten horses and hungry dogs, that he went to the burghers, to the governors, finally to the Emperor, begging for a law against their abuse. He demanded that farmers be forced to treat cattle humanely. . . . He wanted towns and corporations to take time off from levying taxes and scatter crumbs. . . . He pleaded for hostels where strays could be fed and housed, and he raged against the caging of larks.

Phyllis McGinley, *Saint-Watching*

## St Kevin and the blackbird

At one Lenten season, St Kevin, as was his way, fled from the company of men to a certain solitude, and in a little hut that did but keep out the sun and the rain, gave himself earnestly to reading and to prayer, and his leisure to contemplation alone. And as he knelt in his accustomed fashion, with his hand outstretched through the window and lifted up to heaven, a blackbird settled on it, and busying herself as in her nest, laid in it an egg. And so moved was the saint that in all patience and gentleness he remained, neither closing nor withdrawing his hand: but until the young ones were fully hatched he held it out unwearied, shaping it for the purpose.

Helen Waddell, *Beasts and Saints*

## Reverence for life

What does reverence for life say about the relations between men and the animal world?

Whenever I injure life of any sort, I must be quite clear whether it is necessary. Beyond the unavoidable, I must never go, not even with what seems insignificant. The farmer who has mown down a thousand flowers in his meadow to feed his cows, must be careful on his way home not to strike off in thoughtless pastime the head of a single flower by the roadside, for he thereby commits a wrong against life without being under the pressure of necessity.

Those who experiment with operations or the use of drugs upon animals, or inoculate them with diseases, so as to be able to bring help to mankind with the results gained, must never quiet any misgivings they feel with the general reflexion that their gruesome proceedings aim at a valuable result. They must first have considered in each individual case whether there is a real necessity to force upon any animal this sacrifice for the sake of mankind, and they must take the most careful pains to ensure that the pain inflicted is made as small as possible. How much wrong is committed in scientific institutions through neglect of anaesthetics, which to save time or trouble are not administered! How much, too, through animals being subjected to torture merely to give to students a demonstration of perfectly understood phenomena. By the very fact that animals have been subjected to experiments, and have by their pain won such valuable results for suffering men, a new and special relation of solidarity has been established between them and us. From that springs for each one of us a compulsion to do to every animal all the good we possibly can. By helping an insect when it is in difficulties I am thereby attempting to cancel part of man's ever new debt to the animal world. Whenever an animal is in any way forced into the service of man, every one of us must be concerned with the suffering which it has thereby to undergo. None of us must allow to take place any suffering for which he himself is not responsible, if he can hinder it in any way, at the same time quieting his conscience with the reflexion that he would be mixing himself up in something which does not concern him. No one must shut his eyes and regard as non-existent the sufferings of which he spares himself the sight.

Albert Schweitzer, *Civilization and Ethics*

### 'All Heaven in a rage'

A Robin Redbreast in a Cage
Puts all Heaven in a Rage
A dove house fill'd with doves and pigeons
Shudders Hell through all its regions.
A dog starv'd at his Master's Gate
Predicts the ruin of the State.
A Horse misus'd upon the Road
Calls to Heaven for Human blood.
Each outcry of the hunted Hare
A fibre from the Brain does tear.
A Skylark wounded in the wing,
A Cherubim does cease to sing.
The Game Cock clipp'd and arm'd for fight
Does the Rising Sun affright . . .
He who shall hurt the little Wren
Shall never be belov'd by Men.

He who the Ox to wrath has mov'd
Shall never be by Woman lov'd.
The wanton Boy that kills the Fly
Shall feel the Spider's enmity . . .
The Bleat, the Bark, Bellow and Roar
Are Waves that Beat on Heaven's Shore.

William Blake, from 'Auguries of Innocence'


## God's dog

The most characteristic of all Robert Louis Stevenson's utterances
was at Pitlochry in 1881 when he saw a dog being ill-treated. He at
once interfered, and when the owner resented his interference and
told him 'It's not your dog,' he cried out: 'It's God's dog and I am
here to protect it.'

V. Crellin, *Tongues of Men*


## Battery hens

Each little cage
Each little cage
Each and every egg that's laid,
Are put in categories.

That's the life of the hen
The Battery hen
The shining cages
Hygienically clean.

The cruel, hard, short life
The brilliant lights
The spotless floor
For civilised well-mannered hens.

Sally Grant, 13


## The robin's song

God bless the field and bless the furrow,
Stream and branch and rabbit burrow,
Hill and stone and flower and tree,

From Bristol town to Wetherby –
Bless the sun and bless the sleet,
Bless the lane and bless the street,
Bless the night and bless the day,
From Somerset and all the way
To the meadows of Cathay;
Bless the minnow, bless the whale,
Bless the rainbow and the hail,
Bless the nest and bless the leaf,
Bless the righteous and the thief,
Bless the wing and bless the fin,
Bless the air I travel in,
Bless the mill and bless the mouse,
Bless the miller's bricken house,
Bless the earth and bless the sea,
God bless you and God bless me!

Anonymous

# The Riches of the Earth

In most ages men have recorded their admiration for the beauty of the world; and even in prehistoric times the artists who made the paintings and engravings of animals in the caves of France and Spain and Africa leave us in no doubt about their feelings, however practical their purposes may have been. The section starts with a passage from Simone Weil, the French philosopher and teacher, who worked in factory and field as well as experiencing war at first hand in Spain.

*Further reading*: Job 38; Isaiah 35; Psalm 104; Edmund Blunden, 'Nature's Adornings' in *The Midnight Skaters*; John Clare, many poems; Walter de la Mare, 'Fare Well'; James Reeves, 'Voices of the Tree', in *The Password*.

### Ancient and modern attitudes

In ancient times the love of the beauty of the world had a very important place in men's thoughts and surrounded the whole of life with marvellous poetry. This was the case in every nation; in China, in India, and in Greece. . . .

The example of Saint Francis shows how great a place the beauty of the world can have in Christian thought. Not only is his actual poem perfect poetry, but all his life was perfect poetry in action. His very choice of places for solitary retreats or for the foundations of his convents was in itself the most beautiful poetry in action. Vagabondage and poverty were poetry with him; he stripped himself naked in order to have immediate contact with the beauty of the world. . . .

Today one might think that the white races had almost lost all feeling for the beauty of the world, and that they had taken upon them the task of making it disappear from all the continents where they have penetrated with their armies, their trade and their religion. As Christ said to Pharisees: 'Woe to you, for ye have taken away the key of knowledge; ye entered not in yourself and them that were entering in ye hindered.'

And yet at the present time, in the countries of the white races, the beauty of the world is almost the only way by which we can allow God to penetrate us, for we are still further removed from the other two. Real love and respect for religious practices are rare even among those who are most assiduous in observing them, and are practically never to be found in others. Most people do not even conceive them to be possible. As regards the supernatural purpose of affliction, compassion and gratitude are not only rare but have become almost unintelligible for almost everyone today. The very idea of them has almost disappeared; the very meaning of the words has been debased.

On the other hand a sense of beauty, although mutilated, distorted and soiled, remains rooted in the heart of man as a powerful incentive. It is present in all the preoccupations of secular life. If it were made true and pure it would sweep all secular life in a body to the feet of God, it would make the total incarnation of the faith possible.

Moreover, speaking generally, the beauty of the world is the commonest, easiest and most natural way of approach.

Simone Weil, *Waiting on God*

### Lilies in the fields

And why be anxious about clothes? Consider how the lilies grow in the fields; they do not work, they do not spin; and yet, I tell you, even Solomon in all his splendour was not attired like one of these.

St Matthew 6:28, 29

### The snow-storm

His command speeds the snow-storm
and tends the swift lightning to execute his sentence.
To that end the storehouses are opened,
and the clouds fly out like birds.
By his mighty power the clouds are piled up
and the hailstones broken small.
The crash of his thunder makes the earth writhe,
and, when he appears, an earthquake shakes the hills.
At his will the south wind blows,
the squall from the north and the hurricane.
He scatters the snow-flakes like birds alighting;
they settle like a swarm of locusts.
The eye is dazzled by their beautiful whiteness,
and as they fall the mind is entranced.
He spreads frost on the earth like salt,
and icicles form like pointed stakes.
A cold blast from the north,
and ice grows hard on the water,
settling on every pool,
as though the water were putting on a breastplate.

Ecclesiasticus 43:13-20

### An Indian porter's love of flowers

The leader of a Himalayan expedition recalls the action of a native porter:

I saw Matbir take the hatchet and go out for firewood . . . he came back with a bunch of alpine flowers. I had noticed before that Matbir loved flowers, and he had gone back for them now from a need to *give* them to someone. Accordingly, he came to the tent door and gave them to me . . . I accepted them gratefully – blue primulas and rock geraniums, anemones (both the small blue ones and the large white with five big petals and a yellow centre), forget-me-nots and red potentillas); they were indeed most beautiful and I did not hide my admiration. Matbir hovered round the door for a moment to enjoy our enjoyment and then went off to join the coolies. I placed the flowers in a can of water in the centre of our table – a stone slab on crates – where Matbir and we would see them. Before long he whisked off again and presented a second bunch.

A Scottish or English youth of eighteen would not have dared such an act; he is too self-conscious. The charm of a Matbir is that no thought of self enters into the act. It is such freedom that alone makes it good and possible. Altogether, it was a revelation to me of what a man can be like when he is unspoiled: at once firm of eye and bearing, yet unhesitating in his love of men and the world and unembarrassed in showing it. I tried to think of men whom I had met outside the Himalaya, who in unaffected grace of manhood could stand comparison with Matbir. I was unable to think of any.

In our experience of the High Himalaya there occurred nothing to make a more lasting impression on my mind than this trivial incident. Again and again it recurs, accompanied by one or two of its witnessed opposites: Italian sentries of Tobruk staving in a prisoner's face with rifle butts; one pundit of British mountaineering disparaging another; the corpse-like face of a Gestapo agent interrogating me at Mahrisch Trubau. From these I can turn to Matbir and Lampak and feel a respect for man.

W. H. Murray, *The Scottish Himalayan Expedition*

### 'To find the stars'

The author is a South African athlete who succeeded in getting his country excluded from the Olympic Games because it was represented only by whites. Arrested as a political activist, he twice escaped from the South African police, but on the second occasion was shot and caught. Not being allowed to write letters in prison he wrote his letters home in the form of poetry.

I remember rising one night
after midnight
and moving
through an impulse of loneliness
to try and find the stars.

And through the haze
the battens of fluorescents made
I saw pinpricks of white
I thought were stars.

Greatly daring
I thrust my arm through the bars
and easing the switch in the corridor
plunged my cell in darkness

I scampered to the window
and saw the splashes of light
where the stars flowered.

But through my delight
thudded the anxious boots
and a warning barked
from the machine-gun post
on the catwalk.

And it is the brusque inquiry
and threat
that I remember of that night
rather than the stars.

> Dennis Brutus, *Letters to Martha*

### The human soul needs actual beauty

D. H. Lawrence writes about the mining village in which he was born, and the opportunities missed when it was built.

Now though perhaps nobody knew it, it was ugliness which really betrayed the spirit of man, in the nineteenth century. The great crime which the moneyed classes and promoters of industry committed in the palmy Victorian days was the condemning of the workers to ugliness, ugliness, ugliness: meanness and formless and ugly surroundings, ugly ideals, ugly religion, ugly hope, ugly love, ugly clothes, ugly furniture, ugly houses, ugly relationship between workers and employers. The human soul needs actual beauty even more than bread. The middle classes jeer at the colliers for buying pianos – but what is the piano, often as not, but a blind reaching out for beauty. To the woman it is a possession and piece of furniture and something to feel superior about. But see the elderly colliers trying to learn to play, see them listening with queer alert faces to their daughter's execution of *The Maiden's Prayer*, and you will see a blind, unsatisfied craving for beauty. It is far more deep in the men than the women. The women want show. The men want beauty, and still want it.

> D. H. Lawrence, from 'Nottingham and the Mining Countryside' in *Phoenix*

## Any patch of sunlight

Any patch of sunlight in a wood will show you something about the sun which you could never get from reading books on astronomy. These pure and spontaneous pleasures are 'patches of Godlight' in the woods of our experience.

> C. S. Lewis, *Letters to Malcolm*

## 'Long live the weeds'

What would the world be, once bereft
Of wet and of wildness? Let them be left,
O let them be left, wildness and wet;
Long live the weeds and the wilderness yet.

> Gerald Manley Hopkins, from 'Inversnaid'

## The field

It was once an old friend, bright and of emerald green.
A beautiful sight, fresh and litter free.
Surrounded by trees and a running icy brook,
That ran over cobble stones made smooth and dazzling.
One day a huge, yellow, rumbling bulldozer arrived,
A monster of pipes, fumes and noise,
It tore up the cold, dewy, green turf,

Pulled out easily every big tree from the moldy dirt.

Soon the piles of rough, golden brick arrived.
Plus timber, tiles and cement and even the kitchen sink.
Next came the workers with all their might and strength,
Carrying their forks and spades that glinted in the hot sun as they
   worked.

The roads were made, the houses went up,
Ruining the lovely scene completely.
The people slowly, cautiously moved in,
Not knowing what a wonderful field was gone.

> Adrian Brunt, 13

### Walking

To walk abroad is, not with eyes,
But thoughts, the fields to see and prize;
   Else may the silent feet,
      Like logs of wood,
Move up and down, and see no good
      Nor joy nor glory meet.

To walk is by a thought to go;
To move in spirit to and fro;
   To mind the good we see;
      To taste the sweet;
Observing all the things we meet
      How choice and rich they be.

To note the beauty of the day,
And golden fields of corn survey;
   Admire each pretty flower
      With its sweet smell;
To praise their Maker, and to tell
      The marks of his great power.

Observe those rich and glorious things,
The rivers, meadows, woods, and springs,
   The fructifying sun;
      To note from far

The rising of each twinkling star
  For us his race to run.

While in those pleasant paths we talk,
'Tis that towards which at last we walk;
  For we may by degrees
    Wisely proceed
Pleasures of love and praise to heed,
  From viewing herbs and trees.

Thomas Traherne

# Family

Some facets of family life are illumined in this section. The pains and hopes and joy attending birth are universally felt; almost as worldwide are the difficulties between parents and children, resolved by love and understanding. We hear first the adolescents' point of view, and then that of the parents, conscious of being ridiculous and often feeling disappointed. At the end are some reflective poems from writers of varying ages.

*Further reading*: Proverbs 4:1-13; Ecclesiasticus 29:21-4; St Matthew 15:1-9; I John 2:7-14; Ephesians 6:1-4. J. H. Walsh and F. Tomlinson. *Fields of Experience* contains some incisive accounts of adolescent feelings; and Lionel Jackson, *Echoes*, is a verse anthology that opens with a family section.

### Song at birth

My heart is all happy,
My heart takes wing in singing,
Under the trees of the forest,
The forest our dwelling and our mother.
On my thread I have taken,
A little, a very little bird.
My heart is caught on the thread,
On the thread with the bird.

Pygmy

### Prayer before birth

I am not yet born; O hear me.
Let not the bloodsucking bat or the rat or the stoat or the
      club-footed ghoul come near me.

I am not yet born, console me.
I fear that the human race may with tall walls wall me,
      with strong drugs dope me, with wise lies lure me,
      on black racks rack me, in blood-baths roll me.

I am not yet born; provide me
With water to dandle me, grass to grow for me, trees to talk
      to me, sky to sing to me, birds and a white light
      in the back of my mind to guide me.

I am not yet born; forgive me
For the sins that in me the world shall commit, my words
      when they speak me, my thoughts when they think me,
      my treason engendered by traitors beyond me,
      my life when they murder by means of my
      hands, my death when they live me.

I am not yet born; rehearse me
In the parts I must play and cues I must take when
      old men lecture me, bureaucrats hector me, mountains
      frown at me, lovers laugh at me, the white
      waves call me to folly and the desert calls
      me to doom and the beggar refuses
      my gift and my children curse me.

I am not yet born; O hear me,
Let not man who is beast or who thinks he is God
      come near me.

I am not yet born; O fill me
With strength against those who would freeze my
      humanity, would dragoon me into a lethal automaton,
      would make me a cog in a machine, a thing with
      one face, a thing, and against all those
      who would dissipate my entirety, would
      blow me like thistledown hither and
      thither or hither and thither

like water held in the
hands would spill me.

Let them not make me a stone and let them not spill me.
Otherwise kill me.

Louis MacNeice, *Collected Poems*

## Birth

For your sake when I needed them
immediately strangers came
putting all other tasks aside
and so complete was their command
I had no time to understand
that without help you would have died

As kind as was my mother's touch
was the incision of the knife
I do not owe her hands as much
as those that lifted you to life
I did not know that what could kill
could ever be so merciful

How gentle must have been the care
how well they must have guarded me
as I was lying unaware
I have long known people can hate
and did not think that they could be
so tender and considerate

The hands of strangers gave you life
now I can never again feel
as if I were Ishmael
that only solitude is safe
we die but cannot live alone
and owe for everything we own

Karen Gershon, *Selected Poems*

### Birth

It was warm
in the red-velvet
life-supplying
belly of his mother
and his fragile body
slumbered, unencumbered.
Those were the days and nights of
pleasant nothingness, a dream
until
he moved, and then
There was a force,
a thriving, throbbing locomotive,
pulsing, pushing forward,
down the narrow channel,
and,
snapping his naked head,
the first frigid air spat at him.
Why must they force him
from the depth, from the
red bed?

F. M. Turner, 14

### There was a child went forth

There was a child went forth every day,
And the first object he looked upon, that object he became,
And that object became part of him for the day or a certain
    part of the day,
Or for many years or stretching cycles of years . . .

His own parents, he that had fathered him and she that had
    conceived him in her womb and birthed him,
They gave this child more of themselves than that,
They gave him afterward every day, they became part of him.

The mother at home quietly placing the dishes on the supper-
    table,
The mother with mild words, clean her cap and gown, a whole-
    some odour falling off her person and clothes as she walks by,

The father, strong, self-sufficient, manly, mean, angered,
  unjust,
The blow, the quick loud word, the tight bargain, the crafty
  lure
The family usages, the language, the company, the furniture,
  the yearning and swelling heart,
Affection that will not be gainsayed, the sense of what is
The doubts of day-time and the doubts of night-time, the
  curious whether and how . . .

  Walt Whitman

### Authority

In at nine, bed at ten,
It's the same every day, again and again.
And if I'm late just one day in five,
They almost eat me – alive.

And if I laughed or began to sneer,
He would give me a clip, round the ear.
'Don't do that again,' he would say,
It's the same every blinkin' day.

I can't do this, I can't do that,
'Take your shoes off, you'll dirty the mat!
Don't trip up, watch my tea,
Go and switch on the T.V.'

'Take the dog out, do as you're told,
Put your coat on, it's getting cold.
And hurry up, lad, or you'll get a clout,
And post this letter while you're out.

'You're not going out tonight, it's already getting dark,
I'm not having you on this hooliganism lark,
Smashing bottles, windows too,
Next door's son don't do it and nor will you.'

  S. Freestone, 14

### Night scene

Maybe it's fate or just coincidental
But an argument always starts at night.
And in the confusion of tempers and anger
It's on with the coat, a blatant slam of the door
And outside into the night.

The night's such a soothing time
For as you walk swiftly, away from the trouble,
The darkness, the stillness, the quietness, even the coldness,
Slows you down
And, head bowed, you creep along the uneven pavement,
Watching your feet continuously stepping in front of one another.
Trying to concentrate.
But you can't
For there is so much and yet so little happening around you,
That all distracts you.

How dark it all is,
How beautiful the gleaming stars are set in a
Background of nothing.
How cold they look,
How cold it is.
So cold you can see your breath diminishing in silence.
How silent.
How softly the old street lamps throw a soothing
Lightness onto the dark pavements.

But such beauty aids thought.
Thought aids remembrance.
How vile the close coloured curtains are
When the house-lights are burning.
How ridiculous the over-volumed televisions sound.

How maddening the laughter from within four walls gets,
Why do they laugh and mock
The very beauty of the darkness, the stillness,
The quietness.
Who are they to spoil it all?
Why is it that those who suffer, suffer alone?

Time passes by,
The cold becomes unbearable,
And after walking round in one big circle,
You return, unspeaking to the trouble you left.
But in the morning all is forgiven and forgotten.

S. Farnall, 16


## To my mother

Most near, most dear, most loved and most far,
Under the window where I often found her
Sitting as huge as Asia, seismic with laughter,
Gin and chicken helpless in her Irish hand.
Irresistible as Rabelais, but most tender for
The lame dogs and hurt birds that surrounded her –
She is a procession no one can follow after
But be like a little dog following a brass band.

She will not glance up at the bomber, or condescend
To drop her gin and scuttle to a cellar,
But lean on the mahogany table like a mountain
Whom only faith can move, and so I send
O all my faith, and all my love to tell her
That she will move from mourning into morning.

George Barker, *Collected Poems 1930–1955*


## Children's point of view

One girl of 15 told me that she had made a list of all the criticisms that she had received during the past month. These emanated from her parents, her brothers and sisters, her teachers, her school mates and other girl friends, and also from the boys she knew. The list was formidable and many of the criticisms were self-contradictory. They included the following items from her family: inconsistency, unpredictability, arguing, being unreasonable, rude and aggressive manner, bad temper, irritability, moodiness, quarrelsomeness, grumbling and dissatisfaction with everything in the home, dislike of clothes after buying them and refusing to wear them, untidiness, lack of interest in appearance, too much time spent on appearance, always looking in mirror, wanting to use make-up (this during the previous six months), upsetting brothers or sisters by being bossy and interfering, being slow and late for everything, rushing and being slapdash, always wanting to be out with friends, no interest in the home or family, not wanting to help with housework, apparent hostility to parents. Teachers said she was not really trying and complained of her lack of concentration, carelessness in work, not doing homework, always seeming tired, being apathetic, excitable, disturbing in class, noisy in corridors, forgetting books, and generally irresponsible. Friends accused her of moodiness, unpredictability, bossiness, possessiveness, and jealousy, or of wanting other friends; and made criticisms of her appearance and every detail of her behaviour. Boy friends were critical of her appearance, moodiness, unpredictability, going with other boys, jealousy and possessiveness.

No wonder adolescents often feel completely lost and bewildered. Their apparent hostility and resentment usually conceals a deep sense of inadequacy and self-doubt. The more importance they attach to the criticisms of those about them the more they are disturbed by them. It is necessary to realise this, as otherwise the tendency is to become more and more critical, instead of understanding that what they need is to escape from criticism now and then. Naturally the adolescent must to a great extent value itself according to other people's ideas of it.

Doris Odlum, *Journey through Adolescence*

### There's a bunk in the humpy

The bush was too lonely – the life was too slow,
And Johnny, my son, to the city would go:
He knew that his father was lonely and grey,
And he might have gone there without running away.

*Chorus:*   There's a bunk in the humpy – a glass on the shelf,
            Which have never been used since he used them himself,
            And that bunk in the humpy will stand till he comes
            To his father's old hut in the depth of the gums.

'Tis true that my temper was soured long ago,
But old men have sorrows that sons do not know;

I jawed him one day when my temper was stirred,
An' he left his old father with never a word.

Did he think it was kind – did he think it was right
To the lonely old man in the humpy that night?
Who sat with the sound of the rain in his ears,
And thought till his eyes ran a banker with tears?

His mattress and pillow and bluey are there –
He'll never sleep sounder on feathers, I'll swear,
Or eat better stews than I warmed by the blaze
'Neath the old chimney gutter on cold, rainy days.

An' should he come back when the old man is out
He never need linger a moment in doubt:
He'll know where the key of the padlock is hid,
And there's grub in the gin-case for lifting the lid.

> Henry Lawson

## Daddyo

My hearing deadens. My eyes
aren't good in artificial light.
The memory wobbles. But
that's enough of that.

So clearly I remember
what a harsh crass old man
my father seemed
thirty years ago.

But he was the bright boy
from Edinburgh, the medico who won
hundreds of pounds of weighty scholarships.
A big attacking surgeon.

My mind shrank under the barking knife.

Now it's my turn
to be the red-faced fool
that sons hate, tittered at
by sneering miniskirts.

It's strange to wear
a dead man's shoes, to know
exactly where
each one pinches.

Gavin Ewart

## Blaming sons

An apology for his own drunkenness

White hairs cover my temples,
I am wrinkled and gnarled beyond repair,
And though I have got five sons,
They all hate paper and brush.
A-shu is eighteen:
For laziness there is none like him.
A-Hsüan does his best,
But really loathes the fine arts;
Yung and Tuan are thirteen,
But do not know 'six' from 'seven'.
T'ung-tzu in his ninth year
Is only concerned with things to eat.
If heaven treats me like this,
What can I do but fill my cup?

T'ao Ch'ien (A.D. 406), translated by Arthur Waley

## Washington McNeely

Rich, honoured by my fellow citizens,
The father of many children, born of a noble mother,
All raised there
In the great mansion-house, at the edge of town.
Note the cedar tree on the lawn!
I sent all the boys to Ann Arbor, all the girls to Rockford,
The while my life went on, getting more riches and honours –
Resting under my cedar tree at evening.
The years went on.
I sent the girls to Europe;
I dowered them when married.
I gave the boys money to start in business.

They were strong children, promising as apples
Before the bitten places show.
But John fled the country in disgrace.
Jenny died in child-birth –
I sat under my cedar tree.
Harry killed himself after a debauch,
Susan was divorced –
I sat under my cedar tree.
Paul was invalided from over study,
Mary became a recluse at home for love of a man –
I sat under my cedar tree.
All were gone, or broken-winged or devoured by life –
I sat under my cedar tree.
My mate, the mother of them, was taken –
I sat under my cedar tree,
Till ninety years were tolled.
O maternal Earth, which rocks the fallen leaf to sleep!

Edgar Lee Masters, *Spoon River Anthology*

## Parents' point of view

What adolescents fail to realise is that the parents often find them
unpleasing and difficult to live with, and for a time at any rate
have little sympathy with them. Indeed the parents' sympathy is
largely for themselves. They regret the fact that their children
have to grow up and lose their baby charms. It is always something
of a shock to find the formerly dependent and loving child assert-
ing itself and demanding independence. They may feel unwanted
and rejected when the adolescents wish to go out all the time and
spend their holidays with their own friends. Many parents are
resentful and even hostile to their adolescents, especially to their
daughters.

A typical lament is: 'We used to have such happy family holidays at the seaside or in the country. The children were quite
satisfied with our company then, but now we are no longer inter-
esting enough for them. They seem completely bored by us and
are so sulky and moody that they quite spoil the day if we all go
out together.'

Another mother complained that she had always looked forward to the day when her daughter would be a companion to her; but now it was obvious that the girl did not want her, and resented having to go out with her or to spend an evening at home. Fathers are often deeply affronted when their sons stand up to them and oppose their views, and even sometimes get the better of an argument.

Doris Odlum, *Journey through Adolescence*


### The madman

It was in the garden of a madhouse that I met a youth with a face pale and lovely and full of wonder.

And I sat beside him upon the bench, and I said, 'Why are you here?'

And he looked at me in astonishment, and he said, 'It is an unseemly question, yet I will answer you. My father would make of me a reproduction of himself; so also would my uncle. My mother would have me the image of her illustrious father. My sister would hold up her seafaring husband as the perfect example for me to follow. My brother thinks I should be like him, a fine athlete.

'And my teachers also, the doctor of philosophy, and the music-master, and the logician, they too were determined, and each would have me but a reflection of his own face in a mirror.

'Therefore I came to this place. I find it more sane here. At least, I can be myself.'

Then of a sudden he turned to me and he said, 'But tell me, were you also driven to this place by education and good counsel?'

And I answered, 'No, I am a visitor.'

And he said, 'Oh, you are one of those who live in the madhouse on the other side of the wall.'

Kahlil Gibran, *The Wanderer*


### Old age and youth

Yesterday I was young,
Today I thirst for youth.
Yesterday's future evolved
Into shadows of the past.
Years ago I laughed with friends;

Now, I sit alone with experience,
Gnarled, knotted hands search
For the money, the key, the ticket;
The world moves too fast,
And I too slowly.

They moan, they refuse to accept,
They want to be young again.
I abolish them in my mind,
Yet, I would like to understand them.
They live in the past, reality shocks them
They value too highly experience
Gained in a forgotten era.
They are helpless, they crave for rejuvenation.
They are alone and the world moves
Quickly, and I with it.

Sarah Burt, 14

### Fifty years and three

Fifty years and three
Together in love lived we;
Angry both at once
None ever did us see.

This was the fashion
God taught us, and not fear:
When one was in a passion
The other could forbear.

Anonymous

### Beautiful old age

It ought to be lovely to be old
to be full of the peace that comes of experience
and wrinkled ripe fulfilment.

The wrinkled smile of completeness that follows a life
lived undaunted and unsoured with accepted lies.

If people lived without accepting lies
they would ripen like apples, and be scented like pippins
in their old age.

Soothing, old people should be, like apples
when one is tired of love.
Fragrant like yellowing leaves, and dim with the soft
stillness and satisfaction of autumn.

And a girl should say:
It must be wonderful to live and grow old.
Look at my mother, how rich and still she is! –

And a young man should think: By Jove
my father has faced all weathers, but it's been a life!

D. H. Lawrence, *Complete Poems*

# Death

The common fate is an event that everyone must come to terms with, and it may help the forming of a healthy attitude to learn how people of other times and places have regarded and met death. The girl's poem at the end is the effective expression of an honest response to the death of a loved animal.

*Further reading*: II Samuel 12:15-23; I Corinthians 15; Seamus Heaney, 'Mid-Term Break', in *Death of a Naturalist*; D. H. Lawrence, 'The Ship of Death'; Jon Silkin, 'Death of a Son', in *Penguin Modern Poets*, No. 7; Rabindranath Tagore, 'Gitanjali 93', in *Collected Poems*; John Evelyn, *Diary* for 27 January, 1657.

### How Buddha consoled a mother

This is an incident in the life of Buddha, the founder of the religion that bears his name:

One day while he dwelt in Jetavana, there came to his monastery a woman carrying the body of her child. Her name was Kisa Gotami and she had heard of the greatness of the Buddha, his miracles and of the wondrous things he could do.

Kneeling before the Lord she said: 'My babe is dead. O Merciful One! give him life again, I beseech you.'

The Buddha looked at Kisa Gotami and said to her: 'Go, Kisa Gotami, and bring me a handful of black mustard seed from any house where there has been no death and I shall breathe life into your babe's body.'

Happy at the words of the Lord, Kisa Gotami set out for the city, confident that she would soon return with the mustard seeds. But she went from house to house, and everywhere she asked, the reply was: 'Sister, you can take the mustard seeds but death has visited our family and we have mourned our loss.'

Nowhere could Kisa Gotami find a person who had not known the sorrow of losing a dear one. And then the truth dawned on Kisa Gotami. The Lord had in this manner revealed it to her. Now she knew that death was common to all and that all they who are born, must die.

Kisa Gotami went to the burning place and silently cremated the body of her dead child and then she returned to the Lord and said: 'Lord, there is none who has not known the sorrow of death and my suffering is shared by all.'

The Buddha said to Kisa Gotami: 'Come, sit near me, Kisa Gotami, and my words will remove the curtain of illusion that clouds your wisdom. I shall teach you the Law and you will be free of birth and death and the sorrows that are born of them.'

Then the Lord gave the teachings to Kisa Gotami and brought peace and joy to her grief-stricken soul.

Shakuntala Masani, *Gautama, the Story of Lord Buddha*

### Cheerful mourning

When Chuang Tzu's wife died, the logician Hui Tzu came to the house to join in the rites of mourning. To his astonishment he found Chuang Tzu sitting with an inverted bowl on his knees, drumming upon it and singing a song. 'After all,' said Hui Tzu, 'she lived with you, brought up your children, grew old along with you. That you should not mourn for her is bad enough; but to let your friends find you drumming and singing – that is really going too far!' 'You misjudge me,' said Chuang Tzu. 'When she died, I was in despair, as any man might well be. But soon, pondering on what happened, I told myself that in death no new fate befalls us. In the beginning we lack not life only, but form. Not form only,

but spirit. We are blent in the one great featureless, indistinguish-
able mass. Then a time came when the mass evolved spirit, spirit
evolved form, form evolved life. And now life in its turn has
evolved death. For not nature only but man's being has its seasons,
its sequence of spring and autumn, summer and winter. If someone is tired and has gone to lie down, we do not pursue him with
shouting and bawling. She whom I have lost has lain down to sleep
for a while in the Great Inner Room. To break in upon her rest
with the noise of lamentation would but show that I knew nothing
of nature's Sovereign Law.'

> Chuang Tzu, translated by Arthur Waley in *The Way and Its
> Power*

### Safe keeping

During Rabbi Meir's absence from home two of his sons died.
Their mother, hiding her grief, awaited the father's return, and
then said to him:

'My husband, some time since two jewels of inestimable value
were placed with me for safe keeping. He who left them with
me called for them today, and I delivered them into his hands.

'That is right,' said the Rabbi approvingly. 'We must always
return cheerfully and faithfully all that is placed in our care.'

Shortly after this the Rabbi asked for his sons, and the mother,
taking him by the hand, led him gently to the chamber of death.
Meir gazed upon his sons, and realizing the truth, wept bitterly.

'Weep not, beloved husband,' said his noble wife; 'didst thou
not say to me we must return cheerfully when 'tis called for, all
that has been placed in our care? God gave us these jewels; He
left them with us for a time, and we gloried in their possession; but
now that He calls for His own, we should not repine.'

> H. Polano (trans. and ed.), *The Talmud, Selections, and Brief
> Sketches*

### Voluntary death among Eskimos

In many places voluntary death is normal for old men and women
who are burdened with memories of their youth, and who can no
longer meet the demands of their own reputation. Old people kill
themselves to avoid being a hindrance to their kin. Fear of death

is unknown to them, they know only love of life. The Eskimos are themselves unaware of the difficulties of their existence, they always enjoy life with an enviable intensity, and they believe themselves to be the happiest people on earth living in the most beautiful country there is. When an old man sees the young men go out hunting and cannot himself go along, he is sorry. When he has to ask other people for skins for his clothing, when he cannot ever again be the one to invite the neighbours to eat his game, life is of no value to him. Rheumatism and other ills may plague him, and he wants to die. This has been done in different ways in different tribes, but everywhere it is held that if a man feels himself to be a nuisance, his love for his kin, coupled with the sorrow of not being able to take part in the things which are worthwhile, impels him to die.

In some tribes, an old man wants his eldest son or favourite daughter to be the one to put the string round his neck and hoist him to his death. This was always done at the height of a party where good things were being eaten, where everyone – including the one who was about to die – felt happy and gay, and which would end with Angakok conjuring and dancing to chase out the evil spirits. At the end of his performance, he would give a special rope made of seal and walrus skin to the 'executioner', who then placed it on the beam in the roof of the house and fastened it round the neck of the old man. Then the two rubbed noses and the young man pulled the rope. Everybody in the house either helped or sat on the end of the rope so as to have the honour of bringing the old suffering one to the Happy Hunting Grounds where there would always be light and plenty of game of all kinds. There a man can decide whether he wants to go bear hunting, caribou hunting, or fight the walrus in a kayak.

Peter Freuchen, *The Book of the Eskimos*

### Chant

This song was already old when an Italian noted it in the Sudan in 1854.

In the time when Dendid created all things,
He created the sun,
And the sun is born, and dies, and comes again;

He created the moon,
And the moon is born, and dies, and comes again;
He created the stars,
And the stars are born, and die, and come again;
He created man,
And a man is born, and dies, and never comes again.

> Song of the Dinka tribe

### Death in Sicily

This extract from an interview with a Sicilian woman recorded
in one of Danilo Dolci's books suggests the poverty, ignorance
and neglect, against which he has organised successful action:

Antonina was born in Trappeto. She had pneumonia when she was
a child. 'No one stays at school for more than five years, except for
the odd one whose family's got money.' 'Can you do any arith-
metic?' 'Not much.' She never reads newspapers. 'Ever since I
left school I have given up reading newspapers and books. In the
evening we sit and talk among ourselves and say to each other:
"What are we to do for bread tomorrow if we cannot get some
money from somewhere?" And the child needs milk. We make our
own holidays in our own hearts. Where should I find work? A
woman must stay at home, as if she know no better. When I have
time I go to church.'

'Holidays?' 'How do you expect us to have holidays when the
children haven't any clothes to wear.'

'I don't bother my head with what happens in Sicily or the outside world. No one there takes any interest in what we want or
don't want. Christmas and Easter are our holidays. All the other
days of the year are just the same as the next, as long as one has
one's health. There's always something to do in the house. We
don't earn any money, but when one has a family there's always
something to be done in the house. I've lost three boys and a girl.
I'm always having attacks of giddiness. I always feel weak when I
get up in the morning. My religion is a great comfort to me. I'm
very religious and so is my husband. To my mind, religion means
being sorry for others and giving alms to someone who needs
them. My greatest desire? I want a house of my own more than
anything else, because this one is not ours. If one had a house of

one's own, one wouldn't have to listen to the landlord complaining every month when one couldn't pay the rent. I don't ask for any land, because I know that's just an idle dream.

'The eldest girl died when she was one and a half, after a four day's illness, from a *formone* [abscess]. A year and a half later, a boy of six died too. He had a sore throat and the doctor told me it was meningitis, but at Palermo they said it was tetanus. I was pregnant when he died, and the shock affected the unborn baby's heart. Eight days after he was born, his feet swelled up. The doctor told me that his heart was bad. "There's nothing to be done," he said. "The child's bound to die sooner or later." He did die when the doctor came to see him next. Two years later I had another, but as it was wartime there were no doctors to be had. The child got dysentery when he was four months old, and came out in sores all round his mouth. When I put him to my breast he infected me, too, and my milk dried up. I took him to the Children's Hospital and they told me to leave him there. But as I didn't want to leave him there all alone, I took him home again. I took him to the neighbours to feed him, but he died four days later.'

Danilo Dolci, The Outlaws of Partinico

### The death of a shepherd

When I last saw Martha Ierat, then in her eighty-second year, she gave me the following account of her Tommy's end.

He continued shepherding up to the age of seventy-eight. One Sunday, early in the afternoon, when she was ill with an attack of influenza, he came home, and putting his crook aside said, 'I've done work.'

'It's early,' she replied, 'but maybe you got the boy to mind the sheep for you.'

'I don't mean I've done work for the day,' he returned. 'I've done for good – I'll not go with the flock no more.'

'What be saying?' she cried in sudden alarm. 'Be you feeling bad – what be the matter?'

'No, I'm not bad,' he said. 'I'm perfectly well, but I've done work.' And more than that he would not say.

She watched him anxiously but could see nothing wrong with him; his appetite was good, he smoked his pipe, and was cheerful.

Three days later she noticed that he had some difficulty in pulling on a stocking when dressing in the morning, and went to his assistance. He laughed and said 'Here's a funny thing! You be ill and I be well, and you've got to help me put on a stocking!' and he laughed again.

After dinner that day he said he wanted a drink and would have a glass of beer. There was no beer in the house, and she asked him if he would have a cup of tea.

'Oh, yes, that'll do very well,' he said, and she made it for him.

After drinking his cup of tea he got a footstool, and placing it at her feet sat down on it and rested his head on her knees; he remained a long time in this position so perfectly still that she at length bent over and felt and examined his face, only to discover that he was dead.

And that was the end of Tommy Ierat, the son of Ellen. He died, she said, like a baby that has been fed and falls asleep on its mother's breast.

W. H. Hudson, *A Shepherd's Life*

### 'Death, be not proud'

Death, be not proud, though some have called thee
Mighty and dreadful, for, thou art not so;
For those whom thou thinkst thou dost overthrow,
Die not, poor Death, nor yet canst thou kill me.
From rest and sleep, which but thy picture be,
Much pleasure, then from thee much more must flow;
And soonest our best men with thee do go –
Rest of their bones, and soul's delivery!
Thou'rt slave to fate, chance, kings and desperate men,
And dost with poison, war, and sickness dwell;
And poppy or charms can make us sleep as well
And better than thy stroke. Why swell'st thou then?
    One short sleep past, we wake eternally,
    And Death shall be no more: Death, thou shalt die!

John Donne

### 'Even such is time'

The French manuscript from which this poem has been taken records that: 'These verses following were made by Sir Walter Ravleigh the night before he dyed and left att the Gate howse.' The spelling has been modernised.

Even such is time, which takes in trust
Our youth, our joys, and all we have,
And pays us but with age and dust:
Who in the dark and silent grave
When we have wandered all our ways
Shuts up the story of our days.
And from which earth and grave and dust
The Lord shall raise me up I trust.

### Don't go

I moaned and avoided taking you for your regular walks,
I hated to prepare that revolting meaty food.
I never found time to brush your black coat
But why, Queeny, did you run into the road?

I slammed the front door mumbling, 'Now where's that dog?'
There directly in front of me you lay.
Your eyes staring up to the cloudless sky.
Your jaws jarred open showing off yellow teeth.

Blood was pouring from the deep wounds.
Your once well-controlled ears flopped hopelessly into the
    shocking liquid,
Your nose, no more moist, but dry and hard.
I stepped forward shaking, my eyes filling with tears.

Then again I looked towards your body
You were twitching and whimpering, proving that you
    still had the thread of life.
A massive great lump appeared in my throat,
I started to cry.

I reached your body and crouched beside you,
Now, you were stiff, not uttering a sound.
I whispered, 'Queeny, don't go,'
Yet I recognised your death.

Patricia Buck, 15

# Praise

This section amplifies that on 'The Riches of the World'. Ancient Egyptians, Indians, Jews, Christians and Muslims, together with people who have no literature, are all moved by the impulse to praise – God, the Creator, the Sun, Mother Earth . . . Over a span of 3,500 years and in widely separated countries the terms in which they have done so are often similar, for the feelings that moved them are common to human beings. (The last item shows what praise should not be.)

*Further reading*: Psalm 107; C. M. Bowra, *Primitive Song*; Helen Gardner, *Faber Book of Religious Verse*; Willard R. Trask, *The Unwritten Song*; Walter de la Mare, 'The Scribe'; Gerard Manley Hopkins, 'Pied Beauty'.

## Hymn to Aten

This is part of the hymn to the sun, as the one true god, probably by Akhenaten, who came to the throne of Egypt in 1375 B.C.

All cattle rest upon their pasturage,
The trees and the plants flourish,
The birds flutter in their marshes,
Their wings uplifted in adoration to thee.
All the sheep dance upon their feet,
All winged things fly,
They live when thou hast shone upon them.
The barques sail up-stream and down-stream alike.
Every highway is open because thou dawnest.
The fish in the river leap up before thee.
Thy rays are in the midst of the great green sea.

Creator of the germ in woman,
Maker of seed in man,
Giving life to the son in the body of his mother,
Soothing him that he may not weep,
Nurse (even) in the womb,
Giver of breath to animate every one that he maketh!
When he cometh forth from the womb on the day of his birth,

Thou openest his mouth in speech,
Thou suppliest his necessities.
When the fledgling in the egg chirps in the shell
Thou givest him breath therein to preserve him alive . . .

He goeth about upon his two feet
When he hath come forth therefrom.
How manifold are thy works!
They are hidden from before [us]
O sole God, whose powers no other possesseth.
Thou didst create the earth according to thy heart

While thou wast alone:
Men, all cattle, large and small,
All that are upon the earth,
That go about upon their feet;
[All] that are on high
That fly with their wings.
The foreign countries, Syria and Kush,
The land of Egypt,
Thou settest every man into his place,
Thou suppliest their necessities . . .

Translated by J. H. Breasted

### Varuna, the all-knowing God

He knows the path of birds that fly through heaven,
    and, sovereign of the sea,
He knows the ships that are thereon.
True to his holy law, he knows the twelve moons with
    their progeny:
He knows the pathway of the wind, the spreading, high
    and mighty wind;
He knows the gods who dwell above.
Varuna, true to holy law, sits down among his people; he,
Most wise, sits there to govern all.
From thence perceiving he beholds all wondrous things, both
    what hath been,
And what hereafter will be done.

The Rig Veda

### A canticle of the sun

O Most High Almighty Good Lord God, to Thee belong praise, glory, honour, and all blessing.

Praised be my Lord God with all His creatures, and specially our brother the Sun, who brings us the day, and who brings us the light; fair is he and shines with a very great splendour. O Lord, he signifies to us Thee.

Praised be my Lord for our sister the Moon, and for the stars which He has set clear and lovely in heaven.

Praised be my Lord for our brother the Wind, and for air and cloud, calms and all weather by the which Thou upholdest life in all creatures.

Praised be my Lord for our sister the Water, who is very serviceable unto us and humble and precious and clean.

Praised be my Lord for our brother Fire, through whom thou givest us light in the darkness: and he is bright and pleasant and very mighty and strong.

Praised be my Lord for our sister the Earth, the which doth sustain us and keep us and bringeth forth divers fruits – and flowers of many colours and grass.

Praised be my Lord for all who pardon one another for His love's sake, and who endure weakness and tribulation; blessed are they who shall peaceably endure – for Thou, O Most Highest, shall give them a crown.

Praised be my Lord for our sister the death of the body, from which no man escapeth . . .

St Francis


### A mighty River

Lord, Thou art like a mighty River, All-knowing, All-seeing,
And I like a tiny fish in Thy vast waters,
How shall I gauge thy depths?
How shall I reach thy shores?
Wherever I go, I see Thee only,
And when snatched out of Thy Waters I die of separation.
I know not the fisher,
I see not the net
But flapping in my agony I call upon Thee for help.

O Lord Who pervadeth ALL things,
In my fallibility I thought Thou wert far away,
But no deed I do can ever be out of Thy sight;
Thou Who art All-Seeing, all things Thou seest:
I am not worthy to serve Thee,
Nor do I glory in Thy Name.

Thy gifts are my portion,
There is no other door
To which I may go;
This then is the humble prayer
of thy servant, Nanak:
Accept my mind and my body
As devoted unto Thee.

The Lord is near, the Lord is afar,
The Lord is in the mean between these two extremities;
He watcheth His Creation,
He hears His Creation, for He is the Creator;
Nanak, whatever the Lord wills,
That cometh to pass.

> Sikh hymn

### Song to the rainbow

Khwa! Ye! O! Rainbow, O Rainbow!
You who shine on high, so high,
Above the great forest,
Among the black clouds,
Dividing the black sky.

Beneath you have overturned,
Victor in the struggle,
The thunder which growled,
Which growled so strongly in its wrath.
Was it angry with us?

Among the black clouds,
Dividing the dark sky,
Like the knife which cuts a too ripe fruit,
Rainbow, rainbow!

He has taken flight,
The thunder, the man-killer,
Like the antelope before the panther,
He has taken flight,
Rainbow, rainbow!

Mighty bow of the hunter on high,
Of the hunter who chases the herd of clouds,
Like a herd of frightened elephants,
Rainbow, tell him our thanks.

Tell him: 'Do not be angry!'
Tell him: 'Do not be provoked!'
Tell him: 'Do not kill us!'
For we are very frightened,
Rainbow, tell it to him.

Gabon Pygmy song


### For birds

I listen with reverence to the birdsong cascading
At dawn from the oasis, for it seems to me
There is no better evidence for the existence of God
Than in the bird that sings, though it knows not why,
From a spring of untrammeled joy that wells up in its heart.
Therefore I pray that no sky-hurled hawk may come
Plummeting down,
To silence the singer, and disrupt the Song.
That rhapsodic, assured, transcending song
Which foretells and proclaims, when the Plan is worked out,
Life's destiny: the joyous, benign Intention of God.

Arab chieftain


### The responsibility

We are on retreat. Very cold morning, about 8° above. I left for
the woods before dawn, after a conference on sin. Pure dark sky,
with only the crescent moon and planets shining: the moon and
Venus over the barns, and Mars over in the west over the hills and
the fire tower.

Sunrise is an event that calls forth solemn music in the very depths of man's nature, as if one's whole being had to attune itself to the cosmos and praise God for the new day, praise Him in the name of all the creatures that ever were or ever will be. I look at the rising sun and feel that now upon me falls the responsibility of seeing what all my ancestors have seen, in the Stone Age and even before it, praising God before me. Whether or not they praised Him then, for themselves, they must praise him now in me. When the sun rises each one of us is summoned by the living and the dead to praise God.

Thomas Merton, *Conjectures of a Guilty Bystander*

### Miracles

Why, who makes much of a miracle?
As to me I know of nothing else but miracles,
Whether I walk in the streets of Manhattan,
Or dart my sight over the roofs of houses towards the sky,
Or wade with naked feet along the beach just in the edge
   of the water,
Or stand under trees in the woods,
Or talk by day with anyone I love,
Or sit at table at dinner with the rest,
Or look at strangers riding opposite me in the car,
Or watch honey-bees busy around the hive of a summer
   fore-noon,
Or animals feeding in the fields,
Or birds, or the wonderfulness of insects in the air,
Or the wonderfulness of the sundown, or of stars shining
   So quiet and bright,
Or the exquisite delicate thin curve of the new moon in
   spring;
These with the rest, one and all, are to me miracles. . . .

Walt Whitman

### The matchless deed

Strong is the horse upon his speed;
Strong in pursuit the rapid glede,*

Which makes at once his game:
Strong the tall ostrich on the ground;
Strong through the turbulence profound
    Shoots xiphias† to his aim.

Strong is the lion – like a coal
His eye-ball – like a bastion's mole
    His chest against the foes:
Strong, the gier-eagle on his sail,
Strong against tide, the enormous whale
    Emerges as he goes.

But stronger still in earth and air,
And in the sea, the man of prayer;
    And far beneath the tide;
And in the seat to faith assigned,
Where ask is have, where seek is find,
    Where knock is open wide . . .

Glorious the sun in mid career;
Glorious the assembled fires appear;
    Glorious the comet's train:
Glorious the trumpet and alarm;
Glorious the almighty stretched out arm;
    Glorious the enraptured main.

Glorious the northern lights astream;
Glorious the song, when God's the theme;
    Glorious the thunder's roar:
Glorious hosanna from the den;
Glorious the catholic amen;
    Glorious the martyr's gore:

Glorious – more glorious is the crown
Of Him that brought salvation down
    By meekness, called thy Son:
Thou that stupendous truth believed,
And now the matchless deed's achieved,
    DETERMINED, DARED, and DONE.

      Christopher Smart, from *A Song to David*

      *glede*: kite    †*xiphias*: sword-fish

### Psalm for vigour

For hardness of rock
And sharpness and coldness of steel,
For strength of wind
And power of pounding seas,
For blinding downpour of rain,
Sharp biting of frost,
Give thanks to the maker of these.

For the wild seabird's wail
And marshbird's clamour,
The roar of a waterfall's leap from the chasm's brim,
Drumming of thunder, orchestrated splendour,
Praise the creator of all:
Praise Him.

Myra Kendrick.

### The choir-boy

And when he sang in choruses
   His voice o'er topped the rest,
Which is very inartistic,
   But the public like that best.

Anonymous

# II

# Challenge

# Wealth

Ancient Egyptian, Hebrew and Chinese writers and Christians of several periods agree on the dangers of wealth. As they see it, it brings unhappiness, strife, envy, danger, insolence and isolation; it is almost impossible for the rich to lead a normal life and to sympathise with other people. Two poems from the world's richest country offer clear insights, and both are suited to reading aloud. The first is Edgar Lee Masters' 'Washington McNeely' (p. 39); the second is Richard Eberhart's 'An Old Fashioned American Business Man'. In the latter. the business man speaks of his ruthlessness, his cynicism, and his rejection of human feelings, and ends with these words:

> I taught ruthlessness by example
> And hard work and steadfastness.
> Now that the hated grave approaches
> I wish for the love I could not give.

*Further reading*: Ecclesiastes 5:9-20; Ecclesiasticus 13:2-7, 21-3 (the New English Bible version of the Apocrypha is best); St Matthew 19:16-22; St Luke 12:22-34; 'The Loan sharks', a version of St Matthew 11:15-19; Bernard Kops, 'There's a woman down the road,' in *The Dream of Peter Mann*; D. H. Lawrence, 'A Played-out Game', 'The Root of Our Evil'; Louis MacNeice, 'Property'; Carl Sandburg, pp. 98-100 in *Harvest Poems*; J. K. Galbraith, *The Affluent Society*.

## Riches with vexation

Remove not the landmark at the boundaries of the arable land,
Nor disturb the position of the measuring-cord;
Covet not a cubit of land,
Nor throw down the boundaries of a widow . . .
Beware of throwing down the boundaries of the fields,
Lest a terror carry thee off . . .
Better is poverty in the hand of the god
Than riches in a storehouse;
Better is bread, when the heart is happy,
Than riches with vexation.

Egyptian: from *The Teaching of Amenemope*, about 1300 B.C., translated by J. M. Plumley

### Treasure and trouble

Remove not the old landmark, and enter not into the
fields of the fatherless;

For their redeemer is mighty; he shall plead their cause
with thee.

Better is little with the fear of the Lord than great
treasure and trouble therewith.

Better is a dry morsel, and quietness therewith, than a
house full of sacrifices with strife.

Book of Proverbs, from Chs. 23, 15 and 17

### A millionaire looks back

I made me great works; I builded me houses; I planted me vineyards. I made me gardens and orchards, and I planted trees in
them of all kinds of fruits. I made me pools of water, to water
therewith the wood that bringeth forth trees. I got me servants
and maidens, and had servants born in my house: also I had great
possessions of great and small cattle above all that were in Jerusalem before me. I gathered me also silver and gold, and the
peculiar treasure of kings and of the provinces. I got me men
singers and women singers, and the delights of the sons of men,
as musical instruments, and that of all sorts.

So I was great, and increased more than all that were before me
in Jerusalem: also my wisdom remained with me. And whatsoever
mine eyes desired I kept not from them, I withheld not my heart
from any joy; for my heart rejoiced in all my labour: and this was
my portion of all my labour.

Then I looked on all the works that my hands had wrought, and
on the labour that I had laboured to do: and, behold, all was vanity
and vexation of spirit, and there was no profit under the sun.

Ecclesiastes 2:4-11

### Wealth breeds insolence

Stretch a bow to the very full,
And you will wish you had stopped in time;

Temper a sword-edge to its very sharpest,
And you will find it soon grows dull.
When bronze and jade fill your hall
It can no longer be guarded.
Wealth and place breed insolence
That brings ruin in its train.
When your work is done, then withdraw!
Such is Heaven's Way.

Tao Te Cheng (c. 400), translated by Arthur Waley in *The Way and Its Power*

## Christ and the financiers

If we look at the Gospels with the firm intention to discover the emphasis of Christ's morality, we shall find that it did not lie at all along the lines laid down by the opinion of highly placed and influential people. Disreputable people who knew that they were disreputable were gently told to 'go and sin no more'; the really unparliamentary language was reserved for those thrifty, respectable, and sabbatarian citizens who enjoyed Caesar's approval and their own. And the one and only thing that ever seems to have aroused the 'meek and mild' Son of God to a display of outright physical violence was precisely the assumption that 'business was business.' The money-changers in Jerusalem drove a very thriving trade, and made as shrewd a profit as any other set of brokers who traffic in foreign exchange; but the only use Christ had for these financiers was to throw their property down the front steps of the Temple.

Dorothy L. Sayers, *Unpopular Opinions*

## Rich people's food

A rich man once came to the preacher of Koznitz.

'What are you in the habit of eating?' the preacher asked.

'I am modest in my demands,' the rich man replied. 'Bread and salt, and a drink of water are all I need.'

'What are you thinking of!' the rabbi reproved him. 'You must eat roast meat and drink mead, like all rich people.' And he did not let the man go until he had promised to do as he said. Later the hasidim asked him the reason for this odd request.

'Not until he eats meat,' said the rabbi, 'will he realise that the poor man needs bread. As long as he himself eats bread, he will think the poor can live on stones.'

Martin Buber (trans.), Tales of the Hasidim

## Robbing God

Another reason why rich men shall so hardly enter into the kingdom of heaven? A vast majority of them are under a curse, under the peculiar curse of God; inasmuch as in the general tenor of their lives, they are not only robbing God, continually embezzling and wasting their Lord's good, and by that very means corrupting their own souls, but also robbing the poor, the hungry, the naked; wronging the widow and fatherless; and making themselves accountable for all the want, affliction, and distress which they may but do not remove. Yea, doth not the blood of all those who perish for want of what they either lay up, or lay out needlessly, cry against them from the earth? O what account will they give to Him who is ready to judge both the quick and the dead!

John Wesley, Sermon XXIII

## The King and the beans

The mighty King Mahmud of Ghazna, out hunting one day, was separated from his party. He came upon the smoke of a small fire and rode to the spot, where he found an old woman with a pot.

Mahmud said: 'You have as guest today the monarch. What are you cooking on your fire?'

The crone said: 'This is a bean stew.'

The emperor asked her: 'Old lady, will you not give me some?'

'I will not,' she said, 'for this is only for me. Your kingdom is not worth what these beans are worth. You may want my beans, but I don't want anything you have. My beans are worth a hundred times more than all you have. Look at your enemies, who challenge your possessions in every particular. I am free, and I have my own beans.'

The mighty Mahmud looked at the undisputed owner of the beans, thought of his disputed domains, and wept.

Attar of Nishapur, from Idries Shah, The Way of the Sufi

### Poor rich people

I have heard of a man who was angry with himself because he was no taller; and of a woman who broke her looking-glass because it would not show her face to be as young and handsome as her next neighbour's was. And I know another, to whom God had given health, and plenty; but a wife, that nature had made peevish, and her husband's riches had made purse-proud. Because she was rich, and for no other reason, she wished always to sit in the highest pew of the church; and since she could not have it, she egged her husband on to struggle for it. At last she got her husband into a law-suit with an obstinate neighbour, who was just as rich, and had a wife just as peevish and purse-proud; and this law-suit produced more hostility, and actionable words, and more quarrels and law-suits – both of them, you remember, were rich, and fond of getting their own way. Well, this wilful purse-proud law-suit lasted the life of the first husband; and then his wife vexed and blamed, and blamed and vexed, till she too blamed and vexed herself into the grave. Thus the wealth of these poor rich people was cursed into a punishment, because they lacked meek and thankful hearts – for only these can make us happy.

I know a man that had health and riches, and several houses, all beautiful and ready furnished. He would often trouble himself and his family by moving from one to another; and when he was asked by a friend why he moved so often he replied that it was to find content in one of them. However his friend knew his character and told him that if he wanted to find contentment in any of his houses, he must leave self behind – for contentment would never be found except in a meek and quiet soul.

Adapted from Izaak Walton

### Hospitality for horses

When the two brothers, Elimelech and Sussya, were yet wandering about from place to place, poorly dressed and still unknown to fame, they halted at nightfall in Lodmir. The only one who gave them any attention was a poor man, Rabbi Aaron, who welcomed them in his home. A few years later when they had become famous, they arrived in Lodmir with a fine carriage and horses. The richest man in town invited them to stay in his house, but they went instead to the house of Rabbi Aaron, where they had stayed before. When the rich man protested, they replied:

'We are the same persons to whom you paid no attention when we stopped here a few years ago. Hence it appears that it is not so much we who are welcome, as our coach and horses. We are entirely willing to accept your hospitality for the horses.'

L. I. Newman (trans. and ed.), *The Hasidic Anthology*

## Filling up hell

When the Son of God was nailed on the Cross and died, He went straight down to hell from the Cross, and set free all sinners that were in agony. And the devil groaned, because he thought that he would get no more sinners in hell. And God said to him, then, 'Don't groan, for you shall have all the mighty of the earth, the rulers, the chief judges, and the rich men, and shall be filled up as you have been in all the ages till I come again.'

Russian peasant legend in F. M. Dostoievsky, *The Brothers Karamazov*

## The fur coat

Nasrettin Hodja was a Turkish jester who lived in the fifteenth century; stories about him are still endlessly quoted by modern Turks. According to one story he was once invited to a wedding, to which he went in his rather shabby everyday clothes. No one took any notice of him, so he slipped out and went home. There he changed into his best robe and put on an impressive fur coat – and returned to the wedding. He was received with attentive politeness and invited to sit at the most important table, where he was plied with the finest food. Smiling to himself he began to slip the sleeve of his fur coat over the edge of the dishes, saying, 'Have some of this, my fur coat.'

The host and guests nearby were alarmed at this behaviour, and one of them said, 'What are you doing, Hodja Effendi?'

'Oh, I was just inviting my fur coat to have something to eat, since it has been received with such deference and respect! When I came in a few minutes ago without my fur coat, no one took any notice of me. But now I've come back with it on, I'm being overwhelmed with attention.'

# Poverty

Extreme poverty is a cage that prevents people from living. After Simone Weil and D. H. Lawrence have expressed this in their different ways we have examples of the grinding poverty that dehumanises and breeds crime, and of the result of ignorance and stiffly-working bureaucracy even in a welfare state. The economic remedy is suggested by Buddhist teaching – by no means impractical, as it is sometimes thought to be.

*Further reading*: Ecclesiasticus 13:21-3; Bertolt Brecht, 'Song of the Patch and the Overcoat', in *Compact Poets*; Po Chü-i, 'The Charcoal-seller', in *170 Chinese Poems*, translated by Arthur Waley; W. H. Davies, 'When I had money'; Brian Frost, 'Sit Down Strike', in *Citizen Incognito*; C. Day Lewis, 'A Carol'; Edward Thomas, 'The Owl'; Thomas Traherne, 'Poverty'; B. Malamud, short stories; Henry Mayhew, *London Street Life*, ed. R. O'Malley.

## The horror of poverty

Luxury itself represents beauty for a whole class of men. It provides surroundings through which they can feel in a vague fashion that the universe is beautiful, just as St Francis needed to be a vagabond and a beggar in order to feel it to be beautiful. Either way would be equally legitimate if in each case the beauty of the world were experienced in an equally direct, pure and full manner; but happily God willed that it should not be so. Poverty has a privilege. That is a dispensation of Providence without which the love of the beauty of the world might easily come into conflict with the love of our neighbour. Nevertheless, the horror of poverty – and every reduction of wealth can be felt as poverty, even its failure to increase – is essentially a horror of ugliness. The soul which is prevented by circumstances from feeling anything of the beauty of the world, even confusedly, even through what is false, is invaded to its very centre by a kind of horror.

Simone Weil, *Waiting on God*

## Poverty

The only people I ever heard talk about My Lady Poverty
were rich people, or people who imagined themselves rich.
Saint Francis himself was a rich and spoiled young man.

Being born among the working people
I know that poverty is a hard old hag,
and a monster, when you're pinched for actual necessities.
And whoever says she isn't, is a liar.

I don't want to be poor, it means that I am pinched.
But neither do I want to be rich.
When I look at this pine-tree near the sea,
that grows out of rock, and plumes forth, plumes forth,
I see it has a natural abundance.

With its roots it has a grand grip on its daily bread,
and its plumes look like green cups held up to the sun and air
and full of wine.

I want to be like that, to have a natural abundance
and plume forth, and be splendid.

D. H. Lawrence, *Complete Poems*

## Difficult to be human

Danilo Dolci is one of the great men of our time, as an example
to the rest of us. He lives and works among the poorest in Sicily,
bringing justice, hope and a livelihood to people sunk in ignorance,
crime and despair. His efforts to get them to organise, develop
their independence and truly to live have been opposed by the
law, the church and organised crime in the form of the Mafia.
The extracts below come from a short book of vivid sketches of the
Sicilians who need the help Dolci gives; Vincenzo was in prison
awaiting the hearing of his appeal against a four-year sentence
for stealing grass – 'but they keep having to put it off because the
injured party, the man whose grass I picked, never turns up.'

When I was about five I began looking after the animals. They
weren't our animals, though: my father was hired by the year. I
don't know how many months there are in a year. I don't know if
I'm seventeen or nineteen. We could get someone to write home
and ask them to look at the birth certificate. I can count up to

fifty, but I don't understand money because I've lived all my life out in the countryside. I never went into the village, and I never saw another human being, except my father every now and again. My mother doesn't understand money either, and she can't even count. I used to cook herbs and roots and wild cabbages, and eat them.

If you can't get any work, you eat wild greenstuff and herbs. Hunger will drive a man to anything. Sometimes you can't even see out of your eyes. Some people kill themselves – people do terrible things out of hunger. But if only you've got work, you've got everything. If a man's paid a decent wage, he'll do his work properly, and learn to mix with other people, and be able to talk to them without quarrelling. But when there's no work – I tell you, we just go about killing each other.

I stayed out in the countryside and looked after the animals. I used to sleep in the straw. I didn't get undressed at all, I just burrowed into the straw with all my clothes on. I didn't have any blankets or anything. Often I had bare feet, and there were times when I had nothing at all to eat. I was always crawling with lice – covered with them. My boss wouldn't let me drink the cows' milk – if I did he used to beat me with a stick. In the morning I had bread and curds, and in the evening bread and onions, or bread and olives when there were olives.

> Then he described how he would eat raw slugs and snails, and catch and cook over a fire, lit with flints, rabbits, wild dogs and hedgehogs.

Once I had a kid and a lamb that used to follow me around wherever I went. I used to share my bread with them sometimes – if I had any myself, that is . . . I got to love that kid and that lamb terribly . . . And then I had to sell the kid to buy food . . . For two days after that I couldn't eat at all for thinking about it, and I couldn't stop crying.

Danilo Dolci, *For the Young*

## Slavery in Yorkshire

Richard Oastler draws attention to the slavery to which poverty has reduced the people of England, and compares it with the slavery of Negroes in the West Indies. He addresses his Member of Parliament:

True, Sir, the horrors of black slavery were bad enough – its history was indeed a bloody one – but that monster spared its little ones! It did not work even the male adult slaves with such cruel rigour as the white slave master works his youth victims, the little free-born English slaves!

Our ears were never shocked by the recital of such sorrows as the factory child can tell. We never heard from India that little female blacks were worked from twelve to fourteen hours a day – were never allowed to sit, or to recline their weary bodies! and if sleep stole on them unawares, there were no monsters there, to curse and swear, and call them 'idle bitches'! No human fiend so cowardly as to strike them with his heavy fist, and kick them with his clogged feet! Sleep was never driven from the little infant slaves at labour, by a bucket of cold and chilling water, thrown upon their drowsy frames! The strap, with nails inserted, to make it cut the flesh, was not applied to the female children of the slaves, to goad them on to labour! They were not knocked down by billy rollers, and sometimes killed because they were sleepy, after having laboured sixteen hours a day! . . . These little black slave children were not liable, when drowsy at their work, to be suddenly seized by the inanimate machine, and to be dashed lifeless on the spot where they had just laboured! We did not hear of the little slave children being driven, by their unbearable sufferings, deliberately to seek refuge in the grave and absolutely to commit suicide! We heard not of their parents being idle, and unemployed, carrying the little sufferers to and from their labour! or of their dying as they paced their weary journey homewards! We heard not of their widowed mothers feeding the infants who earned their food, weeping in anguish over them because they had not strength to eat, but as their mothers fed them fell asleep, between each spoonful of porridge their mother gave them, with the food unmasticated in their mouths! We heard not then of the waking slumbers on a widow's pillow, the nightly portion of the mother of a factory child – who, as she sleeps, or seems to sleep, still dreads the approach of early morn, which opens daily to new scenes of anguish; her first duty . . . is to rouse her child from sleep, to break her rest, to tell her that the bell is ringing, and she must rise, not to worship her Maker, not to improve her mind, not to gambol in the fields, but to earn her own and her parents' food . . .

Richard Oastler, *Slavery in Yorkshire*, a pamphlet (1831)

### Hearts are trumps

The Rabbi at Poznan received a letter from a poor woman, a mother of six small children, in which she stated that she had no money to feed her large family, inasmuch as her husband was ill. She added that undoubtedly more money changed hands at one card game at the club of merchants than her husband earned in an entire year.

The Rabbi therefore went to the club and asked permission to join the game. As soon as he sat at the table, and the cards were dealt, the Rabbi threw the woman's letter on the table, and called: 'Hearts are trumps.'

The merchant read the letter, and gave to the Rabbi all the money in the bank of the game, so that he might present it to the destitute woman.

L. I. Newman (trans. and ed.), *The Hasidic Anthology*

### Poverty means crime in England

All children in those days [the middle of the nineteenth century] were regarded as the 'possessions' of their parents – indeed the law of the land took that view – and bad parents and other evil people regarded girls as more valuable 'possessions' than boys. This was because they were weaker, more easily bullied, thrashed and cowed, more effective for begging purposes and less readily suspected as thieves. There might certainly be found fewer girls wandering on their own, but their fate in the hands of evil 'owners' – bad parents or strangers – could be infinitely worse.

In his daily paper, for instance, Dr Barnardo read such stories as these: two little girls, brought before a magistrate charged with being found begging, wept bitterly – explaining that unless they went out begging and brought home money their mothers would beat them and give them nothing to eat. While they begged in one place the mother of one of them went off on a begging round of her own, carrying a baby, returning from time to time to the children to collect what coppers they had gathered in. Most of the proceeds went on gin.

Late one night, crossing Westminster Bridge, a man heard a six-year-old girl pleading in terror with a great hulking fellow who was threatening to throw her over the parapet into the water. This passer-by reported what he had heard to a policeman, who went to investigate. It was discovered that the bully was a professional beggar of notoriously evil habits, an idle, dissolute vagabond who for years had been in the habit of buying children whom he took on tramps round the country for begging purposes. Nothing could be discovered about the parents of the little girl. Perhaps she had been stolen, perhaps she had been sold.

In the year 1878 a six-year-old girl was the subject of a question in the House of Commons, because she had been sent to Newgate Prison. Her offence was passing counterfeit money on the instructions of her mother. The Minister ruled that the magistrate who had sent the child to prison had done a perfectly proper thing, but that it would be rather better for such very young children to be sent to the workhouse instead of prison!

Gladys Williams, *Barnardo: the Extraordinary Doctor*

### Poverty means homelessness

The following case typically illustrates the kind of problems which arise when an individual is socially and financially handicapped (i.e. with limited income and resources) and personally handicapped (in this case mental illness). It also shows that neither a realistic nor a desirable choice of accommodation was available.

*Case A*  A widow in her forties with a background of admissions to mental hospitals and continuing out-patient care was evicted from her unfurnished flat, apparently for rent arrears, while in hospital. She was therefore not present at the court hearing. The bailiffs had come the previous day to take possession and in doing so had locked up both her personal possessions and furniture in her flat.

The night before seeking help she had spent in a waiting room at Waterloo Station. She needed immediate shelter – none was available through either the local welfare department or through the mental welfare department. The only possible shelter available would be in a hostel.

The next day she was seen again, very distressed and also upset about her hostel experience. She felt it had been a dreadful place and she had been expected to bath and wash her hair before being admitted. The police had taken her there from the railway station.

She was helped by the Citizens' Advice Bureau to make practical arrangements to ensure that her widow's pension continued, and that arrangements could be made whereby she could get a grant to cover the cost of storing her possessions. Her name was entered on the local authority housing list, and her landlord was approached on her behalf to allow her access to her belongings.

What is significant is that although this woman, because of sickness, was particularly handicapped and therefore highly vulnerable to housing difficulties, only one type of emergency accommodation was available for her, and this increased her anxieties and impaired still further her capacity to cope. Furthermore, no constructive plans for her future could be put into effect to reverse her social situation – one in which she was homeless and without realistic hope of finding further unfurnished accommodation. It is a small step from the present stage to one in which her personal possessions and furniture are lost to her altogether.

John Grieve and others, *Homelessness in London*

### Cause of poverty

Poverty is the cause of immorality and crimes such as falsehood, theft, violence, hatred, cruelty, etc. Kings in ancient times, like governments today, tried to suppress crime through punishment ... This method can never be successful. Instead the Buddha suggests that, in order to eradicate crime, the economic condition of the people should be improved: grain and other facilities for agriculture should be provided for farmers and cultivators; capital should be provided for traders and those engaged in business; adequate wages should be paid to those who are employed. When people are thus provided for with opportunities for earning a sufficient income, they will be contented, will have no fear or anxiety, and consequently the country will be peaceful and free from crime.

Because of this, the Buddha told lay people how important it is to improve their condition. This does not mean that he approved of hoarding wealth with desire and attachment, which is against his fundamental teaching, nor did he approve of each and every way of earning one's livelihood. There are certain trades like the production and sale of armaments, which he condemns as evil means of livelihood.

From the examples given above, one could see that the Buddha considered economic welfare as requisite for human happiness, but that he did not recognise progress as real and true, if it was only material, devoid of a spiritual and moral foundation. While encouraging material progress, Buddhism always lays stress on the development of the moral and spiritual character for a peaceful, happy and contented society.

W. Rahula, *What the Buddha Taught*

### The big rug

That so many of the poor should suffer from cold what
    can we do to prevent?
To bring warmth to a single body is not much use.
I wish I had a big rug ten thousand feet long,
Which at one time could cover up every inch of the
    City.

Po Chü-i (772-846), translated by Arthur Waley

### Awkward questions

Theologians and philosophers have no special expertise at all, except in the asking of awkward questions, and a certain acquaint-once with the answers that men in past generations have offered themselves. But this is precisely why they are needed now, to ask us what our objects are, what we are aiming at, what sort of society we really want to create, what sort of people we really want to be.

The point I am trying to make is excellently illustrated by the moon landings. Nothing could demonstrate better the capacity of human beings to accomplish what they set their hearts on, and their equal capacity to set their hearts on the wrong things. The moon landings, are, of course magnificent. But to the under-privileged, undernourished two-thirds of the world they are a magnificent irrelevance. We are clever enough to reach the moon, but not sensible enough to share out the world's resources with anything approaching equity.

Henry McKeating, *Living with Guilt*

### Poverty and blindness

A blind man is a poor man, and blind a poor man is;
For the former seeth no man, and the latter no man sees.

Friedrich von Logau

### The only acceptable form

To a people famishing and idle, the only acceptable form in which God can dare appear is work and promise of food and wages.

M. K. Gandhi

### Getting used to it

There was a young man who had inherited the riches of several generations of his family. Not knowing how to deal with money, he spent it rashly, and within a year he had nothing left.

And then there happened what is usual in such cases: all his friends deserted him, and he was at his wits' end till he remembered the elderly sage, Nasrettin Hodja. He sought out the old man and told him what had happened. 'What is to become of me, Hodja Effendi? I have no friends and no money left.'

'Don't worry, my son,' advised the Hodja. 'You'll soon be right again. You just wait and see.'

The young man cheered up at once. 'Do you mean that I am going to get rich again?'

'No, that isn't at all what I meant. What I meant was that you will get used to being poor and friendless.'

Turkish story

# Colour

The passages that follow present extremes of feeling, from the active contemptuous suppression and exploitation that make up the policy of South Africa and Rhodesia to cold detachment. A book such as this is not concerned with programmes, which considered in a short space would inevitably be dangerously simplified, but with attitudes, including those that will lead to improvement. The poems by James Kirkup and J. H. Thomas point to such attitudes, and the second one though so brief contains a most relevant truth: even in South Africa people of any colour can regard each other as human beings in a context, such as working at a common task, which does not require them to feel hostility.

*Further reading*: St Matthew 12 (46-50) and 22 (35-40); Cosmas Desmond, *The Discarded People*; G. Moore and Ulli Beier, *Modern Poetry from Africa*; A. Luthuli, *Let My People Go*; Dennis Brutus, *Letters to Martha*; E. L. Masters, 'Shack Dye', in *Spoon River Anthology*; Roy Fuller, 'The White Conscript and the Black Conscript', in *Penguin Modern Poets*, No. 18.

### Slavery in America

American slavery is distinguished from all other forms of slavery because it dehumanized the Negro. In Greece and Rome, for example, slaves preserved dignity and a measure of family life. Our institution of slavery, on the other hand, began with the break-up of families on the coasts of Africa. Because the middle passage was long and expensive, African families were torn apart in the interest of selectivity, as if the members were beasts. In the ships' holds, black captives were packed spoon fashion to live on a voyage lasting two to six months in a space for each the size of a coffin. If water ran short, or famine threatened, or a plague broke out, whole cargoes of living and dead were thrown overboard. The sheer physical torture was sufficient to murder millions of men, women and children. But even more incalculable was the psychological damage.

Of those families who survived the voyage, many more were ripped apart on the auction block as soon as they reached American shores. Against this ghastly background the Negro family began family life in the United States. On the plantation the institution of legal marriage for slaves did not exist. The masters might direct mating, or if they did not intervene, marriage occurred without sanctions. There were polygamous relationships, illegitimacies, abandonment and the repetitive tearing apart of families as children, husbands or wives were sold to other plantations. But these cruel conditions were not yet the whole story . . .

The liberation from slavery in 1863, which should have initiated the birth of a stable Negro family life, meant a formal legal freedom, but as Henrietta Buckmaster put it, 'Four million black people in the South owned their skins and nothing more.' With civil war still dividing the nation, a new inferno engulfed the Negro and his family. Thrown off the plantations, penniless, homeless, still largely in the territories of their enemies and in the grip of fear, bewilderment and aimlessness, hundreds of thousands became wanderers. For security they fled to Union Army camps that were unprepared to help. One writer describes a mother carrying a child in one arm, a father holding another child, and eight other children with their hands tied to one rope held by the mother, who struggled after Sherman's army and travelled hundreds of miles to safety. All were not so fortunate. In the starvation-induced madness some Negroes killed their children to free them of their misery.

Martin Luther King, *Chaos or Community?*

### The runaway slave

The runaway slave came to my house and stopt outside,
I heard his motions crackling the twigs of the woodpile,
Through the swung half-door of the kitchen I saw him limpsy and
    weak,
And went where he sat on a log and led him in and assured him,
And brought water and fill'd a tub for his sweated body and
    bruised feet,
And gave him a room that enter'd from my own, and gave him
    some coarse clean clothes,
And remember perfectly well his revolving eyes and his awkward-
    ness,

And remember putting plasters on the galls of his neck and
   ankles;
He stayed with me a week before he was recuperated and passed
   north,
I had him sit next me at table, my fire-lock leaned in the corner.

       Walt Whitman

### Except for the Negroes

One hundred years of delay have passed since President Lincoln
freed the slaves, yet their heirs, their grandsons, are not fully free.
They are not yet free from the bonds of injustice. They are not
yet freed from social and economic oppression, and this nation,
for all its hopes and all its boasts, will not be fully free until all
its citizens are free. We preach freedom round the world, and we
mean it, and we cherish our freedom here at home, but are we to
say to the world and, much more importantly, to each other that
this is a land of the free except for the Negroes; that we have no
second-class citizens except for the Negroes; that we have no class
or caste system, no ghettoes, no master race except with respect
to Negroes?

       President J. F. Kennedy, *Address to the American People* at the
       White House on 11 June 1963

### Black shadows

    in memory of Martin Luther King

I can hear from New Orleans
Funeral jazz.

Memphis, Nashville, Atlanta
Blow horns of grief.

All the jazzbands of the South
Trumpet your murder.

What has our world become? Are we all mad?
Good man, forgive us.

When I look at your calm face, I see
The courage of your death.

It is our shame
That such courage was necessary.

You knew that bullet from a white rifle
Would one day seek your flesh.

You walked in danger every day
With sad humility.

Not wishing to be chosen thus by fate,
Yet knowing you must drink that cup.

Your wife and children weep now
For a man who was more than a father.

You were a father to all of us.
We did not know it till you were gone.

Now we understand your gentleness
Too late. Why must we hate?

Why must we kill our brothers?
Why suffer this shame of wars upon wars?

You who told us war and violence are bad
Died of war and violence.

You were a man of peace and mercy,
But received neither.

Let us raise no monument to you
But human peace and mercy.

What has our world become? Are we all mad?
Good man, forgive us.

James Kirkup

### Worse than serfdom

I suppose that anyone who has lived in Sophiatown – or one of
the 'Native Urban Areas' of South Africa – could write a book
about the pass laws and nothing else. It would be a very terrible
book, but it would not cause the slightest ripple of disturbance
in South Africa. And, of course, there are not so very many
Europeans who have had the privilege of living in Sophiatown.

No. It is not so much the hatreds, the fears, the brutalities which are the basic social evils of our country – it is the ignorance, and with it the acceptance of the evil.

So I could tell you the story of Jonas – of Jonas who was home from school for his summer holidays and who was arrested one morning and charged with being a vagrant. When I heard about it it was already late afternoon and by the time I had reached the police station he was waiting in the yard before being locked up for the night. 'Where was your school pass?' I asked him. 'They tore it up.' Luckily the waste-paper basket was still there: luckily I found the pass – in four pieces. And when I refused to surrender it to the sergeant in the charge office, I was arrested myself. But at least I had the satisfaction, a few days later, of a complete apology, cap in hand (and not metaphorically either) of the commandant who later became Commissioner of the South African Police. Yet, for every boy like Jonas whose arrest was reported to me, there are a thousand who have no one to care: a thousand, for whom a torn-up pass might mean ten days in prison, the loss of a job, the beginning of that swift and terrible journey into crime. For another consequence of the pass laws – a consequence known to every intelligent South African at all interested in penal reform – is that it leads to an absolute contempt for the law. If it is a crime to be in the street without a pass, without a bit of paper in your pocket: and if that crime is punished automatically with a fine that you cannot pay or a sentence of imprisonment – well, why not commit a crime that is worth while? You stand as good a chance of getting away with it as the next man. You stand the chance, too, of making something for yourself. The magistrates' courts, every day of the week, are crowded with pass-offenders. Even if, as is generally the case, the magistrate is a just man and an honest, he has no alternative but to administer the law as if he were in care of a turnstile at a football ground. 'Charge' 'Section 17 – vagrancy.' 'Guilty or Not Guilty?' The prisoner looks bewildered; the interpreter impatiently snaps out the words again in Xosa or Zulu or Tswana. 'Not Guilty,' and a fumbling attempt to explain why his pass is out of order: a brief intervention by the official who attends the court on behalf of the pass-office authorities. 'Thirty shillings or ten days.' The prisoner is bundled down the steps to the cells, and another takes his place.

His case has taken two minutes. If he is fortunate a friend will pay his fine. If not he will remain in prison till his sentence, and very probably his job, is finished. And so a vast force of able-bodied men is, in fact, compulsorily confined in a building supported to house half the number: of men who, for the most part, are simply technical offenders, but who are in South Africa criminals.

In spite of a most excellent and, incidentally, expensive Commission on Penal Reform, whose report included the most damning exposure of the dangers to society inherent in the system I have described, the system still goes on. The Report of the Commission was tabled in the House of Assembly over five years ago, but nothing so constructive as penal reform can find a place on the agenda . . . particularly when it concerns the effects of the Pass Laws on crime. It is not crime that matters, it is control. And to have that control: to know that any native can be stopped in the street and questioned: can be turned out of bed at night or in the early hours of the morning: can be arrested first and questioned afterwards – to have that control, why, that is proof of supremacy: that is 'baasskap': that is our solution of the racial problem. At least it is part of our solution. The only serious defect in the system is that the real criminal always has a pass – he can buy one for £15 any day of the week, and it is well worth the money.

But all these things have been said, have been written about, have been part of every discussion on racial problems for the past twenty years and more. And even though it may happen only once in a while, every European citizen of Johannesburg experiences sooner or later the arrest of his houseboy or the disappearance of his cook. It is part of the pattern of life. And, on the whole, it is a pattern which is wonderfully acceptable – for it carries within it the great idea, of course: of power, of supremacy for whiteness. It is so comforting, too, to the conscience to be able to go and pay the fine, or sign the admission of guilt and bring Jim back again to his job in the kitchen. It must (surely it must) fill his heart with gratitude to the missus or the baas, to know that they will take that trouble: to know that they really want to be just. ('But I must remember to deduct 30s. from his wages this month, to cover the fine.')

Every citizen experiences it. But every African boy lives in the shadow of it from the moment he leaves the classroom behind him for the last time. And it does not matter, either, what position in society he reaches. He is never beyond its grasp. It is indeed the shadow – his own black shadow that is with him always. So a young African priest, a member of my own Community just back from his ordination in England, and wearing the habit of his order, was arrested and handcuffed at nine o'clock one morning and brought to me at the priory because he had no pass. The European policeman who brought him was a tall, callow, gawky youth who stood in front of me, hands on hips, cigarette drooping wet from the corner of his lips. And when I was angry and turned him off the premises he said: 'I'll arrest every bloody kaffir in this place if they break the law . . .' And when, that afternoon, I went to report the incident to the Commandant he was furious that the story had already appeared in the afternoon edition of the *Star*. But I have long learned that my only weapon in such cases is publicity, and so I explained to him. I was not surprised at his anger, either, for I had expected it. But I was surprised, when, after a few minutes of fierce rebuke (we were alone in his office), the Commandant suddenly said, gently and wearily: 'As a matter of fact, Father, you are quite right. If I could leave the force tomorrow I would. But it's my livelihood and my profession. So what can I do?'

One of the terrible things that happens, after a while, to all of us in South Africa is the acceptance, unwilling or otherwise, of a situation which cannot be justified on any moral principle, but which is so universal, so much a part of the whole way of life, that the struggle against it seems too great an effort. And this attitude affects the African as much as the European. For so long have passes been woven into existence itself; for so long has it been the right and the duty of every policeman to stop, to search and to question anyone, anywhere at any time, that the resistance and the will to resist have almost died. And I am as guilty in this respect as anyone else. For, although I get angry when the boys in my school are arrested on their way to the shops (and what school-master in any country would need to spend hours of his time issuing and collecting passes?), yet I pay their 'admission of guilt'. I become part of the system. I accept it. Even, sometimes, I get exasperated when one of my own employees fails to produce the necessary papers – exasperated because it will mean for me, as well as for him, hours of wasted and profitless effort. It is easier to obey: easier to be guilty of connivance at an evil, easier, even to oneself, 'Well, perhaps it's not so bad after all . . . it's the law . . . they're used to it . . . why worry?'

'Why worry?' If the instances I have quoted were just isolated moments, the kind of things that happen in any society through the failure of the individual, or the weakness of that human nature which is the basis of society, perhaps there would be no need to worry. At least the Christian in this world is warned often enough to regard himself as a 'stranger and pilgrim . . . with no continuing city'. And the priest – if he is even feebly aware of his purpose and function – knows well enough that man is a frail and wayward creature.

Unfortunately it is not the isolated cases of cruelty, of sordid motive or of plain stupidity which made the indictment of the pass laws so grave a matter. It is the whole foundation upon which they, like the policy of apartheid itself, rest. For, basically, the underlying assumption of the pass laws is just this – that discrimination is justifiable and even commendable if it ensures the permanent superiority of our race over another: if it ensures control, 'baasskap', domination.

And from this assumption, or perhaps as the origin of it, there flows that other even more deadly thing – the depersonalisation of man. This most characteristic modern phenomenon – the submerging of the individual in the mass – is nowhere more manifest than in South Africa to day. And it is nowhere more clearly or more devastatingly exampled than in the operation of the pass laws. A man is a native. A native must carry a pass. A pass is his title to existence, his guarantee (so slender and so precious) of temporary freedom, his only excuse to authority for being where he is and doing what he does. In other words, man is reduced, because he is black, to an integer, a fingerprint in a file, a thing rather than a person. But a sentient thing, threatened and fearful because of the shape of the society of which he is a part.

I pray God I may never forget nor weary in fighting against it, for it seems to me that as a Christian, and above all as a priest, my manward task is always and everywhere the same: to recognise in my brother more than my brother: more even than the personality and the manhood that are his: my task is to recognise

Christ Himself. And I cannot, therefore, stand aside when it is He whom men treat contemptuously in the streets of the city.

'I was in prison, and ye visited me not . . .'

Trevor Huddleston, *Naught for Your Comfort*

## Hypocrite

She spoke of heaven
And an angelic host;
She spoke of God
And the Holy Ghost;
She spoke of Christ's teachings
Of man's brotherhood;
Yet when she had to sit beside a Negro once –
She stood.

Elizabeth Hart

## The number eight

The number eight
Rolled to a stop by the concrete shelter.
A negro embarked,
And people stared for a split second
Then returned to their talking,
But more quietly.
He sat beside a woman, who turned away
To stare with cold embarrassment through the window.
Suddenly a little boy turned in his seat,
And asked, 'Why are you black?'
' 'Cos I spend a lot of time in the sun,' replied the negro.
No one laughed.
He smiled.
Then sat, ashamed.

Alan Rodgers, 17

## Martin Luther King

Martin Luther King, the grandson of a slave, was a Baptist pastor who received a Nobel Peace Prize and was murdered at the age of thirty-nine.

The reasons for his award and for his early death were the same. Against his will he came to be regarded as the champion of the negroes in the Southern States of America for voting rights, fair pay and the right to use the same schools, buses, restaurants and places of entertainment in the same way as whites. He preached and practised non-violence not because it was easier than violence, but because it was right; and so he guided the student movement for racial integration along non-violent lines. It was this movement that adopted as its Marseillaise a negro church hymn 'We Shall Overcome' – originally sung by black textile workers, its new popularity among students has made it world-famous.

He was imprisoned a score of times on trumped-up charges, and for years lived under the shadow of assassination, as his supporters were beaten up and sometimes killed. For example in the early days pairs of black and white volunteers would board interstate buses in order to desegregate them. In her book on her husband Mrs King writes: 'This . . . seemed to infuriate southern reactionaries beyond all reason. Bands of raging whites attacked the buses . . . The riders were hauled off, beaten up and thrown into jails. In Anniston, Alabama, a roaring crowd attacked a Greyhound bus, smashed its windows with iron bars, punctured the tyres, and threw an incendiary bomb into it. The bus was destroyed.' In 1965 black men and women and a few whites started a demonstration march in favour of voting rights. Again in Mrs King's words:

'The marchers were ordered to halt and given two minutes to turn back. At the end of less than a minute of dead silence, during which the troops put on gas masks, Major John Cloud shouted, "Troopers, forward!" His sixty men charged into the defenceless column of demonstrators, clubs swinging. Twenty people were knocked flat; others knelt to pray. The troopers charged again, throwing tear-gas grenades. Then Sheriff Clark shouted to his mounted posse, "Get those goddam niggers! Get those goddam white niggers!" The horsemen charged . . . Sixteen people were hospitalised; fifty others were hurt.'

He was probably influential in the election as President of J. F. Kennedy, whose administration got a civil rights bill through Congress in 1963, but success did not make him less humble. He did not want to be idolised, disliked travelling in expensive cars, and forbade his own organisation to reproduce his picture. Moderate men like Martin Luther King make it possible for changes and reforms to be effected without violence, but when they are murdered, as he was, or ruthlessly suppressed as they are in South Africa, a backward step is taken which makes it difficult for social and economic justice to be established without a phase of bloodshed.

Editor

## Colour

Red, black, white or yellow,
What does it matter?
If you work,
You are my brother.

J. H. Thomas, *Doves for the Seventies*

### Trevor Huddleston

The priest who defied a government

Trevor Huddleston, born at Bedford in 1913, comes of a religious family; one of his ancestors was the Restoration priest who received Charles II into the Roman Catholic church on his deathbed. He had the conventional education of the middle class at Lancing and Oxford, and it was during his Oxford vacations, spent with the hop-pickers in Kent, that he became interested in missionary work. After visits to Ceylon and India he was ordained, and for two and a half years was curate of a railway parish at Swindon. Then he joined the Community of the Resurrection, an English monastic order, and in 1943 was sent to be priest in charge of the Community's mission in Sophiatown, a depressing shanty town on the outskirts of Johannesburg, now destroyed. During the thirteen years he spent there his name became a legend; his immense success with black Africans was due to his sense of humour and joy in life, both of them characteristic of Africans.

Naturally his work for Africans caused him to be regarded as a danger to a government, some members of which supported the Nazis in the 1939–44 war. A cabinet minister said of him publicly that 'in the middle ages people like Huddleston would have been burned at the stake'. And a senior official of the South African government wrote to Huddleston 'that he deserved to be drummed out of the country or strung up from the nearest lamp-post as a renegade'.

The police persecuted him by searches, and by photographing his audiences row by row. He has been accused of being an agitator, to which his reply was 'The Christian always is, if he is true to his calling'. But an African student said of him 'I wish he was black'.

After a spell as bishop in another part of Africa, he became Bishop of Stepney, and since his return he has taken part in many interviews and given many lectures and broadcasts. His aim always is to get world opinion to make its voice heard before South Africa is lost to Christianity, for in his words 'Racialism in any form is an attack not only on the nature of man, but upon the nature of God himself.'

Editor

# Violence

Obviously the topic forms part of other themes presented here – War and Prisons for example. The extracts that follow lay bare the roots of some forms of violence – racial, economic, and political; and other remaining passages point to some causes and remedies, including those that lie within the individual.

*Further reading*: Proverbs 16:1-18; St Matthew 5; Aldous Huxley, *Ends and Means*; John Singleton, *Violence*; Robin Richardson, *Frontiers of Inquiry*; Carl Sandburg, 'Wilderness', in *Collected Poems*.

### How violence erupts

Colin McGlashan is a freelance journalist who won the Journalist of the Year award in 1968.

I'd like to describe an incident typical of many I saw while riding with police in Chicago, a riot that didn't quite happen. It began when an armed night-watchman detained a Negro youth he thought had stolen a car battery. Five other Negro youths stood watching. Two detectives arrive in a crime car. Before getting out, they call a squad car to help them. They know this is a dangerous area. The previous night, after a similar incident, a mob wrecked a supermarket.

When the squad car arrives, one of the detectives is pointing a riot shotgun at the youths; the other has drawn his revolver. The suspect refuses to be arrested, and backs away. He shouts that he is innocent. He looks very frightened. He is probably afraid the police will beat him up, also that he will lose face with his friends if he submits.

Two officers grab him and put him in a car. Suddenly, he struggles free and jumps out. One detective thrusts an automatic rifle against his chest. In defiance, the youth rips open his shirt and shouts 'Go on, kill me, you obscenity!' The detective starts slamming the muzzle of the rifle into the boy's stomach. The other five youths rush forward and start fighting. They are unarmed. The police have a total of eight revolvers, a rifle and a shotgun. However, they radio a general 'officer needs assistance' call.

Inside one or two minutes, this produces seven squad cars, sirens wailing, each with two policemen. None of them knows what has happened, merely that a colleague is in trouble in a bad area. They can easily identify the 'enemy' – the enemy is black. They rush in waving revolvers, shotguns and truncheons. There is now a general melée: both sides are shouting obscenities. A crowd is gathering. The six youths, several covered in blood, are thrown into squad cars and all the police leave.

Rumours are now spreading fast among the people flocking on to the streets. One version is that the police killed a youth, another that they beat up a Negro girl. Someone is shouting obscenities about 'the pigs!' The members of the local street gang start gathering. Community workers desperately find out what really happened so they can calm the people.

Back at the station, the police are also angry. There is a lot of violent talk, led by one of the sergeants. They decide to deal with the situation by a show of force – a tactic adopted following the 1967 riots. Twenty riot cars are sent out, each with four heavily-armed officers, to patrol the area, the uproar dies down.

As an outside observer, the first thing that came through to me was the fear on both sides. Next was the absence of any attempt at discussion or conciliation; both sides were determined to be strong. Lastly, the stereotypes symbolised by the sub-human epithets; 'pigs' on the one side, 'niggers' on the other.

This incident happened in 1968, and there are two postscripts. The first is that the youth *was* innocent, as the police later admitted. The second is that this summer – following a new pattern becoming common in black neighbourhoods and elsewhere – two white policemen are shot dead from ambush in the same area, perhaps 50 yards away.

> Colin McGlashan, 'The Roots of Violence' in *Christian Action Journal* (February 1971)

### Institutional violence

Chicago is one of the richest cities in the world. Yet one medical research unit has estimated that 600 Negro babies die in Chicago every year from the effects of malnutrition, rat-bites and lead poisoning. The lead poisoning comes from chewing the old, flaking paint and plaster in the ghetto apartment blocks; it causes brain damage or death. There is, of course, a law compelling landlords to repair crumbling walls. There is also a law forbidding them to allow the temperature of an apartment to fall below 65 degrees in winter. When I lived in Chicago, on the South Side, which is the largest Negro ghetto in the world, a baby died from exposure a few streets away. The landlord had dismantled the heating system in an attempt to force the family out. He was fined a hundred dollars or so.

This is institutionalised violence, and it wears many, many faces. As Mrs Coretta King, widow of Dr Martin Luther King, once described it: 'Starving a child is violence. Suppressing a culture is violence. Neglecting school children is violence. Punishing a mother and her family is violence. Discrimination against a working man is violence. Ghetto housing is violence. Ignoring medical needs is violence. Contempt for poverty is violence. And the lack of will-power to help humanity is a sick and sinister form of violence.'

Institutional violence is the city authorities in Chicago refusing to apply for a Federal programme of free food parcels for the hungry. It is also white policemen looking the other way when a Mafia drug peddler sells heroin to teenagers. More subtly, it is black children going to a school where the teachers and the textbooks reflect a white suburban world from which they are excluded, a world that tells them that they are failures, written off. Perhaps most savagely, it is psychological castration.

There is a familiar domestic situation where the husband who has had a bad day at the office comes home and vents his anger and frustration on his wife. He says all the things he couldn't say to his boss.

To the black man living in an American ghetto, *every* day is a bad day at the office. If he has a job, it's often below his abilities and badly-paid. The average earnings of Negro university graduates are lower than those of whites who only went to high school.

When he comes home, he is confronted with the evidence of his powerlessness, his failure as a man. There is the area in which he is forced to live. There are the potholed streets he can't get the authorities to mend, the overflowing dustbins he can't get them to clear. He can't get the landlord to repair his home. He can't afford proper medical care for one of his children, who is ill. (For all its expensive and sophisticated medicine, the United States is 18th in the league table of nations in infant mortality). He can't pay the hire-purchase on his furniture; he can't stop the local white-owned supermarket selling rotten meat; he can't stop despising himself.

It is no accident that a recurrent theme in black American culture is that expressed by singer Otis Redding, when he promises his girl anything in the world if only she will give a little *respect* when he comes home.

Institutional violence like this produces three kinds of violence: violence in the family; violent crime against members of the same community; finally, *political* violence, when – as so eloquently described by Frantz Fanon, writing about Algeria – the violence of the community turns outwards against the common enemy.

All three are common in the Third World as in the American ghettoes. It is as though some force has created a special breed of man, who can be found in Algiers, or in Harlem, Calcutta or Kingston, Jamaica; Mexico City or Manilla. What they have in common is powerlessness. And a man who is powerless is a violent man, however meekly he is forced to behave. He dreams of being strong and attacking his enemies. The greater the powerlessness, the greater the violence. Slave revolts and jail riots are noted for their savagery.

White America calls them riots. Young black America calls them rebellions. How do they start? Most have happened after trivial incidents involving white policemen. Watts and Newark after minor traffic offences, Detroit following a raid on an unlicensed club.

Colin McGlashan, in the article quoted above

### Diluting responsibility

Tolstoy replies to the objection that Christ's teaching is visionary because it is not natural to man:

Who will deny that to murder or torture, I will not say a man, but to torture a dog or kill a hen or calf is contradictory and distressing to man's nature? (I know people who live by tilling the land, and who have given up eating meat merely because they had themselves to kill their own animals.) Yet the whole structure of our lives is such that each man's personal advantage is obtained by inflicting suffering on others, which is contrary to human nature. Not a single judge would decide to strangle with a rope the man he condemns to death from the bench. Not a single magistrate would make up his mind himself to take a peasant from his weeping family and shut him up in prison. None of our generals or soldiers, were it not for discipline, oaths of allegiance, and declarations of war, would, I will not say kill hundreds of Turks and Germans and destroy their villages, but would even decline to wound a single man. All this is done thanks to a very complex state and social machinery the purpose of which is so to distribute the responsibility for the evil deeds that are done that no one should feel the unnaturalness of those deeds. Some men write the laws; others apply them; a third set drill men and habituate them to discipline, that is to say, to senseless and implicit obedience; a fourth set – the people who are disciplined – commit all sorts of deeds of violence, even killing people, without knowing why or wherefore. But a man need only, even for a moment, free himself mentally from this net of worldly organisation in which he is involved to understand what is really unnatural to him.

A. Tolstoy, *What I Believe*

## 'If you've never been . . .'

If you've never been in a concentration camp
If you've never been tortured
If your best friend has never denounced you
And you've never crawled out of a heap of corpses
After surviving execution by a miracle
If you don't know the theory of relativity
And tensor calculus
If you can't do a ton on a motorbike
If you've never killed the girl you love on orders from outside
If you can't build transistor radios
If you've never been in any kind of mafia
And can't forget yourself and shout 'hurray' with the others
If you can't hide from an atomic blast in two seconds
If you can't dress at the expense of food
If five of you can't live in five square metres
And don't even play basketball
– Man, the 20th century's not for you!

Artyomy Mikhailov, translated by Keith Bosley, in *Russia's Other Poets*

## Molecular biology

The organic chemistry of human blood
Is, I am told, an extremely complex business.
The individual atoms of each molecule
Stretched end to end
Would reach halfway across the solar system.

Moreover, its geometry in three dimensions
Permits it to be held in quite a modest compass.
Three hundred millions (to the power of two or three)
Subsist in a single droplet on your finger.

Maybe, if they realised what ingenuity
Had gone into the details of its composition,

Human beings would be a little less careless
About the spilling of it.

Quintin Hogg

### Is violence ever justified?

There are certainly instances when injustice cries out to heaven
for repayment. When an entire population, deprived of very es-
sentials, live in such dependence that all initiative and responsibility are forbidden them, as well as all possibility of cultural progress and participation in social and political life, great is the
temptation to rise up with violence against such offences against
human dignity.

We are aware, nevertheless, that revolutionary aggression – except when men are subjected to clear and prolonged tyranny which
could constitute a grave threat to basic human rights and seriously
harm the common good of a country – can give rise to new in-
justices, provoke fresh disorders and cause further ruin. One must
not fight a genuine evil at the price of incurring worse disasters.

Pope Paul VI, in an Encyclical

### Unlived life

It would seem that the amount of destructiveness to be found in
individuals is proportionate to the amount to which expansiveness
of life is curtailed. By this we do not refer to individual frustra-
tions of this or that instinctive desire but to the thwarting of the
whole of life, the blockage of spontaneity of the growth and expression of man's sensuous, emotional, and intellectual capacities.
Life has an inner dynamism of its own; it tends to grow, to be
expressed, to be lived. It seems that if this tendency is thwarted the
energy directed towards life undergoes a process of decomposition
and changes into energies directed towards destruction. In other
words: the drive for life and the drive for destruction are not
mutually independent factors but are in a reversed interdepen-
dence. The more the drive towards life is thwarted, the stronger
is the drive towards destruction; the more life is realised, the less
is the strength of destructiveness. Destructiveness is the outcome
of unlived life.

Erich Fromm, *The Fear of Freedom*

### The cure for football violence

As a nation we are churning out kopsful of school leavers, hopeless, hellbent for nowhere, begging for a cause to latch in to – crying out for the promised land. And in the footsteps of Wesley and Booth stride Stein and Shankly and Revie, down from the mountain. 'Thou shalt have no gods but our gods' they cry, scattering multi-coloured photos, car stickers, pop records and similarly stupefying paraphernalia about them. In tiny bedrooms shrines are erected and players are beatified at the flash of a £200,000 cheque. But footballers, bless 'em, aren't divine. They can't always produce the goods and while their bewildered and betrayed disciples rampage, up in the boardrooms the wailing and gnashing of teeth is wondrous to behold.

We must be aware of our responsibilities as a society for the creation of soccer's violent minority. The solution isn't in dogs – or the cat for that matter. The phenomenon hasn't arisen from the lowering of moral standards or the relaxing of discipline or the lack of parental control. It is the result of one soul-crushing disease – frustration. Any sec. mod. teacher will describe it to you. He watches its cancerous growth, sucking away the kids' vibrance, perverting their ideals and diverting their natural exuberance and energy in truculent aggression. When he finally kicks them out at 16 they head straight for the terraces. 'No respect for anything' we mutter in the comfort of the stands as they mass and sway to their anthems.

No respect? When has anyone shown them any respect? Society certainly doesn't. Its standards and its values aren't designed for them. So why should they respect them? If we really want to go a long way towards removing violence from both in and out of football we can make a start tomorrow. And it's not with cock-eyed measures like bigger jail sentences, the birch, or even manacles beneath the stands. We must begin to revolutionise our education system, revising its priorities, directing them towards the individual, his aspirations, emotional needs, his talents and his dreams . . . and not the demands of a system which requires only his labour.

Things would soon start to happen. For a start, those expert exploiters of youthful energies, 'pop' music and 'pop' soccer, would soon feel the pinch. As the kids found their feet and them-

selves they'd see them for the phoney myths they are and revert
to regarding football as only a game. But as things stand these are
only pipe dreams. The realists tell us that it's not just the game,
it's a multi-million pound enterprise. And as such it has the right
to exploit the market to the hilt. And if that market didn't exist
we'd all go up the spout . . . or so they say . . .

They can't have their cake and eat it, those soccer barons and
all their camp followers . . . the publishers, sports manufacturers,
mug makers, pennant painters, peanut vendors and rosette sales-
men. Soccer mania is a two-edged sword and we'd have a happier,
healthier and safer place to live in if both were permanently
blunted.

> Colin Welland, from 'How to Disarm the Football Hooligans', in
> *The Observer*

### Thug

School began it.
There he felt
the tongue's salt lash
raising its welt

on a child's heart.
Ten years ruled
by violence left him
thoroughly schooled,

nor did he fail
to understand
the blow of the
headmaster's hand.

That hand his hand
round the cosh curled.
What rules the classroom
Rocks the world.

> Raymond Garlick, *Doves for the Seventies*

**Playing it cool**

How to Keep out of a Fight

Playing it cool
Will keep you out of a fight without losing face.
But shooting your mouth off
    Will get another guy all teed up,
        And he will climb all over you.
Sometimes what a square says may be right
    And he may know something.
        It might be a good idea to listen.
A hood is always sounding off,
    Mostly about things he don't know anything about.
God is everywhere keeping watch
    And he is ready to help you.
But a fool don't pay no attention –
    He thinks
        Nobody knows anything but him.

> Proverbs 15:1-7, version by young American delinquents, re-
> corded by Carl Burke in *God is for real, Man*

**Avoid hatred and anger**

> The verses below come from a collection of the sayings of Buddha
> that contains the essence of the Buddhist faith.

'He abused me, he beat me, he defeated me, he robbed
me' – in those who harbour such thoughts hatred will never
cease.

'He abused me, he beat me, he defeated me, he robbed
me' – in those who do not harbour such thoughts hatred
will cease.

For hatred does not cease by hatred at any time: hatred
ceases by love – this is an old rule.

The world does not know that all must come to an end
here; but those who know it, their quarrels cease at once.

Let a man leave anger, let him forsake pride . . .

He who holds back rising anger like a rolling chariot,
him I call a real driver; other people are but holding the
reins.

Let a man overcome anger by love, let him overcome evil
by good; let him overcome the greedy by liberality, the
liar by truth!

Beware of bodily anger, and control thy body! Leave the
sins of the body, and with thy body practise virtue!

Beware of the anger of the tongue, and control thy tongue!
Leave the sins of the tongue, and practise virtue with thy
tongue!

Beware of the anger of the mind, and control thy mind!
Leave the sins of the mind, and practise virtue with thy
mind!

> The Dhammapada, about 477 B.C., translated by F. M. Müller

# War

The mass media give us all the war they can, but the effect is both
to trivialise what they report and to desensitise their viewers and
readers. Young people are often fascinated by war, and up to a
point this reflects their coming to terms with it; they see and hear
much about it at secondhand, but not often in a way that helps
them.

The section sheds light on the character and futility of war. A
resounding opening would be the lament of David for Jonathan
in Book II of Samuel, 1:19-27, for even the poem of a warring
people seems to realise the futility of warfare, with its tolling
refrain 'How are the mighty fallen' and the significant conclusion.
The Brecht poem mentioned below, cool and detached about those
who looted Europe and about their fate, also reads well aloud.
Prose and other poems convey the indiscriminate cruelty and
inefficiency of war.

*Further reading*: II Samuel 1:19-27; Micah 4:1-5; I John 3;
poems of Wilfred Owen, Isaac Rosenberg, Anthony Rye, and
Siegfried Sassoon; Denise Levertov, 'What Were They Like', in

*The Sorrow Dance* and in *Voices*; J. Michie, 'Dooley is a Traitor', in *Possible Laughter* and in anthologies; 'In a Huai village after the fighting', in *Penguin Book of Chinese Verse*; Richard Eberhart, 'The Fury of Aerial Bombardment'; 'Brotherhood of Men', in anthologies and *Collected Poems*; Bertolt Brecht, 'What Did the Soldier's Wife Receive?', in *Compact Poets*.

### Where was God?

And where was God
When war broke out?
Where was he, not to hear them shout?
Where was God when aloud they cried?
Where was God when they died?
Where was God when blood was spilt?
Was he asleep
Or was he awake
Or was he fighting the devil?

D. Williamson, 15

### The meaning of Hiroshima

In approaching Hiroshima there is nothing to suggest that one is about to enter a place of tragedy. We turned inward from the coast, bumped over a trestle bridge, and were suddenly in the town. To me the sight was something of an anti-climax. I had already seen so much of desolation, and this place looked no different from the rest; nor was I much impressed when I recollected that in this city alone one hundred thousand people had died. This reaction, which is very general, was not, I think, due to any lack of emotional sensitivity; it would seem that the human mind is incapable of comprehending things on such a scale. The experience of a single human being who has survived can affect one much more than the evidence of mass extinction. It was not until much later that I realised the full significance of Hiroshima, the consequences of which will remain with its destroyers long after the city has been rebuilt. We can never make amends; and to talk of giving Japan the benefits of western civilisation is to disregard the mockery. Material help we can of course give; but I doubt if we ever find any moral justification for the decision to abandon the principles for which the war was fought. That, it now seems to me, is what we really did on 6th August 1945. There was not even the excuse of military expedience; the war was, for all practical purposes, already won and would have ended in a matter of weeks. Tokyo and the other Japanese cities can have had not the slightest doubt of this. Moreover, the official report of the United States Strategic Bombing Survey has made it quite clear that the atomic bomb dropped on Hiroshima had no effect whatever on the military progress of the war. In no circumstances is it possible to justify the further use of this weapon, only three days later, on the port of Nagasaki.

John Morris, *The Phoenix Cup*

### Nations are made of people

There is no such thing, in the sense of its being a real living entity, as 'England' or 'Germany'. There are so many Englishmen or Germans, an individual, every one of them, like you or me: these, and the physical territory in which they live, the mountains and valleys and pastures, the cities and townships and villages, of their several homelands. That is all: unless you care to add the non-human creatures, every one of them again individual, and the works of art and historical monuments and ruins – and something which we call the national character or maybe the national tradition, something we have to be terribly careful about in our thinking and feeling. For 'the national character', also, is devoid of independent existence: it does not float about in a vacuum, divorced from the solid people who partake of or exhibit it. In brief, there is nothing but the physical landscape – and men. Individual men, individual Englishmen or Germans: for to talk about 'The English' or 'The Germans' is only another way of talking about 'England' or 'Germany'.

Now the fact that we have forgotten all this (or have never realized it, owing to our easy acceptance, from earliest child-hood, of labels that personalize abstractions) allows us to commit such unspeakable abominations against our fellow human beings as might otherwise have been impossible. I remember being most vividly aware of this during the second world war. Night after night that dreadful voice on the air, either coldly matter-of-fact or with the faintest ring of triumph in it, advised us that so many tons of high-explosive or incendiary bombs had been dropped on Germany. Germany! They had been dropped, not on that mythical entity, not on that figment of the imagination or rather of thought-lessness, but on German men, German women and German children (never mind the cities and houses, the bridges and docks): living torches, forty thousand of them, had been flinging themselves into the canal at Hamburg, fathers and mothers had been spattered with the brains of their children. But that was not how we thought of it, if we thought at all: we were doing it, as the announcer told us, to 'Germany'. And *we* were not doing it either, for the personalization works both ways: 'England' was doing it.

Victor Gollancz, *The New Year of Grace*

### Effects of warfare

The American writer Mary McCarthy visited Vietnam to report on the war; and here she describes how a group of German volunteers, the Catholic Knights of Malta, took her to some of the refugee camps set up by the American forces fighting there. First they showed her a cowshed used as a leper hospital for seventy people, and then in her words:

The Knights of Malta gave me a quick tour of the Hue madhouse, known as the 'psychiatric wing' of the hospital. Here conditions were more terrible than in the leprosarium. A few sane children of insane mothers were roaming about the dirty, untended female ward: a depressive sat howling on her bed. Rusty torn screens, fly-spattered walls. There was no sign of a nurse; no patients had been washed or combed. At the entrance to the dangerous ward, old tin cans were lying in the mud. A madman stared out of a peephole; the place was locked, and no one could go in because, at least today, there were no attendants . . .

Seeing the Hue leper house and this bedlam somewhat readied me for the 'temporary' refugee camps I was shown the next day. The first of these camps was about six months old and contained 1,500 people. As I walked with a German doctor through rows of communal huts, we came to a stagnant duck pond, about ten or fifteen feet wide, in which some ducklings in fact were swimming amid floating tin cans and other refuse. This was the water facility – the *only* water for drinking, washing, and cooking, to supply 700 people. On the other side of the camp, which was divided in

two, was another duck pond, perhaps slightly larger, which served
the remaining 800. There were no sanitary facilities of any kind;
we saw women and children squatting; garbage was strewn in
front of the huts, which had earth floors and inflammable old
straw roofing . . .

The misery and squalor of that first camp is hard to convey,
partly because the eye shrinks from looking too closely at it, as
though out of respect for the privacy of those who are enduring
such disgrace. The women stood massed in their doorways to
watch us pass; some approached the doctor and asked for medicine. But mostly they just watched us, defying us, I felt, to watch
*them*. Skin diseases were rampant, especially among the children,
diseases of the scalp, eye diseases, gross signs of malnutrition, bad
teeth, stained by betel-chewing and reduced, often, to stumps.
Most of the refugees (as usual women and children and a few
grandfathers) were dirty – how could they wash? . . . The daily
food allowance of ten piastres per family, supplemented irregu-
larly by a little rice, said the doctor, was below subsistence require-
ments. Some families had begun straggly little vegetable patches
– mainly lettuce plants, cabbage and mustard – that were growing
haphazardly amidst the refuse. This would help a little. And there
were a few pigs, chickens, and the ducklings. But except for this
spasmodic gardening, there was no work for these people – no
fields they could plant, nothing . . .

Of all the Westerners I saw in Vietnam, only these German
boys and girls (in particular, Wolfgang, the electrician) showed
gentleness and compassion with the small, fragile Vietnamese,
stroking a leper's shoulder, respectfully helping an old man
scramble up to show the writing on a Buddhist altar. 'You gimme
cigarette!' a very small Vietnamese boy said to a young Knight,
who refused and added in apology: 'It is not good that they smoke.'

Mary McCarthy, *Vietnam*

### The Buddhist view of war

The world today lives in constant fear, suspicion, and tension.
Science has produced weapons which are capable of unimaginable
destruction. Brandishing these new instruments of death, great
powers threaten and challenge one another, boasting shamelessly

that one could cause more destruction and misery in the world than the other.

..They have gone along this path of madness to such a point that, now, if they take one more step forward in that direction, the result will be nothing but mutual destruction along with the total destruction of humanity.

Human beings in fear of the situation they have themselves created, want to find a way out, and seek some kind of solution. But there is none except that held out by the Buddha – his message of non-violence and peace, of love and compassion, of tolerance and understanding, of truth and wisdom, of respect and regard for all life, of freedom from selfishness, hatred and violence.

You will say this is all very beautiful, noble and sublime, but impractical. Is it practical to hate one another? To kill one another? To live in eternal fear and suspicion like wild animals in a jungle? Is this more practical and comfortable? Was hatred ever appeased by hatred? Was evil ever won over by evil? But there are examples, at least in individual cases, where hatred is appeased by love and kindness, and evil won over by goodness. You will say that this may be true, practicable in individual cases, but that it never works in national and international affairs. People are hypnotised, psychologically puzzled, blinded and deceived by the political and propaganda usage of such terms as 'national', 'international', or 'state'. What is a nation but a vast conglomeration of individuals? A nation or state does not act, it is the individual who acts. What the individual thinks and does is what the nation or the state thinks and does. What is applicable to the individual is applicable to the nation or the state. If hatred can be appeased by love and kindness on the individual scale, surely it can be realised on the national and international scale also. Even in the case of a single person, to meet hatred with kindness one must have tremendous courage, boldness, faith and confidence in moral force. May it not be even more so with regard to international affairs? If by the expression 'not practical' you mean 'not easy', you are right. Definitely it is not easy. Yet it should be tried. You may say it is risky trying it. Surely it cannot be more risky than trying a nuclear war.

W. Rahula, *What the Buddha Taught*

### The other time

He killed a man
In a drunken brawl;
They tried him, hanged him.
That was all.

But he left his wife
Nearly penniless.
She was raven-haired,
She was glamorous,

She had swooned in court,
She had caused a stir.
And the editor of
The *Sunday Blare*,

Aware of his readers'
Appetite
And judging she should
Be worth a bit,

Hurried a snooper
Round to her house
With an offer she thought
Quite fabulous,

If she'd lend her picture,
Lend her name
To story about
Her life with Him.

They'd write it up
From what she said.
Did she understand?
She understood.

'I never had much,
I've still less now,
I need the money.
The answer's No.'

As he rose to go
He noticed a medal,

Mounted and framed,
Above the mantel.

And asked her about it.
Where was it won?
When did he get it?
What had he done?

'Oh, that,' she said.
'They pinned that on
The other time
He killed a man.'

Peter Appleton

### Soldiers

Soldiers who wish to be a hero
Are practically zero,
But those who wish to be civilians,
Jesus, they run into millions.

Anonymous

### No Justafacation

There is just one thing I should like to say, about those monuments
they have erected to the men that fell in cruell and greedy war.
They have put on them 'For God and Cuntry'. The People think
wen they read them words that a good God ment that his human
beins should be murdered for the lust of Nations, and there Greed.
The Bible tell us that he that slay is a murderer, so it is hard to
see that there is a justification for that 'For God and Cuntry',
Every man have a right to live they say. Now they talk about dis-
arment, yet still the cuntrys go on making mashiens for the purpose of murdering there fellow men . . . Stand beside the Mothers
and wives and se there tears, and then read them words, and I say
there is no Justafacation, not for them words.

Written down by an old Norfolk poacher, who had lost a son in
war, recorded in L. Rider Haggard, *I Walked By Night*

## Massive obliteration

We should look with terror at any human activity which makes it impossible for us to perform the works of mercy. War does just that. In times of old, the works of mercy were merely interrupted for the duration of the hostilities. Modern war literally reverses the works of mercy. Rather than feed the hungry, we scorch the earth from which the hungry are fed; rather than clothe the naked, we raze the plants where clothing is manufactured; rather than shelter the shelterless, we destroy, in minutes the shelter that man patiently built for himself and his kind; rather than give drink to the thirsty, we bomb reservoirs serving great cities; rather than heal the sick, we kill them in their beds in homes and hospitals; rather than ransome the captive, we make captives of as many of our opponents as possible. This is the face of modern total war, even of 'conventional' war. Nuclear war, by vaporizing the human being so that he is no more than a shadowy outline on a Hiroshima sidewalk, makes all the works of mercy impossible.

In the United States alone, nearly fifty billion dollars annually goes into the bottomless pit of the nuclear deterrent and that loathsome thing known as overkill. These are the resources that the family of man needs for its health, its educational improvement, its dignity. Here again there is a massive obliteration of the works of mercy, as Pope John XXIII and Pope Paul VI have so eloquently pointed out to the world.

Dorothy Day in *The Catholic Worker*

## No army is the key to peace

A letter arrives stamped with the slogan 'The U.S. Army, key to peace.' No army is the key to peace, neither the U.S. Army nor the Soviet Army nor any other. No 'great' nation has the key to anything but war. Power has nothing to do with peace. The more men build up military power, the more they violate peace and destroy it.

Thomas Merton, *Conjectures of a Guilty Bystander*

# Prison

Prisons have always been cruel places; they represent a form of violence that can damage mind and spirit as well as the body. Some of the cruelty is unintentional, caused by lack of thought, lack of knowledge and lack of imagination; in the case of imprisonment in war or for political reasons at all times it is often intentional. Even when the prisoners are those against whom society needs protection and for whom it is difficult to feel sympathy, it has to be remembered that the punishment falls on relatives and dependants as well as on the man found guilty, and that it may last long after his release.

*Further reading*: Dennis Brutus, *Letters to Martha*; D. J. Enright, 'What became of what's his name?', in *Unlawful Assembly*; Sidney Keyes, 'Europe's Prisoners'; Po Chü-i, 'The Prisoner', in *170 Chinese Poems*, translated by Arthur Waley; F. Villon, 'Epitaph in form of a Ballad', translated by A. C. Swinburne; John Bunyan, *Grace Abounding* (for his own imprisonment); *The Pilgrim's Progress*, Part 1 (for the encounter with Giant Despair); A. Camus, short story, 'The Guest'; Walt Whitman, pp. 649, 650 in *Complete Verses and Selected Prose*; Y. Yevtushenko, *Precocious Autobiography*.

## Elizabeth Fry

In the 1820s it was too easy for the poor and unfortunate to be thrown into prison; employers and the wealthy classes simply had too much power over those who had to work for them. The prisons were foul beyond description and the penalties savage. Among the great reformers was the Norfolk Quaker, Elizabeth Fry, who succeeded in getting the authorities to apply common sense to the horrors of imprisonment and transportation; she found the latter almost as terrible in its effects as the death penalty. This is an account of one of the problems she dealt with:

'Easy migration to a milder climate' was what one member of the House of Lords had called transportation, and he even hinted that criminals rather looked forward to being sent to New South Wales. Perhaps this was why the women in Newgate always got drunk the night before they were taken to the transport which waited at Deptford; they rioted furiously, singing and shouting, breaking windows and smashing furniture. They wreaked the only kind of vengeance that they could think of on the scene of their misery, protesting as best they could at what was to be done to them. The following day, drunk or sober, weary or still resisting, they were put in irons, loaded into open carts, and trundled down to the river while the mob, which must have contained many in danger of a similar fate, hooted and pelted them. When they reached the Thames they were joined by others, who had escaped being drawn through the London streets, but had often suffered in other ways from the casual cruelty of the system. Everyone was anxious to save expense, and so the prisoner might have travelled the length or breadth of England on top of a coach, or have been run into the Thames on a local fishing-smack. The turnkeys who brought them were afraid of the consequences of losing them; as a result they shackled their prisoners, not just with handcuffs, but often with iron hoops about the waist and leg, joined together by chains. When several women had to be sent at once they were sometimes chained together, so that if one of them needed to come down from the top of the coach the whole clanking team was obliged to descend. They brought with them for the voyage what they could carry in a bundle, and in the past no one had cared how little it was; a few had their babies with them; others had seen the last of their children. But what could women expect in a world where Sir Samuel Romilly could record how he was told by a Duke at a dinner party that a private in the Guards, a man sixty years old, had been sentenced to three hundred lashes – and the sentence had been carried out?

John Kent, *Elizabeth Fry*

## from **The Ballad of Reading Gaol**

The vilest deeds like poison weeds
   Bloom well in prison-air:
It is only what is good in Man
   That wastes and withers there:
Pale Anguish keeps the heavy gate,
   And the Warder is Despair.

For they starve the little frightened child
   Till it weeps both night and day:
And they scourge the weak, and flog the fool,
   And gibe the old and gray,
And some grow mad, and all grow bad,
   And none a word may say.

Each narrow cell in which we dwell
   Is a foul and dark latrine,
And the fetid breath of living Death
   Chokes up each grated screen,
And all, but Lust, is turned to dust
   In Humanity's machine.

The brackish water that we drink
   Creeps with a loathsome slime,
And the bitter bread they weigh in scales
   Is full of chalk and lime,
And Sleep will not lie down, but walks
   Wild-eyed, and cries to Time.

But though lean Hunger and green Thirst
   Like asp with adder fight,
We have little care of prison fare,
   For what chills and kills outright
Is that every stone one lifts by day
   Becomes one's heart at night.

With midnight always in one's heart,
   And twilight in one's cell,
We turn the crank, or tear the rope,
   Each in his separate Hell,
And the silence is more awful far
   Than the sound of a brazen bell.

And never a human voice comes near
   To speak a gentle word:
And the eye that watches through the door
   Is pitiless and hard:
And by all forgot, we rot and rot,
   With soul and body marred.

                 Oscar Wilde

### The Southern freedom movement

The southern states of America have always treated negroes as third-class citizens, with severe restrictions on their use of schools, restaurants, buses and cinemas; and when white students organised protests they were beaten up and arrested by the police. Here Bob Zellner of the Student Non-Violent Coordinating Committee relates an experience:

On a Saturday afternoon in February Chuck McDew and I went to visit Dion Diamond, a SNCC field secretary, who was confined in the East Baton Rouge Parish Jail, Louisiana. When told we could not visit Dion, we got permission to bring him some books and fruit. We returned with the articles and were promptly arrested for vagrancy and criminal anarchy, carrying a sentence of ten years at hard labour, and placed under $7,000 bond apiece.

I was cursed and shoved into an open cell block with 65 other white prisoners. The police brought papers to the other prisoners with stories saying that Chuck McDew and Bob Zellner were subversive integrationists and were trying to overthrow the government of the state of Louisiana. They incited the other prisoners, most of them Southerners, to beat me up. For four days I faced men with sharpened razor blades who said they would eventually castrate me and 'pin me to my mattress.' Finally our lawyers forced the police to remove me from the open cell block. The police, announcing unceremoniously 'you're goin' to the hole' pushed me into a 5' by 7' cell with a five-inch square puncture in the steel door for ventilation.

I didn't know that Chuck too was in solitary and I wondered where he was and how he was faring. Suddenly I heard his voice at my shoulder calling in a loud whisper, 'Bob, is that you?' I put my ear to a grate in the ceiling, then jumped down to the small vent in the door, realizing his voice was coming from there. There was Chuck's face reflected in a piece of metal on the stone wall across from my cell. He was in the cell next to me. 'Chuck, are you all right?' . . . 'Yes, you?' . . . 'Fine.'

Then we sang. As the police pounded on the door threatening to whip us, we sang 'Woke Up This Morning With My Mind On Freedom.' Even after they turned the heaters on and blasted us with unbearable heat for seven days, we continued to sing.

G. and C. Carawan, *We Shall Overcome*

### Prisoners of the Japanese

Guards were stationed at several points around the perimeter of the camp; others patrolled at regular intervals. They could be eluded. But if a man broke through where was he to go? A thousand miles of jungle was the strongest fence that could surround any camp. To be caught outside meant death. Of those who attempted escape there is no record of any surviving.

Death called to us from every direction. It was in the air we breathed – it was the chief topic of our conversation. The rhythm of death obsessed us with its beat – a beat so regular, so pervasive, so inescapable that it made Chungkai a place of shadows in the dark valley.

Dying was easy. When our desires are thwarted and life becomes too much for us, it is easy to reject life and the pain it brings, easier to die than to live. It is an easy thing to adopt a philosophy of despair: to say, 'I mean nothing; there is nothing; nothing matters; I live only to die.' Those who decided they had no further reason for living, pulled down the shades and quietly expired. I knew a man who had amoebic dysentery. Compared to the rest of us, he was in good condition. But he convinced himself that he could not possibly survive and he did not.

As conditions steadily worsened, as starvation, exhaustion, and disease took an ever-growing toll, the atmosphere in which we lived was increasingly poisoned by selfishness, hatred, and fear. We were slipping rapidly down the scale of degradation. In Changi the patterns of army life had sustained us. We had huddled together because of our fears, believing there was safety in numbers. We had still shown some consideration for one another. Now that was gone, swept away. Existence had become so miserable, the odds so heavy against us, that nothing mattered except to survive.

When a man lay dying we had no word of mercy. When he cried for our help, we averted our heads. Everyone was his own keeper. It was free enterprise at its worst, with all the restraints of morality gone. Our captors had promised to reduce us to a level 'lower than any coolie in Asia'. They were succeeding all too well. Although we lived by the law of the jungle, the strongest among us still died, and the most selfish, the most self-sufficient, the wiliest and cleverest, perished with the weak.

Little acts of meanness, suspicion, and favouritism permeated our daily lives. Even the drawing of our meagre ration was a humiliating experience. To get our meals we formed a line in our huts. Our server would dip his can into the rice bucket and dump its contents on our mess tins. Another server would ladle out a watery stew of green leaves. We mistrusted not only the ones we could see, but also the ones we could not see. How much were the helpers in the cookhouse holding back? How much were they stealing for themselves? Suspicion gripped us.

The minute roll call was over in the evening, Japanese cooks would bring out swill pails and set them on the ground. Then they would stand back, fold their arms, and look on with self-satisfied smiles while prisoners pushed, kicked, and shoved one another out of the way as they fought for scraps from the enemy table. One evening a wretch broke away and stumbled towards me. In his hand he clutched a soggy mess of rice and stew. Bits of gravy dripped through his fingers. He had turned his back on the others, lest they should see what he had and be tempted to rob him. A wolfish leer contorted his face as he craftily licked at his spoils. He considered himself lucky.

'Rather than do that,' I thought to myself, 'I'd die!'

He passed me at a kind of trot, like an animal going to his lair, except that an animal would have had more dignity.

Ernest Gordon, *Through the Valley of the Kwai*

### Booked for prison

Each of us in here – we're each of us booked for prison, like we're all booked for the graveyard: we all come to it in the end. We quarrel, and fight, and kill each other, and end up either here in prison or else in the graveyard. And when a man is let out of prison, he isn't reformed, you know: he goes out more of a savage that when he came in. He'll go and seek out his enemy, and say to him: 'You've stained my honour – and now you're going to pay for it!' and he kills him. And unless there are spies around, he'll get away with it.

A young man in prison, reported in Danilo Dolci, *For the Young*

### The rat race

The Rat Race is a cruel race
And crooked are the rules,
You'll never be a millionaire
Unless you win the pools.
   Will somebody tell me how?

My standards keep on going up,
It's like the posters say,
I smoke a better cigarette
(A penny more to pay)
   Will somebody tell me how?

You can't afford to worry now,
For worry, it can kill,
And if you're over forty
Then you'd better buy a pill.
   Will somebody tell me how?

The Rat Race is a cruel race,
'Relax' the doctor said,
But how the hell can you relax?
You've got to keep ahead.
   Will somebody tell me how?

And now the rent is going up,
I cannot pay the bill,
Where shall I find a hundred quid
Unless I rob the till,
   (And so I rob the till)

'The more you have the more you want
It's time you understood'
(The old judge said) 'that you have never
Had it quite so good'.
   Will somebody tell me how?

The chaplain came into my cell,
He told me not to grieve,
For blessed are the poor (he said),
I wish I could believe.
   Will somebody tell me how?

I climb up on my prison bed
To look out thro' the bars,
A bloody great advertisement
Has blotted out the stars!

                Sydney Carter, *Songs of Sydney Carter in the Present Tense*, Book 2

### Out of prison

There was a knock on the door,
I went to open it;
The rain hurled in.
A man stood there –
Elderly, dishevelled,
In a suit that did not fit.
I brought him in to dry himself.

He said he wanted money,
I asked 'What for?'
And so it all came out.
He had been in prison,
A friend of mine
Had told him I would help.

What circumstances had brought
Him into crime I never asked;
Was it, I secretly asked,
Only inadequacy?
Only that failed marriage –
Or was it some
Hereditary complaint?
At any rate, I tried to help.
Away he went, into the back streets,
Looking for work and lodgings.

Here the city would cloak his shame,
Here he could seek that job,
Here it would show by blank refusals
Rejection for its misfits.

There are numerous like him,

On probation,
Out of prison,
On the dole,
Whose lives are stunted, under-grown,
Made outcasts because they disrupt,
Startle our settled and secure
Behaviour patterns.

And yet when we ignore
The man knocking on the door,
We ignore you –
For through the prisoner –
And the outcast –
You are to be found,
Disclosing yourself to us
In electrifying power
Which terrifies by its humanity
And baffles by its breadth.

Brian Frost, *Citizen Incognito*

### Inner freedom

What is personal freedom? It is essentially something *inside* a
man: the presence of something in a man's soul, not the absence of
such outer restrictions as the walls of a prison or Acts of Parliament that he must obey or take the consequences. To be free is
to be at rest in the depths of one's being, whatever people and
circumstances may be doing to one . . .

Consider actual imprisonment. People who go to prison for
refusing to do something they think wrong – conscientious ob-
jectors, for instance – are far freer, in the deepest sense, than
people who do something they think wrong for fear of going to
prison . . .

It is even possible, for human beings of the rarest quality, to
remain free under torture. I know of one or two who did so in a
Nazi concentration camp: and Jesus Christ was so utterly free on
the Cross (except, perhaps, for a passing moment of despair) that
he could pray for his tormentors. No one, on the other hand, can
possibly be free when the torturer is his own guilty conscience.

The meaning of inner freedom becomes clear if we think about its opposite, inner slavery. Inner slavery is nothing but preoccupation with self. A man totally preoccupied with himself is a total slave: he spends his entire life in a prison far narrower than any ever built of bricks or mortar or stone. We all know from our own experience that this is the case: we are all partially imprisoned, for none of us is completely free from the selfishness that *is* our imprisonment. Or certainly very few of us. But there are kinds, as well as degrees, of preoccupation with self, and they vary, or may vary, at different periods in our lives.

Victor Gollancz, *The New Year of Grace*

### No deterrent

We have been punishing criminals, often with ferocious cruelty, for centuries and no evidence has ever been produced to show that punishment is an effective deterrent. On the contrary, there is plenty of evidence to suggest that violence inflicted on criminals by society only tends to embitter the criminal and make him all the more determined to take his revenge. And so much violence inflicted on criminals has borne no relation to any offence committed by the criminal; its nature has been more that of a crime committed by society itself.

Michael De-la-Noy, *Delinquency and Guilt*

### Experimental prison

They give you time to think – they reduce the temperature for you, reduce the hostility between the staff and the prisoners, so that you don't all the time have to be plotting and scheming how you can get your own back on them. Nobody really bothers you here, they don't have all those petty restrictions which most other places have, where you've got to ask permission for every little thing you want to do. Like, for instance, having a bath: if you feel like having a bath here you go and have one, twice a day if you want to. Or if you want to go in the library and look at the papers, or stay in bed on a Sunday morning, it's left to you.

These are small things, but they do mean a lot when you're in for a long time. They remind you that you're still looked on as a human being, however diabolic what you've done outside is in the eyes of society. And you'll get non-uniformed members of the staff coming along and sitting down where you're working, just to have a chat with you. They ask how your wife and kids are, whether you're reading any good books at the moment, or they'll tell you about a trip they had to London, where they went, who they saw, what shows are on at the theatre, that sort of thing. And they do it for nothing, they're not trying to worm a bit of information out of you or sound you out about something they suspect is going on.

There's some right funny geezers among the doctors, you know. One of them, he's a little old guy and dead sincere he is. 'Look', he says, 'I know I can't prevent you carrying on with crime when you go out, and I'm not even going to try to discuss with you things like what's right and what's wrong. All I want you to do is to think about your behaviour in terms of "wise" and "unwise", and try and sort out what makes you happy and what makes you unhappy. I don't expect you to leave here changed from a crook into a dead-straight citizen. I'll be quite satisfied if when you go out you've become a happier and better-adjusted criminal.'

I thought he was having me on, the first time he said it. But he's not. It makes you think, doesn't it? I've never met geezers like that before.

Quoted in Tony Parker, *The Frying Pan*

# Refugees

Refugees are the tragic victims of almost every violent conflict; and early scriptures, Hebrew, Egyptian and Mesopotamian, seem to have recognised this and therefore laid down rules for their treatment. The psalm quoted refers to the forced removal by Nebuchnezzar II of Jewish craftsmen to Babylon after the capture of Jerusalem in 597 B.C.; and it is followed by examples in prose and verse from various periods and countries.

*Further reading*: W. H. Auden, 'Refugee Blues'; Bertolt Brecht, 'Children's Crusade, 1939'; Brian Frost, 'Refugee Home', in *Citizen Incognito*; Herbert Read, 'Refugees', p. 49 in *Collected Poems*; Ian Serraillier, *The Silver Sword* (fictional counterpart of

*The Cigarette Sellers of Three Crosses Square*); the Vietnam
shelves in any library.

### Ye were strangers

And if a stranger sojourn with thee in your land, ye shall not vex
him. But the stranger that dwelleth with you shall be unto you as
one born among you, and thou shalt love him as thyself; for ye
were strangers in the land of Egypt.

> Leviticus 19:33-4

### Do not neglect a stranger

Do not neglect a stranger with thy oil-jar,
That it be doubled before thy brethren.
God desires respect for the poor
More than the honouring of the exalted . . .

> Egyptian: from *The Teaching of Amenemope*, about 1300 B.C.,
> translated by J. M. Plumley

### By the rivers of Babylon

By the rivers of Babylon,
There we sat down, yea, we wept,
When we remembered Zion.
We hanged our harps
Upon the willows in the midst thereof.
For there they that carried us away required of us a song,
And they that wasted us required of us mirth, saying,
'Sing us one of the songs of Zion.'
How shall we sing the Lord's song
In a strange land?
If I forget thee, O Jerusalem,
Let my right hand forget her cunning.
If I do not remember thee,
Let my tongue cleave to the roof of my mouth;
If I prefer not Jerusalem above my chief joy.

> Psalm 137

### The little cart

Chen Tzu-lung (born in 1607) was a soldier involved in the Chinese civil wars of the mid-seventeenth century. Here he describes the flight of a husband and wife from a town menaced by the advancing Manchus; they find the whole countryside deserted.

The little cart jolting and banging through the yellow haze
    of dusk.
The man pushing behind: the woman pulling in front.
They have left the city and do not know where to go.
'Green, green, those elm-tree leaves: *they* will cure my hunger,
If only we could find some quiet place and sup on them together.'

The wind has flattened the yellow mother-wort:
Above it in the distance they see the walls of a house.
'*There* surely must be people living who'll give you something
    to eat.'
They tap at the door, but no one comes: they look in, but the
    kitchen is empty.
They stand hesitating in the lonely road and their tears fall
    like rain.

Chen Tzu-lung, translated by Arthur Waley

### An army of children

When the Germans invaded Poland and occupied Warsaw, they concentrated the whole Jewish population in a small district, with several families crowded into a flat. The area was surrounded by high walls and barbed wire, isolating it from the rest of the town and from the Polish inhabitants. Warsaw was split into two sections: the Jewish and the Polish or Aryan one.

Soon the death penalty was introduced for crossing the ghetto walls. Inside the ghetto opportunities for earning a living fell to a minimum. Under the system of enforced pauperisation, the face of the ghetto changed rapidly, while terror and slave labour for the 'new masters of the world' reduced morale. Hunger increased from day to day. The official rations were less than sufficient and food smuggled from the Aryan side very expensive.

Tne special treatment devised by the Germans – they cut off the water supply, stopped refuse collection, etc. – brought on an epidemic of typhus. Hundreds died daily from hunger and disease. The situation deteriorated rapidly when the German authorities resettled thousands of destitute Jews from the neighbouring towns and villages in the ghetto.

But the people had to live and eat somehow, and it was then that the children's army of little smugglers set out for the Aryan side. Stealing across the walls and barbed wire, they emerged into the Polish streets and from there smuggled food to the starving ghetto. Some of them begged for a bowl of soup, a crust of bread or a few coins with which they could buy food for the rest of their families. Many of the children were hunted and shot by the Germans and fell under the ghetto walls. Their places were taken by others, since this was the only way to keep their families alive.

When the ghetto was liquidated a group of children escaped and led an adventurous and independent existence on the Aryan side of Warsaw. Sentenced to death, hounded and harried at every step, they found a way of surviving in the jungle of the occupation. They knew how to defend themselves and how to fight for their existence. They knew – unlike so many adults – how to help each other.

Growing in number, they lived at first by begging, by singing in the streets or by casual labour, and later by selling cigarettes on the Three Crosses Square. They were very brave. Some of them used to smuggle food and arms to the ghetto and took part in the uprisings of 1943 and 1944. These were the luckiest; of more than 20 children, the majority have survived.

Joseph Ziemian, *The Cigarette Sellers of Three Crosses Square*

### Refugees from Hungary

On retiring from her work for the Save the Children Fund, Mary Hawkins described some of her experiences. Here she relates what happened when thousands of people fled into Austria when Russian tanks enabled Communists to take over.

The refugees who were crossing the border in large numbers every night were being sheltered and fed by the Austrians in houses, schools and barns, but the stocks of food were now completely exhausted and there was no more accommodation. The country was quite unprepared for such an overwhelming disaster.

The Einser Canal bridge had been blown up by the Russians so the crossing had to be made in a rubber dinghy, or by swimming. No easy feat in the freezing water in the middle of winter. On the Austrian side of the frontier at various points, including the canal, vehicles driven by volunteers were waiting to pick up the refugees and take them to the village two miles away. Mothers and children were brought to our centre and the others went to the Austrian Red Cross.

We were allotted two rooms in the village kindergarten, and in the largest room deep straw covered the floor with blankets laid on top. On arrival the refugees were given dry clothes, hot drinks and food, and they slept as long as possible. They arrived exhausted, cold and hungry, some having travelled for many miles from the eastern side of Hungary, and there were often stories of hardship and tragedy. Small children were carried on the father's back in sheepskin bags which kept them warm and dry, but unfortunately nearly all the children under five had to be given heavy doses of bromide to ensure their silence at the critical part of the journey when passing the border guards. Many had been given an overdose. These were sent to the Red Cross for treatment and returned to us to be given sweet coffee and kept awake, which naturally they hated. Sometimes adults and older children arrived suffering from frostbitten feet and hands, another serious condition needing immediate attention.

Those for whom the journey was most difficult were the children over five years old – too heavy to be carried and too young to be able to keep up the pace on the long walk. Nevertheless they usually arrived in the centre in good spirits and many of them had shown great fortitude. There was a twelve-year-old boy who had had to leave his home as he was on the black list, accused of throwing an explosive into a Russian tank in Budapest. His father was a cripple and could not make the journey and the mother must stay with him, but she urged Miklos to go alone as his life was in danger. He was captured and put on a train for deportation to the east, but escaped and made the long journey from the eastern frontier to reach Austria. Many others like him were not so fortunate.

One family consisting of father, mother, three boys of 3, 5 and 7 years and a baby girl of three months set out from the Roumanian border only to be captured because the baby cried when passing near a guard. The father and baby were imprisoned and the mother sent back home with the three boys. She attempted the journey a second time and finally arrived in Andau safely, having walked sixty miles in six days, carrying the three-year-old boy, with the other two struggling along beside her. For this family there was a happy ending. A farmer in Andau heard that a woman had arrived with three children after being separated from her husband and baby. Only two weeks before the farmer had taken a man with a small baby and helped him to get to Vienna. Names were checked and it proved to be the same family; the farmer looked after the mother and her boys until the father was contacted and could arrange to fetch them.

Mary Hawkins, in *The World's Children* (December 1972)

### Refugees in West Bengal

They lay on the cold stone floor, a hundred men, women and children, retching and shaking, their terrified eyes fixed on the back entrance of the hospital where the corpses were piling up. Cramped in the tiny village hospital, some only half alive, they are all victims of the cholera epidemic sweeping through the refugee camps of West Bengal.

It is not pleasant to see a hundred people dying of cholera when one knows that there are huge stocks of medicine in the world which could have saved them or could at least have eased their agony. With neither mattresses nor blankets they die on the hard floor of this improvised hospital in the south of the Nadia district. A dying baby still clings to its mother's body. An old man coughs and dies a foot away from my feet.

A young doctor with tears in his eyes points to the street where thousands of refugees are huddled under umbrellas and on straw mats in the rain. 'I only have the equipment and medicine to save a few,' he says. 'The only thing I can do now is to bring them inside so they don't die in the rain.'

It was the same grim story in the northern region of Nadia. The official death toll has risen to 1,700 deaths but officials from West Bengal's health services, who escorted me to the cholera-affected refugee camps near Bethuadahari village, about 90 miles north of Calcutta, claim that as many as 5,000 have died since last Sunday.

'Many doctors are still playing down the statistics because they feel that they might be held responsible for the outbreak,' an official explains. 'But I can tell you that we have already hired 15 lorries to transport bodies in the northern towns of Shikarpur and Karimpur.'

The town of Karimpur near the border has been hit hardest by the disease. 'We are burning them in huge communal graves but we cannot cope with the number of deaths,' says the young official, Rishikesh Choudhury. 'The bodies are still lying in the streets and the vultures are eating them. This will spread the epidemic.' His fears are echoed by officials in all parts of the district. The disease has already claimed 200 lives in the huge refugee camp near the town of Kalyani, 40 miles north of Calcutta. You know you are approaching the Kalyani refugee camps before you see them. You can smell them.

An estimated 100,000 Bengalis have been accommodated in these makeshift camps. There is no sanitation nor any permanent shelter and thousands of refugees are crouching under crude straw mats or umbrellas in fields flooded by the monsoon rains. As the reports of the cholera epidemic spread through the town the local inhabitants are beginning to place handkerchiefs over their mouths and noses as they pass the huge camps.

We drive to the north passing a never-ending stream of refugees on the roads. Some are too tired to walk and are squatting under trees in the rain. We arrive at the village hospital at Bethuadahari and it is the same story . . .

Peter Hazlehurst, in a *Times* report, 4 June 1971

**Krishna**

News photographer Mark Edwards found Krishna alone, quite deserted, in a muddy corner of a reed hut in a refugee camp. Even the other children in the hut were ignoring him. His matchstick body was covered in sores. He had probably never seen a European before, but the presence of Edwards elicited only a bored glance. Beckoned, he followed him to a War on Want doctor. Krishna had TB, scabies and quite a lot else. Left alone, he would die; with treatment, he had some hope. His mother was found, and the party set off by jeep back to the War on Want hospital near

Dum Dum. Through an interpreter the story unfolded. The boy's father had suffered from the same sores, and had died. His mother, convinced that the disease was leprosy, had banished the child from the family. It was difficult to believe, but credible nevertheless. Although leprosy can be treated, it is still dreaded in parts of Asia as it was in Biblical times. Isolated, the boy had gradually starved. And the more he starved, the more the deficiency diseases ate into his body.

Krishna was impassive and expressionless throughout a somewhat painful bathing. When he was handed a banana, he hesitated to accept it, as if frightened that it would be snatched away in some cruel tease. It was two or three days before he confidently accepted food, and then he ate it passionately, like a starved dog. While he ate he refused to acknowledge the presence of anyone else.

More importantly than being starved of food, he'd been starved of love; the battle to get a smile out of Krishna became a crusade. The smile came the day the nurse put a bracelet of sticking plaster round his wrist, and drew a watch-dial on it. Soon he was demanding to be picked up by anyone who had a moment to spare, and carried piggy-back. One day Krishna's mother came and demanded his return. The hospital had to agree. Last reports were that she brought him to hospital regularly for injections.

War on Want report in *Frontline*

### Refugees

Stumbling, limping, crying and frightened,
They come, pouring into the camp:
Terrified, hurt, shoeless and ragged,
They come for safety and food;
Starved and diseased, uncared for, bewildered,
They arrive for sanctuary and refuge;
Each one, homeless, friendless, parentless,
They slowly, wearily come.

Hopeful and longing, wistful and wanting,
They come in threes and fours;
Many have sores, are ill and fevered,
They come for medical aid;

Unclothed, forgotten, scorned and repulsed,
They come both young and old;
Each without money, shelter or warmth,
They slowly, wearily come.

Though the camps be full,
And conditions poor,
They are welcomed, clothed and fed,
So the fortunate ones have found a haven,
A shelter plus a bed.

Jane Hillsdon

# III

# Response

# Love 1

A sense of reverence forms part of all the great religions, and also of beliefs that are tantamount to a kind of religious faith, such as the humanism of Julian Huxley, for whom 'the spirit of love and reverence' must hold all together. The extent to which among different peoples the feeling of reverence emerges in the form of praise was suggested by the examples in the section on Praise in Part I, in which men are seen 'to know and love God'. In the Christian and some other religions the second great commandment enjoins that we should love our neighbour; therefore this and the next two sections include passages from different periods in which the injunction is expressed, and examples given of the ways in which it has been put into practice.

*Further reading*: I John 4; Caryl Houselander, 'Soeur Marie Emilie', in *The Flowering Tree*; N. Kazantsakis, *God's Pauper* (St Francis); A. Schweitzer, *My Childhood and Youth*.

### Holding all together

For man to live fully it is necessary for him, as for every other organism, to be adapted to his surroundings; but man can do so on a new level, denied to other organisms, in the world of mind. His life, if it is to be the best life possible, must be seen, felt and practically lived in its relation to the rest of the universe. If he fails to take account of any essential of reality, or if he misinterprets it, woe to him: the omission or the mistake will bring its retribution.

To this task of relating his life to the rest of reality he must bring all his powers; but the mortar which must hold all together if the construction is to hold is the spirit of love and reverence. Such a construction so held together is a true and developed religion.

That is what orthodox theism means when it says that the knowledge and love of God is the first duty of man.

Sir Julian Huxley, *Religion Without Revelation*

### The way to know God

I always think that the best way to know God is to love many things. Love a friend, a wife, something, whatever you like, but one must love with a lofty and serious intimate sympathy, with strength, with intelligence, and one must always try to know deeper, better, and more.

Vincent van Gogh, a letter to his brother Theo

### The right answer

On one occasion a lawyer came forward to put this test question to him: 'Master, what must I do to inherit eternal life?' Jesus said, 'What is written in the Law? What is your reading of it?' He replied, 'Love the Lord your God with all your heart, with all your soul, with all your strength, and with all your mind; and your neighbour as yourself.' 'That is the right answer,' said Jesus; 'do that and you will live.'

St Luke 10:25-8

### True piety

It is not piety, that you turn your faces
   to the East and to the West.
    True piety is this:
To believe in God, and the Last Day,
the angels, the Book, and the Prophets,
to give of one's substance, however cherished,
   to kinsmen, and orphans,
the needy, the traveller, beggars,
   and to ransom the slave,
to perform the prayer, to pay the alms.
And they who fulfil their covenant
when they have engaged in a covenant,
   and endure with fortitude
   misfortune, hardship and peril,
these are they who are true in their faith,
   these are the truly godfearing.

The Koran, translated by A. J. Arberry

### St Francis's love for all creatures

When he washed his hands he chose a place where the washing-water would not afterwards be trampled underfoot. When he was obliged to walk over rocks he walked with fear and reverence for the love of him who was called a rock, and when he recited that verse of the psalm where it says: 'Thou hast raised me on the Rock', he used to say with great devotion: 'Thou has raised me beneath the feet of the Rock'. He told the brother who got wood for the fire not to cut down the whole tree but to cut it in such a way that some part remained and part was cut. He also made this order to a brother who was in the friary where he was staying. He told the brother who tended the garden not to plant all the space in the garden entirely with vegetables but to leave some part of the soil where he might grow flowering plants which in their season might produce their brothers the flowers.

> Rosalind B. Brooke, trans. and ed., *The Writings of Leo, Rufino and Angelo*

### Not enemies, but people

In '41 Mama took me back to Moscow. There I saw my enemies for the first time. If my memory is right, nearly twenty thousand German war prisoners were to be marched in a single column through the streets of Moscow.

The pavements swarmed with onlookers, cordoned off by soldiers and police.

The crowd were mostly women – Russian women with hands roughened by hard work, lips untouched by lipstick and thin hunched shoulders which had borne half the burden of the war. Every one of them must have had a father or a husband, a brother or a son killed by the Germans.

They gazed with hatred in the direction from which the column was to appear.

At last we saw it.

The generals marched at the head, massive chins stuck out, lips folded disdainfully, their whole demeanour meant to show superiority over their plebeian victors.

'They smell of eau-de-cologne, the bastards,' someone in the crowd said with hatred.

The women were clenching their fists. The soldiers and policemen had all they could do to hold them back.

All at once something happened to them.

They saw German soldiers, thin, unshaven, wearing dirty blood-
stained bandages, hobbling on crutches or leaning on the shoulders
of their comrades; the soldiers walked with their heads down.

The street became dead silent – the only sound was the shuffling
of boots and the thumping of crutches.

Then I saw an elderly woman in broken-down boots push herself
forward and touch a policeman's shoulder, saying: 'Let me
through.' There must have been something about her that made
him step aside.

She went up to the column, took from inside her coat something
wrapped in a coloured handkerchief and unfolded it. It was a crust
of black bread. She pushed it awkwardly into the pocket of a
soldier, so exhausted that he was tottering on his feet. And now
suddenly from every side women were running towards the
soldiers, pushing into their hands bread, cigarettes, whatever they
had.

The soldiers were no longer enemies.

They were people.

> Yevgeny Yevtushenko, *A Precocious Autobiography*

### Real charity

We call it charity, when men give away what they do not want
themselves in order to patch up evils and ameliorate bad conditions which their greed, slackness, or stupidity have helped to
create. This is not charity, and it is blasphemy to call it by that
splendid name. We call it charity when we give a poor devil half
a crown to get shut of him and rid ourselves of the sight of his
misery; that is blasphemy too. Real charity is not easy, it is always
hard; it means that we must be ready to take time, trouble and
infinite pains to create life. The business man who seeks to give
good value for money, who prides himself on his fellow workers
in the business, and whose aim is to see that by efficiency and
energy his business produces and sustains fine life, he is the charit-
able man. Our faith is that God is Charity – that His Charity is so

great that he spares himself no suffering and no agony in order to create in the world fine life. We are meant to be like him.

G. A. Studdert Kennedy, *The New Man in Christ*

### The ring

A poor man came to Rabbi Schmelke's door. There was no money in the house, so the rabbi gave him a ring. A moment later, his wife heard of it and heaped him with reproaches for throwing to an unknown beggar so valuable a piece of jewelry, with so large and precious a stone. Rabbi Schmelke had the poor man called back and said to him: 'I have just learned that the ring I gave you is of great value. Be careful not to sell it for too little money.'

Martin Buber (trans.), *Tales of the Hasidim*

### Witnesses

What I command you is to love one another. If the world hates you, remember that it hated me before you . . . a servant is not greater than his master. If they persecuted me they will persecute you too . . . indeed the hour is coming when anyone who kills you will think he is obeying God's will.

St John 15

The preacher of a sermon on the text above emphasised that no age had more martyrs than ours; and he went on:

Who are today's witnesses to Christ's limitless love? Many of the Christians of Russia, suffering but unbroken, are among the most impressive. They do not hate their rulers, but their rulers fear their freedom of spirit. Some of the greatest writers of modern Russian literature are among them.

Many more are simple, humble people. Peasants and priests and bishops who go on loving at great cost to themselves. Communist Russia is the richer for their free lives, free in prison as well as out of prison.

But we are wrong if we think that persecution is at its worst in countries which call themselves communist. Far greater is the tragedy where tyranny and oppression are committed by those who claim to be Christians.

If the Soviet Union is impressive in its many witnesses today, so is the world's other frightening great power, the United States. In Martin Luther King it has produced perhaps this generation's most inspiring martyr, dedicated to brotherhood at any cost and dying in the certainty of the ultimate victory of love over hate. But there are many more Americans, in and out of prison, carrying the torch of freedom and humanity. The Berrigan brothers, two Catholic priests, imprisoned for their passionate protest against the Vietnam war, are among the best known.

> from a sermon by the Rev. Paul Ostreicher, reported in *The Times*

### Nursing with love

Mrs Eva Engholm's hobby is caring for ill and wounded birds till they are fit for release. Here she writes of the secret of success:

On the second of my two visits to Joan Hicks at the Ashington Bird sanctuary, when she was already ill in bed, I confessed to her that I had – in desperation – nursed a baby plover in my hand for five nights. 'That's it,' she said, 'that's what saved him; they *must* be loved.' And indeed mere efficiency is no substitute for love. As a teacher one has experienced the truth of this in human affairs; the warm-hearted, if feckless slum-mother who spanks and loves her brood, is rewarded by the fierce loyalty of her children, while the efficient mother methodically 'treating' her child according to the textbook of psychology is frequently punished by the hostility of a problem child. Equally important is the attitude of the 'nurse' or 'rescuer' of birds. If efficiency is no substitute for love, neither is hygiene. The most efficient 'rescuer' working along irreproachably hygienic lines and surrounded by the most glamorous equipment is no substitute for love, for love does not work according to theories but is absorbed in learning from the object of the love. I hasten to add this is not meant to be a plea or an excuse for inefficiency or *lack* of hygiene; it is a question of putting first things first, and in the sphere of feeling, priority must be given to the emotional attitude of the rescuer. As in all else it is motivation that counts; birds exist in their own right, they are not quaint or amusing things nor yet pieces of property to be owned. Above all they are not experimental material to exercise a rescuer's lust for power. Rescuer and rescued should meet on equal terms.

Eva Engholm, *Company of Birds*

### Albert Schweitzer

The way in which he was different from most of us showed at an early age. He was son of the pastor in an Alsatian village, and when he went, well-fed and well-clothed, to school he found that many of the children were often cold and hungry. So he gave up his expensive clothes so that he might be dressed no better than they were. Other differences soon appeared. After studying music in Paris, he went to Strasbourg University to study theology, and at the age of twenty-eight became Principal of the Theological Faculty there. At this point, when he could have had a brilliant career in several directions – music, theology, philosophy – he completely abandoned the idea of success. He had read a report on starvation and disease in the Congo, and decided to take the full medical training of six years in order to go to the Congo and set up a hospital there.

He and his wife went to Africa in 1913 and started their hospital at Lambaréné – where he died fifty-two years later at the age of ninety. A war meant that he and his wife had to go back to France to be interned as enemy aliens; and he made several trips to Europe to lecture and give organ recitals of Bach's music to raise funds for his hospital. As his achievement became known visitors came from all over the world, and he himself received numerous honours, culminating in the Nobel Peace Prize for 1952. Despite all sorts of obstacles – the jungle, the difficult tropical climate, famine, prolonged absences – the hospital was a success from the start in that it attracted thousands of patients at once. But some of the visitors were shocked by what they saw. Instead of a hygienic European or American type hospital, run on rather military lines, they found something much more like an African village with people and animals wandering about and at the centre a number of physicians caring for the sick. This was what Schweitzer intended, for he felt that the Africans would not come to the forbidding efficient institution that many hospitals appear to be. He always encouraged a patient to bring one or two relatives to cook for him.

This intensely powerful man is remembered not only for practising what he preached (cf. St Matthew 10 and 11), and thus repaying with good some of the evil done to the Congolese by the Europeans who had cruelly exploited them. His books on Bach and Jesus are true additions to our knowledge, but his idea of Reverence for Life is what catches the imagination of the young today, when the taking of life, human and animal, is seen more clearly for what it is. Again, some people thought that at Lambarené the doctrine was carried too far, when they found that insect pests were left alone and building was stopped to avoid damage to an ants' nest.

An anecdote from the early days: Schweitzer, without previous experience and only a knowledge of anatomy to help, had to do operations with simple anaesthetics. The working of the latter was described by an African: 'First the white man kills the sick man. Then he cures him. And then he wakes him up.'

Editor

## The difference

In Korea there is a legend about a native warrior who died and went to heaven. 'Before I enter,' he said to the gate-keeper, 'I would like you to take me on a tour of hell.' The gate-keeper found a guide to take the warrior to hell. When he got there he was astonished to see a great table piled high with the choicest foods. But the people in hell were starving. The warrior turned to his guide and raised his eyebrows.

'It's this way,' the guide explained. 'Everybody who comes here is given a pair of chopsticks five feet long, and is required to hold them at the end to eat. But you just can't eat with chopsticks five feet long if you hold them at the end. Look at them. They miss their mouths every time, see?'

The visitor agreed that this was hell indeed and asked to be taken back to heaven post-haste. In heaven, to his surprise, he saw a similar room, with a similar table laden with very choice foods. But the people were happy; they looked radiantly happy.

The visitor turned to the guide. 'No chopsticks, I suppose?' he said.

'Oh yes,' said the guide, 'they have the same chopsticks, the

same length, and they must be held at the end just as in hell. But
you see, these people have learned that if a man feeds his neighbour, his neighbour will feed him also.'

Anonymous

# Love 2

### When the heart is happy

Injure not a man, with pen upon papyrus –
O abomination of the god!
Bear not witness with lying words,
Nor seek another's reverse with thy tongue.
Make not a reckoning with him who hath nothing,
Nor falsify thy pen.
If thou hast found a large debt against a poor man,
Make it into three parts,
Forgive two, and let one remain,
In order that thou shalt find thereby the ways of life.
Thou wilt lie down – the night hasteneth away – lo, thou art in the
    morning;
Thou hast found it like good news.
Better is praise for one who loves men
Than riches in a storehouse;
Better is bread, when the heart is happy,
Than riches with contention.

Egyptian: from *The Teaching of Amenemope*; about 1300 B.C.
translated by J. M. Plumley

### A little with righteousness

How do ye say, 'We are wise, and the law of the Lord is with us?'
Lo, certainly in vain he made it; the pen of the scribes is in vain.

Jeremiah 8 : 8

Better is a little with righteousness than great revenues without right.

Proverbs 16 : 8

Better is a dry morsel, and quietness therewith, than a house full of sacrifices with strife.

Proverbs 17 : 1

## Love

I may speak in tongues of men or of angels, but if I am without love, I am a sounding gong or a clanging cymbal. I may have the gift of prophecy, and know every hidden truth; I may have faith strong enough to move mountains; but if I have no love, I am nothing. I may dole out all I possess, or even give my body to be burnt, but if I have no love, I am none the better.

Love is patient; love is kind and envies no one. Love is never boastful, nor conceited, nor rude; never selfish, not quick to take offence. Love keeps no score of wrongs; does not gloat over other men's sins, but delights in the truth. There is nothing love cannot face; there is no limit to its faith, its hope, and its endurance.

Love will never come to an end. Are there prophets? their work will be over. Are there tongues of ecstasy? they will cease. Is there knowledge? it will vanish away; for our knowledge and our prophecy alike are partial, and the partial vanishes when wholeness comes. When I was a child, my speech, my outlook, and my thoughts were all childish. When I grew up, I had finished with childish things. Now we see only puzzling reflections in a mirror, but then we shall see face to face. My knowledge now is partial; then it will be whole, like God's knowledge of me. In a word there are three things that last for ever: faith, hope, and love; but the greatest of them all is love.

St Paul, I Corinthians 13

## The widow's offering

Once he was standing opposite the temple treasury, watching as people dropped their money into the chest. Many rich people were giving large sums. Presently there came a poor widow who dropped

in two tiny coins, together worth a farthing. He called his disciples
to him. 'I tell you this,' he said: 'this widow has given more than
any of the others; for those others who have given had more than
enough, but she, with less than enough, has given all that she had
to live on.'

St Mark 12:41-4

### Show kindness

Show kindness to your parents, and to kindred and to orphans,
and to the poor and to neighbours who are your kinsmen, and to
neighbours that are strangers, and to your familiar companions,
and to the wayfarer; and to whatever your right hand possesses (be
they your slaves or servants or horses or other domestic animals),
for this is what God loves; and He does not love the vain boasters
and the selfish, and does not like those who are niggardly themselves and bid others to be niggardly, and hide away that which
God of His bounty has given them, saying to the poor and needy
'We have not got anything'.

The Koran

### Prayer half granted

The wife of the Rabbi of Roptchitz said to him: 'Your prayer was
lengthy today. Have you succeeded in bringing it about that the
rich should be more generous in their gifts to the poor?'

The Rabbi replied: 'Half of my prayer I have accomplished.
The poor are willing to accept them.'

L. I. Newman (trans. and ed.), *The Hasidic Anthology*

### November third

Bending neither to the rain
Nor to the wind
Nor to snow nor to summer heat,
Firm in body, yet
Without greed, without anger,
Always smiling serenely.
Eating his four cups of rough rice a day

With bean paste and a few vegetables,
Never taking himself into account
But seeing and hearing everything,
Understanding
And never forgetting.
In the shade of a pine grove
He lives in a tiny thatched hut:
If there is a sick child in the east
He goes and tends him:
If there is a tired mother in the west
He goes and shoulders her rice sheaves:
If there is a man dying in the south
He goes and soothes his fears:
If there are quarrels and litigation in the north
He tells them, 'Stop your pettiness.'
In drought he sheds tears,
In cold summers he walks through tears.
Everyone calls him a fool.
Neither praised
Nor taken to heart.

That man
Is what I wish to be.

> Miyazawa Kenji

## Alms

Give unto all, lest he whom thou deniest,
May chance to be no other man, but Christ.

> Robert Herrick

## Jesus to supper

Two old people had invited the Lord to supper, and he was late
coming. They kept the supper hot and waited and waited, but still
he didn't come.

Directly an old beggar came to the door and asked for something to eat. The old woman thought, 'Well, I'll let him have my
part.' They were so poor they hardly had enough for the three of
them. She went ahead and fed the beggar, and he thanked her and
left.

They still waited and waited and kept looking out the door. Then a little ragged boy came along. He looked cold and sort of starved, so they took him in. The old man told his wife, says, 'I'm not much hungry. He can have my supper.'

So they fed the boy and let him sit and get warm. Tried to get him to stay the night but he said he couldn't, and when he left the old man got a coat for him so he'd keep warm.

They kept the fire going and kept Jesus' supper ready. And finally they looked out and saw him coming. They went to meet him at the gate, said 'We waited so long! We were afraid you'd never come.'

The Lord took their hands, says, 'I've already been here twice.'

An American folk tale from the Southern Mountains

### The leper on the Umbrian Plain

One day Francis was riding on the Umbrian Plain, on his way home to Assisi. Though he too was struggling with God and destiny, he was still a rich man's son, and was fashionably dressed and riding a gaily caparisoned horse. Then suddenly his horse shied under him, and he looked up to see the sight that he most feared in all the world, a leper. Then happened for him, as for us also, a tremendous event, for Francis, fighting down his loathing and his fear, dismounted from his horse, and going to the leper, put money into his hand. Then impelled by some power that had overcome his fear, he took the hand and kissed it, putting his lips to the leper's flesh. And the leper, seeing that Francis was afire with love, took hold of him and gave him the kiss of peace and Francis kissed him also. Then Francis mounted his horse and rode back to Assisi with joy. From that day onwards he began to visit the lepers in the lazar house of Assisi, bringing them gifts and kissing their hands. He wrote in his will, 'the Lord Himself led me amongst them, and I showed mercy to them, and when I left them, what had seemed bitter to me was changed into sweetness of body and soul'.

*A Legend*: Francis remounted his horse and rode away. Then suddenly he turned round, but there was no one to be seen on the road at all. Then he knew that he had kissed the Lord.

*The Little Flowers of St Francis of Assisi*

### The fur coat

A man died and was brought before the Heavenly Court. His sins and good deeds were placed on the scales, and the sins far outweighed the good deeds. Suddenly a fur coat was piled on the scale containing the good deeds, and this side becoming heavier, the man was sent to Paradise. He said to the Angel who escorted him: 'But I cannot understand why the fur coat was brought in.' The Angel replied: 'One cold winter's night you travelled on a sled and a poor man asked for a ride. You took him in, and noticing his thin clothes, you placed your fur coat on him to give him warmth. This act of kindness more than offset your transgressions.'

L. I. Newman (trans. and ed.), *The Hasidic Anthology*

### Love is kind and cool

Listen, you guys, if I came there blasting and sounding off and didn't do it because I really cared about you, all I'd be is a great big noise. And if I was the smartest guy in the world and I knew what was gonna happen tomorrow to you and if I had enough faith in God to tell the building to get outta the way and I didn't do it because I really cared about you then I'm a zero. And if I gave away everything I got and didn't do it because I cared about you, then it wouldn't make no difference at all.

Don't you know that the most important thing in the world is love? It's always kind and cool. It never gets shook up, it never sounds off. It never gets mad at people and nasty at them. It never tries to get its own way and it never feels good when things go wrong for the next guy. But it always feels good when things go right for him. Don't you know that love always sticks by a guy? That it's always got lots of hope and it never, never gives up? Everything else will get done in someday. But love will always stick around. You remember when you were just a little cat, how you used to fight with your brothers and your sisters, and the only one you could ever think about was yourself? Well, now you are grown up and it's time to see yourself. And the most important things you can see in yourself are faith and hope and love, and the best of all is love because it never goes away. And that's about all I got to say to you, 'cause that's most important of all.

I Corinthians 13, version by young American delinquents, recorded by Carl Burke, in *God Is Beautiful, Man*

### St Martin of Tours

With London's most famous church dedicated to him and thousands of people named after him, St Martin must be reckoned a popular saint. There is some reason for this. Born in Hungary about 315, he was brought up at Pavia in Italy, and at sixteen was forced by his father to join the army. One bitter winter day while at Amiens he was stopped by a half-naked beggar who asked for money. But he had no money with him, so he drew his sword and cut his long military cloak in two, throwing one half of it over the shivering beggar. That same night he was led to recognize Christ in the beggar man, for he had a dream in which he saw Christ making known this act of charity to a group of angels, wearing the half cloak and telling them where it had come from. In an excellent poem, 'St Martin and the Beggar', Thom Gunn tells a different story in which Martin meets the beggar again that evening in the inn; and the beggar says to him

You recognised the human need
Included yours, because
You did not hesitate, my saint,
To cut your cloak across;
But never since that moment
Did you regret the loss.

My enemies would have turned away,
My holy toadies would
Have given the cloak and frozen
Conscious that they were good.
But you, being a saint of men,
Gave only what you could.

Soon after the encounter with the beggar Martin was baptized a Christian.

So far the story is a fairly ordinary one; there are hundreds of unknown people every year who do as much. Of greater importance is the next event we hear of in the life of Martin written by a friend; this was when he asked for his discharge from the army, saying, 'I am Christ's soldier; I am not allowed to fight'. This stand was in line with much Christian teaching of the period, when a number of the great fathers took the sixth commandment to mean what it said, and preached that it was always wrong to kill.

Accused of cowardice, he retorted by offering to stand between the opposing lines – as Buddhist monks and nuns have done today in the Vietnam war.

However he was given his discharge, and then founded a religious community. Made Bishop of Tours in 370, he worked long and hard as a missionary, visiting every part of his diocese on foot or donkey-back. It is also recorded that he stood out against the Emperor Maximus when he condemned some Spaniards to death on the ground that they had practised magic. As the worker of various supposed miracles he had constant visitors, who became a nuisance. So with his eighty monks he retired to a monastery on the Loire, surrounded by high cliffs; and there they lived in wooden huts and cells hollowed out of the rocks.

Editor

# Love 3

### Thy neighbour

The passage below comes from *The Teaching of Amenemope*, which belongs to the Egypt of perhaps 1300 B.C. This work and the Hebrew *Book of Proverbs* have so much in common that it seems likely that there existed in the Near East a common stock of proverbs from which both drew. Mircea Eliade notes that the Moon is the symbol of the god who presided at the Judgement of the Dead when a man's heart was weighed against the feather of Truth; and he compares lines 18, 20 and 21 respectively with Proverbs 24:29; Deuteronomy 33:27; and Proverbs 25:21. Readers will have noticed the contrast between the attitude of lines 17-21 and the eye-for-an-eye morality of the time; the Egyptian teaching looks forward to that of Christ, cf. St Matthew 5:39ff.

Guard thyself against robbing the wretched
And against being puissant over the man of broken arm.
Stretch not forth thy hand to repel an old man,
Nor prevent the aged from speaking.
Let not thyself be sent on a wicked mission,

Nor love him who hath performed it.
Cry not out against him whom thou hast injured,
Nor answer him back to justify thyself.
He who hath done evil, the river-bank abandons him,
And his flooded land carries him away.                          10
The north wind cometh down that it may end his hour;
It is united to the tempest;
The thunder is loud, and the crocodiles are evil.
O hot-head, what is thy condition?
O Moon, arraign his crime!
Steer that we may ferry the wicked man across,
For we shall not act like him –
Lift him up, give him thy hand;
Leave him in the hands of the god;
Fill his belly with bread that thou hast,                       20
So that he may be sated and may cast down his eye.

from *The Teaching of Amenemope*, translated by J. M. Plumley

### Do them a good turn

Tiru-Valluvar was an Indian sage who lived about 100 B.C. and compiled a complete guide to public and private conduct, written in couplets packed with meaning in an easily-remembered form. Here are two of his sayings:

Even when another has injured him in his hate, the man who is pure in heart returns not the injury.

How shall a man punish them that have injured him? Let him do them a good turn and make them ashamed in their hearts.

### When was it?

Then the king will say to those on his right hand, 'You have my Father's blessing; come, enter and possess the kingdom that has been ready for you since the world was made. For when I was hungry, you gave me food; when thirsty, you gave me drink; when I was a stranger you took me into your home, when naked you clothed me; when I was ill you came to my help, when in prison you visited me.' Then the righteous will reply, 'Lord, when was it that we saw you hungry and fed you, or thirsty and gave you drink, a stranger and took you home, or naked and clothed you? When did we see you ill or in prison, and come to visit you?' And the king will answer, 'I tell you this: anything you did for one of my brothers here, however humble, you did for me.'

St Matthew 25 : 35-40

### Neighbourhood

Any human being is a neighbour who needs aid.

Very often misery is unrelieved because it is not clamorous. When we hear of great numbers of people lying half dead on the roadside, the very magnitude of their need is apt to make us feel that we can do little and, therefore, might be excused from doing anything.

Some French people in a small village decided to honour a doctor who had served them for fifty years. A large vat was placed in the village square and everyone was asked to bring in a little wine. The plan was to give the whole vat, when filled, to the doctor. Each person said to himself, 'The little that I give will amount to nothing.' So each one brought a little water and poured it into the vat. In the end, the doctor had nothing.

Fulton J. Sheen, *Guide to Contentment*

### Enemy cares for enemy (seventeenth century)

A Sikh, Kanihya by name, was reported to his religious leader, or Guru, for having committed the 'sin' of giving water to the wounded on the battle-field, irrespective of whether they were friend or foe. To test him, the Guru in all innocence questioned him about his so-called misconduct.

The Sikh replied: 'You it was who taught me to see no enemy, no evil, no "otherness" in any man. When I served the wounded, it is you that I served in all of them. How could I know that one was my enemy and another my friend, when you are in the hearts of all?'

Based on Gopal Singh, *Religion of the Sikhs*

### Enemy cares for enemy (eighteenth century)

A few days ago some hundred English, who had been prisoners in France, were landed at Penzance by a cartel ship. Many of these passed through Redruth going home, but in a most forlorn condition. None showed more compassion to them than the French.* They gave them food, clothes, or money, and told them, 'We wish we could do more, but we have little for ourselves here.' Several who had only two shirts gave a naked Englishman one. A French boy, meeting an English boy, who was half naked, took hold of him and stopped him, cried over him a while, and then pulled off his own coat and put it on him!

John Wesley, *Journal*, 18 September 1757

*The French referred to were prisoners of war, themselves hardly well provided.

### Enemy cares for enemy (twentieth century)

The following is an extract from a letter received from an Austrian Jew now in the British Pioneer Corps. He is attached to a hospital receiving German wounded. He had been for nine months in the concentration camps of Dachau and Buchenwald: he had been hung by the wrists to a tree and had once nearly died of gangrene, Jews at that time not being allowed medical attention in concentration camps. He also has reason to believe that his old mother was taken to Poland two years ago:

'This is being written in the solitude of a ward in which I am guarding wrecked members of the Herrenvolk. It is so strange a situation that I can hardly describe what I am feeling. Loneliness is perhaps the only word for it. These are men who set out to conquer the world, and they and their kind have done unspeakable things to me and my kind, and I am supposed to hate them with all my strength, and would be right to do so according to recognised standards of human behaviour. But I cannot hate, or is it that in the face of suffering hatred is silent? So it happens that the guard is turned into a nurse, and if a man, from losing too much blood, goes out of his mind and stammers incoherently, I have to talk him to sleep again. And it sometimes happens that men try to hold my hand when I have helped them. That makes me feel lonely.

'Only a few lines. It is midnight, and I am going off duty after having had a busy time with that man who lost so much blood that he went crackers. He had an operation and blood transfusion, and I was the only one able to talk to him. In the end he obeyed my orders instantly with "Jawohl, Herr Doktor!" Once he said "Sie sind so ein feiner Mensch"* and then "Sie sind zu mir wie ein Vater."† What shall I make of that? I can only draw one conclusion, which is that I am a terribly bad soldier and I am somehow glad about it.

'The man I wrote about has died. The doctors fought for his life as if he were a celebrity.'

*Left News* (November 1944)

*'You are a good man!'   †'You are like a father to me.'

## Enemy cares for enemy (twentieth century)

We found ourselves on the track with several car-loads of Japanese wounded. These unfortunates were on their own and without medical care.

No longer fit for action in Burma, they had been packed into railway cars which were being returned to Bangkok. They had been packed up and dropped off according to the make-up of the trains. Whenever one of them died en route he was thrown off into the jungle. The ones who survived to reach Bangkok presumably would receive some kind of medical treatment. But they were given none on the way.

They were in a shocking state. I have never seen men filthier. Uniforms were encrusted with mud, blood and excrement. Their wounds, sorely inflamed and full of pus, crawled with maggots. The maggots, however, in eating the putrefying flesh, probably prevented gangrene.

It was apparent why the Japanese were so cruel to their prisoners. If they didn't care a tinker's damn for their own, why should they care for us?

The wounded men looked at us forlornly as they sat with their heads against the carriages, waiting for death. They had been discarded as expendable, the refuse of war. These were the enemy. They were more cowed and defeated than we had ever been.

Without a word most of the officers in my section unbuckled their packs, took out part of their ration and a rag or two, and, with water canteens in their hands, went over to the Japanese train.

Our guards tried to prevent us, bawling, 'No goodka! No goodka!' But we ignored them and knelt down by the enemy to give water and food, to clean and bind up their wounds. Grateful cries of '*Aragotto*!' (Thank you!) followed us when we left.

An allied officer from another section of the train had been taking it all in.

'What bloody fools you are!' he said to me.

'Have you never heard the story of the man who was going from Jerusalem to Jericho?' I asked him . . .

'But that's different,' the officer protested angrily. 'That's in the Bible. These are the swine who have starved us and beaten us. These are our enemies . . .' He gave me a scornful glance and, turning his back, left . . .

I regarded my comrades with wonder. Eighteen months ago they would have joined readily in the destruction of our captors had they fallen into their hands. Now these same officers were dressing the enemy's wounds.

Ernest Gordon, *Through the Valley of the Kwai*

### More than love

An anecdote, which gives yet another manner of regarding love: Dick Sheppard, the beloved, tempestuous, and eccentric vicar of St Martin-in-the-Fields, was asked by a freind how he could possibly love a certain person, to which Sheppard replied, 'I do more than love him, I positively like him!'

Alan Paton, *Instrument of Thy Peace*

### The Thief's gratitude

A thief in his old age was unable to ply his 'trade' and was starving. A wealthy man, hearing of his distress, sent him food. Both the rich man and the thief died on the same day. The trial of the rich man occurred first in the Heavenly Court; he was found wanting and sent to Purgatory. At the entrance however an Angel came hurrying to recall him. He was brought back to the court and learned that his sentence had been reversed.

The thief whom he had aided on earth had stolen the list of his iniquities.

L. I. Newman (trans. and ed.), *The Hasidic Anthology*

## Danilo Dolci

Danilo Dolce, after training as an architect, went and worked with peasants and fishermen at Trappeto in Sicily, one of the most wretched and depressed places that could be. 'I found myself', he writes, 'in one of the most miserable and blood-drenched areas in the world: with tremendous unemployment, widespread illiteracy, and Mafia violence reaching nearly everywhere. The people were bitter and discontented . . . Faced with the problems of a half-starving and desperate population, the State, instead of giving it the employment and the schools which it needed – actions which would have built up solid trust – responded by imprisoning or killing whoever uttered a protest.' And he describes the hopeless ignorance in which the people were sunk: 'Water in winter runs down the hillside and is wasted in the sea, and in the summer fields that might produce food for all lie parched and yellow; but how can you plan to build a dam if you have never heard of a dam? Manure is burned in heaps on the outskirts of many villages; how can you put it to good use if you do not know how to rot it and turn it into a valuable resource? Topsoil slides down from un-planted slopes, improperly cared-for crops and livestock produce low yields, while a large part of the population, often superstit-iously regarding these evils as punishment from on high, stand around with their hands in their pockets.'

So Dolci organised first a study and action centre, which acted as a stimulus for fresh undertakings and the formation of a workers' union and agricultural co-operatives. Dams and schools were built, and the people learned how to escape from poverty and the power of the Mafia – though the latter in its opposition to Dolci seems to have had the help of the legal system and at times of the Church as well. He has several times been recommended for a Nobel Peace Prize, and he well deserves one; many people see him as one of the most hopeful and admirable figures in action today. (Please see also p. 68.) One of his innovations was the 'strike in reverse'. When the authorities neglected to provide work, he and 700 others repaired a road which had long been in disrepair; and for this crime Dolci and 22 others were arrested, tried and imprisoned. At his trial he said, 'I would like to point out that no one took so much as a penknife with him to cut his bread . . . this was meant to be a symbol of a new spirit. The people understood its meaning – that the days of the machine-gun were finished, and that true revolution was born from within. There was to be an end of shooting'.

Editor


### Elizabeth Pilenko

Elizabeth Pilenko came from a wealthy family in the south of Russia, and in 1914 became a keen socialist revolutionary. A few years later she went to Paris, and being revolted by the excesses of the Russian revolution she joined a religious order of the Russian Orthodox Church, and was known as Mother Maria. However, she was not the traditional Russian Orthodox religious. She was accused by some of neglecting the long services and the traditional contemplation. 'I must go my way,' she said. 'I am for the suffering people.' In the early morning she was at the markets buying cheap food for the people she fed, bringing it back in a sack on her back. She was a familiar figure in the slum, in her poor black habit and her worn-out men's shoes.

The many Russian refugees in France in those days were stateless persons, many of them poverty-stricken, without privilege, without claim on any of the services which the country provided for the poor. Mother Maria worked among the poorest. She discovered that Russians who contracted tuberculosis were lying in a filthy hovel on the banks of the Seine into which the Paris police used to throw those syphilitic wrecks which they picked up along the riverside. With ten francs in her pocket she bought a château and opened a sanatorium.

Then she found that there were hundreds of Russians in lunatic asylums all over Europe. They had just 'disappeared' into these institutions, where no questions were asked about them. She raised a public outcry and got many of them released. In those days the Russian congregations in and around Paris were living examples of what the early apostolic communities must have been. They were real homes for the poor and the unwanted. Russians living in tenements could find there comfort and friendship. The Churches had their own labour exchanges, clinics and many other services, and the convent, over which Mother Maria presided, was central to their life.

When the German occupation took place Mother Maria summoned her chaplain and told him that she felt that her particular duty was to render all possible assistance to persecuted Jews. She knew that this would mean imprisonment and probably death, and she gave him the option of leaving. He refused. For a month the convent was a haven for Jews. Women and children were hidden within its walls. Money poured in to enable them to escape from France and hundreds were got away. At the end of a month the Gestapo came. Mother Maria was arrested and sent to the concentration camp at Ravensbruck. Her chaplain was sent to Buchenwald, where he died of starvation and overwork.

The story of her life in the camp is only now being pieced together. She was known even to the guards as 'that wonderful Russian nun', and it is doubtful whether they had any intention of killing her. She had been there two and a half years when a new block of buildings was erected in the camp, and the prisoners were told that these were to be hot baths. A day came when a few dozen prisoners from the women's quarters were lined up outside the buildings. One girl became hysterical. Mother Maria, who, had not been selected, came up to her. 'Don't be frightened', she said. 'Look, I shall take your turn', and in line with the rest, she passed through the doors. It was Good Friday, 1945.

*Christian News Letter*, 17 April 1946


√    **The Jericho road\***

A man went up on the Jericho road –
He went up all alone.
He was beaten up and left for dead,
And all his money had gone.

*Chorus*:   Who is neighbour to this fellow?
            Who'll stop to share his load?

Who gives a damn for the nameless man
On the other side of the road?

A religious man came along that way
With a great deal on his mind,
He was so concerned about higher things
He left the poor fellow behind.

Then a second traveller came that way,
He stopped to see him there;
But he thought of the danger and hurried on –
It had given him quite a scare.

At last a Samaritan came along,
A real outsider was he,
He stopped and tended the wounded man
And took him to a hostelry.

From the Congo to Calcutta streets
Little children cry for food,
But an affluent world still passes by
On the other side of the road.

A negro living in a Southern State
On the wrong side of the track,
Must he wait for a Muslim to say to him
'Be proud because you're black!'?

The Jericho road runs through our world
From Cape Town to Notting Hill;
And the Christ who told of the nameless man
Is asking his question still.

Geoffrey Ainger, *More Songs from Notting Hill*

*See St Luke 10:25-37 for the original story.

# Peace

The second of two well-known passages from the Old Testament presents the peaceful occupation of agriculture as the positive alternative to war. The idea that there is a natural order of things is a thread running through the poetry of centuries, and it is found acceptable today when the possible destruction of our habitat is a common topic. It appears for instance in a modern poem, 'Nightmare for Future Reference' by Stephen Vincent Benét, who puts these words into the mouth of a biologist:

We know a great many things and what do we know?
We think we know what finished the dinosaurs,
But do we? Maybe they were given a chance
And then it was taken back. There are other beasts
That only kill for their food. No, I'm not a mystic,
But there's a certain pattern in nature, you know,
And we're upsetting it daily. Eat and mate
And go back to the earth after that, and that's all right.
But now we're blasting and sickening earth itself.
She's been very patient with us. I wonder how long.

*Further reading*: Isaiah 11:1-9; Proverbs 16 and 17; St John 14:27; Romans 13 (8-12) and 14 (16-21), Walter de la Mare, 'An Old Cannon', in *A Choice of de la Mare's Verse*; D. H. Lawrence, 'The Combative Spirit', in *Complete Poems*; Carl Sandburg, 'Forgotten Wars', in *Complete Poems*; and Roger Schutz, the Prior of Taizé, *Violent for Peace* – very good on his discussions with young people, protest, and getting the economic foundations secure.

## Help in trouble

God is our refuge and strength,
A very present help in trouble.
Therefore will we not fear, though the earth be removed,
And though the mountains be carried into the midst of the sea;
Though the waters thereof roar and be troubled,
Though the mountains shake with the swelling thereof.
There is a river, the streams whereof shall make glad the city of
  God,
The holy place of the tabernacles of the most High.
God is in the midst of her; she shall not be moved:
God shall help her, and that right early.

The heathen raged, the kingdoms were moved;
He uttered his voice, the earth melted.
The Lord of hosts is with us;
The God of Jacob is our refuge.
Come, behold the works of the Lord,
What desolations he hath made in the earth.
He maketh wars to cease unto the end of the earth;
He breaketh the bow, and cutteth the spear in sunder;
He burneth the chariot in the fire.
'Be still, and know that I am God:
I will be exalted among the heathen,
I will be exalted in the earth.'
The Lord of hosts is with us;
The God of Jacob is our refuge.

> Psalm 46

### Swords into plowshares

He shall judge among many people, and rebuke strong nations afar off; and they shall beat their swords into plowshares, and their spears into pruning-hooks: nation shall not lift up a sword against nation, neither shall they learn war any more. But they shall sit every man under his vine and under his fig tree; and none shall make them afraid; for the mouth of the Lord of hosts hath spoken it.

> Micah 4:1-4

### Compassion the driving force of action

To talk of maintaining peace through the balance of power, or through the threat of nuclear deterrents, is foolish. The might of armaments can only produce fear, and not peace. It is impossible that there can be genuine and lasting peace through fear. Through fear can only come hatred, ill-will and hostility, suppressed perhaps for the time being only, but ready to erupt and become more violent at any moment. True and genuine peace can prevail only in an atmosphere of amity, free from fear, suspicion and danger.

Buddhism aims at creating a society where the ruinous struggle for power is renounced; where calm and peace prevail away from conquest and defeat; where the persecution of the innocent is vehemently denounced; where one who conquers himself is more respected than those who conquer millions by military and economic warfare; where hatred is conquered by kindness, and evil by goodness; where enmity, jealousy, ill-will and greed do not infect men's minds; where compassion is the driving force of action; where all, including the least of living things, are treated with fairness, consideration and love; where life in peace and harmony, in a world of material contentment, is directed towards the highest and noblest aim, the realisation of the ultimate truth, Nirvana.

W. Rahula, *What the Buddha Taught*

### The case of William Penn

William Penn, the Quaker, was granted land in the New World by King Charles II in return for a large sum of money which the King owed him. It was called Sylvania because of its forests and the King insisted on adding the name Penn. The Charter of Pennsylvania empowered Penn to make war on the Indian savages, but Penn refused to build any forts or to have cannon or soldiers in his province.

It was prophesied that all his settlements would soon be destroyed. But Penn took no notice of these prophecies. He set about founding his capital city which he named Philadelphia, the City of Brotherly Love. He made friends with the Indians and they arranged that all quarrels should be settled by a meeting of six white men and six red men. The Indians enjoyed equal citizenship with the white men and an equal choice of land. When William Penn died they mourned him as their friend.

After Penn's death, while every other colony in the New World was constantly attacked by the Indians, Pennsylvania was perfectly free from attack as long as they refused to arm themselves. Many years later the Quakers were outvoted in the State and the colony gave way to pressure on them from the other States and began to spend money in building forts and to train soldiers against possible aggression. They were immediately attacked.

E. B. Emmott, compiled from *The Story of Quakerism*

## A lesson from the primitives

The history of civilized nations justifies a most pessimistic view of human nature. But Geoffrey Gorer observes that

There are, however, a few rays of hope, a few societies where men seem to find no pleasure in dominating over, hurting or killing the members of other societies, where all they ask is to be at peace and to be left in peace. These societies are, of course, small, weak, technologically backward, and living in inaccessible country; only so could they survive the power-seeking of their uninhibited neighbours.

Among these gentle societies are the Arapesh of New Guinea; the Lepchas of Sikkim in the Himalayas (whom I studied); and, most impressive of all, the pygmies of the Ituri rain-forest in the Congo, studied by Colin Turnbull. These small societies (there are several others) living in the most inaccessible deserts and forests and mountains of four continents, have a number of traits in common, beside the fact that they do not dominate over, hurt or kill one another or their neighbours, though they possess the weapons to do so. Many of them, including the pygmies and the Lepchas until a couple of generations ago, rely almost exclusively on hunting for their protein food.

What seem to me the most significant common traits in these peaceful societies are that they all manifest enormous gusto for concrete physical pleasures – eating, drinking, sex, laughter – and that they all make very little distinction between the ideal characters of men and women, particularly that they have no ideal of brave, aggressive masculinity.

Men and women have different primary sexual characteristics – a source of endless merriment as well as of more concrete satisfactions – and some different skills and aptitudes. No child, however, grows up with the injunctions, 'All real men do . . .' or 'No proper woman does . . .' so that there is no confusion of sexual identity: no cases of sexual inversion have been reported among them. The model for the growing child is of concrete performance and frank enjoyment, not of metaphysical symbolic achievements or of ordeals to be surmounted. They do not have heroes or martyrs to emulate or cowards or traitors to despise; their religious life lacks significant personalized gods and devils; a happy, hardworking and productive life is within the reach of all.

Geoffrey Gorer, in *Man and Aggression*

### 'The sword sung on the barren heath'

The sword sung on the barren heath,
The sickle in the fruitful field;
The sword he sung a song of death,
But could not make the sickle yield.

William Blake


### The letter

This letter, gentlemen, is to your politicians,
Your men in high positions – please read it if you can.
When I woke up today, orders were waiting for me
To go and join the army, at once without delay.
I shall not, gentlemen, that's why I write this letter
To say that men had better refuse to fight again.
My words are blunt, I'm sure; I don't mean to upset you,
I only want to let you know that we are sick of war.

I've seen for many years how they have killed the others,
Seen brothers snatched from brothers and children lost in tears;
Mothers with swollen eyes weep while the rich not caring
Too busy profiteering grow fat on crimes and lies.
I've seen the prisoners, what did they do to merit
The sapping of the spirit, this test of what they were.
Tomorrow I'll be gone, I'll slam the door behind me
On all that may remind me of cruelty and wrong.

Then I will make my way around the world and travel
To fight out against evil and this is what I'll say –
It's good to be alive for all mankind are brothers
In this land and all others, so help your brothers thrive.
If blood is to be shed, shed yours you politicians,
You men in high positions and be it on your heads.
Follow me if you will. Call out your men and arm them.
Tell them I will not harm them, disarmed I'm safe to kill.

This letter, gentlemen, is to your politicians,
Your men in high positions – please read it if you can.
When I woke up today, orders were waiting for me
To go and join the army, at once without delay.

I shall not, gentlemen, that's why I write this letter
To say that men had better refuse to fight again.
My words are blunt, I'm sure; I don't mean to upset you,
I only want to let you know that we are sick of war.

Anonymous

## Share our resources

By world standards everyone in our society, even the old-age
pensioners who have been so shamefully neglected, is rich beyond
the dreams of avarice. In Nigeria, one of the more prosperous
states of tropical Africa, the average income per head of the
population is still under £30 a year. Something like two-thirds of
mankind are hungry; it has been said, though these things are
impossible of measurement, that half are starving in that their
lives are cut short because they have not enough food to build up
resistance. They are prey to every disease except stomach-ulcers,
which are the privilege of the pursuit of wealth; nothing else causes
so much anxiety. What does community mean in this context? We
have not begun to share our resources. The poorer nations are
still contributing more to us than we are to them: overall the flow
is from them to us.

John Ferguson, in the Alex Wood Memorial Lecture (1971)

## A way out

The more I have reflected on the experience of history the more
I have come to see the instability of solutions achieved by force
. . . But the question remains whether we can afford to eliminate
force in the world as it is without risking the loss of such ground as
reason has gained . . . There is at least one solution that has yet to
be tried – that the masters of force should be those who have
mastered all desire to employ it . . . If armed force were controlled
by men who have become convinced of the wrongness of using
force there would be the nearest approach to a safe assurance
against its abuse. Such men might also come closest to efficiency in
its use, should the enemies of civilisation compel this. For the more
complex war becomes, the more its efficient direction depends on
understanding its properties and effects; and the deeper the study

of modern war is carried the stronger grows the conviction of its futility.

Sir Basil Liddell Hart, *Why Don't We Learn From History?*

## Peace

My soul, there is a country
　Far beyond the stars,
Where stands a winged sentry
　All skilful in the wars:
There, above noise and danger,
　Sweet Peace sits crown'd with smiles,
And One born in a manger
　Commands the beauteous files.
He is thy gracious Friend,
　And – O my soul awake! –
Did in pure love descend
　To die here for thy sake.
If thou canst get but thither,
　There grows the flower of Peace,
The Rose that cannot wither,
　Thy fortress, and thy ease.
Leave then thy foolish ranges;
　For none can thee secure
But One who never changes –
　Thy God, thy life, thy cure.

Henry Vaughan

## Asoka

One of the uncommon exceptions to the historian's dictum, 'Power corrupts, and absolute power tends to corrupt absolutely. Great men are almost always bad men' (Lord Acton, *Historical Essays and Studies*):

He was Emperor of India about 300 to 232 B.C., and almost all that we know of him comes from the inscriptions that he had carved on rocks and stone pillars all over his empire. What little else concerns him comes from tradition, one being that he murdered ninety-nine of his brothers and sisters; this probably records a war of succession with one of his brothers. When he became emperor in 273 B.C. he behaved in the manner expected of such people, acting in an autocratic way, running a large court, and indulging in the usual hobbies – war, hunting and feasting; thousands of birds and animals were consumed every day in the imperial kitchens.

He had been reigning eight years when he decided to conquer the kingdom of Kalinga, and he succeeded, at a frightful cost. One of the rock edicts records that in this war 'men and animals, numbering one hundred and fifty thousand were carried away captive from that country, as many as one hundred thousand were killed there in action, and many times that number perished'. This so much horrified him that he became a Buddhist, attracted by the insistence of the faith on the sanctity of human life. He took full Buddhist vows after two years, and then spread over his kingdom the Buddhist teaching about piety, right living and morality; this was summed up in the word 'dharma'. One of the rock edicts says that it involves 'proper courtesy to slaves and servants, obedience to mother and father, liberality to friends, acquaintances and relatives . . . and abstention from the slaughter of living beings'. The massacre of birds and animals in the royal household was stopped; a daily maximum of two birds and one animal was to be allowed, but not as a regular affair. He carried this further later in his reign, for one of his edicts, this time on a pillar, declares a long list of animals exempt from killing, including parrots, mynahs, wild geese, bats, mango-tree ants, terrapins, tortoises, rhinoceroses and so on. Husks containing living beings were not to be burnt, and the burning of forests was regulated.

He wished all religions to live in harmony, replaced hunting expeditions by pilgrimages, and declared an amnesty for prisoners in nearly every year of his reign. He appointed a corps of civil servant missionaries to spread Buddhist principles around his empire, and told his officials to be kind to the border tribes he had conquered. In his reign of forty years there was peace at home and with other countries. He had roads built, trees planted, and hospitals started. Although his empire crumbled away within sixty years of his death, he set an example of a long and peaceful reign, and did much to establish Buddhism as one of the world's chief religions.

Editor, based on D. C. Sircar, *Inscriptions of Asoka*

### A new way of life

A nation, following the way of Christ, might feel called upon to adopt a policy of total disarmament. But it would do so, in the first instance, not with the deliberate purpose of courting martyrdom, but with the conviction that the best safety from the perils against which nations arm is to be found in a new national way of life, which would remove causes of provocation and lead progressively to reconciliation and peace. It would risk everything on the conviction that God's way would work. But such a nation must also be willing, if necessary, to incur the risk of national martyrdom by refusing to equip itself against the possibility of aggression. And it may be that the world must wait for its redemption from warfare until one nation is ready to risk crucifixion at the hands of its possible enemies. It might lose its own national life; but it would set free such a flood of spiritual life as would save the world.

G. H. C. MacGregor, *The New Testament Basis of Pacifism*

### Free the world from fear

But vain the sword and vain the bow,
They never can work war's overthrow.
The Hermit's prayer and the widow's tear
Alone can free the world from fear.

For a tear is an intellectual thing,
And a sigh is the sword of an angel king,
And the bitter groan of the martyr's woe
Is an arrow from the Almighty's bow.

William Blake, from 'The Grey Monk'

### Brotherhood of man

What's the world to you?
Much. I was born of woman, and drew milk,
As sweet as charity, from human breasts.
I think, articulate, I laugh and weep,
And exercise all functions of a man.
How then should I and any man that lives
Be strangers to each other? Pierce my vein,

Take of the crimson stream meandering there,
And catechise it well; apply thy glass,
Search it, and prove now if it be not blood
Congenial with thine own: and, if it be,
What edge of subtlety canst thou suppose
Keen enough, wise and skilful as thou art,
To cut the link of brotherhood, by which
One common Maker bound me to the kind?

William Cowper, from 'The Task'

# Religion 1

The first of the next three sections records some religious experiences, from that of John Clare to contemporary examples.
The passage from Douglas Hyde's book could be followed by the
account of St Paul's conversion in Acts 19:1-19; as a communist,
Douglas Hyde was at least a potential persecutor of Christians,
and St Paul was an active harrier of heretics, and an approving
witness of the lynching of St Stephen.

Thoughts about the nature of religion from religious men and
women are included in the next section, which starts with a
Hebrew meditation that is especially acceptable today in its re-
fusal to localise or personify God. It is followed by other views
on the nature of true religion and by some statements of the
humanist belief that man must find in his own resources a faith
to hold on to in living – a belief to which the Sikhs and some
Christians today seem to approach very closely; 'It is through the
man in the world that God is seen and realised in the world'
(Gopal Singh, *The Religion of the Sikhs*). Please see also Isaiah
58:3-9.

The third section contains illustrations of what religions involve
in practice; it comes out clearly that the existence and the power
of religion are to be found in the ordinary relationships of men
with one another. Religion is shown in various examples as
tolerant, life-bringing and working for good; and a few comic
examples show the absurdity of narrow and exclusive sectarianism.

### The king of kings

A Jewish legend puts these words into the mouth of God, addressing his people:

When I show myself to you I am not like earthly kings for whom their servants clear the highways and display hangings wherever they go, and kindle the lights for them and beautify their houses. I myself stretch out the heavens, whose blue is above your heads, and I myself kindle my great light, the sun, and I spread out over all the highways and on every mountain and hill and over all the valleys hangings of green, and flowers of sweet fragrance. Today you shall know and reflect on it in your hearts, that there is none like unto me among all the kings of the earth, for my power is without end and my loving kindness is for ever and ever.

J. B. Levner, *The Legends of Israel*, translated by Joel Snowman

### The fields was our church

I had plenty of leisure, but it was the leisure of solitude, for my Sundays were demanded to be spent in the fields at horse or cow tending. My whole summer was one day's employment as it were. In the fields I grew so much into the quiet love of nature's preserves that I was never easy but when I was in the fields passing my sabbaths and leisure with the shepherds and herd boys, as fancies prompted – sometimes playing at marbles on the smooth-beaten sheep tracks or leapfrog among the thymy molehills; or running into the woods to hunt strawberries; or stealing peas in churchtime (when the owners were safe), to boil at the gipsies' fire, who went half-shares at our stolen luxury. We heard the bells chime, but the fields was our church, and we seemed to feel a religious piety in our haunts on the sabbath – while some old shepherd sat on a molehill, reading aloud some favourite chapter from an old fragment of a Bible, which he carried in his pocket for the day. A family relic – which possessed on its covers and title pages in rude scrawls genealogies of the third and fourth generations; when aunts, mothers and grandmothers died; when cousins etc were married and brothers and sisters born. Occupying all the blank leaves in the book and title pages, which leaves were preserved with a sacred veneration though half the contents had been suffered to drop out and be lost.

John Clare, *Autobiography*

### Intoxicated with delight

My memory takes me back to a time when the delight I experienced in all natural things was purely physical. I rejoiced in colours, scents, sounds, in taste and touch; the blue of the sky, the verdure of earth, the sparkle of sunlight on water, the taste of milk, of fruit, of honey, the smell of moist or dry soil, of wind and rain, of herbs and flowers; the mere feel of a blade of grass made me happy; and there were certain sounds and perfumes, and above all certain colours in flowers, and in the plumage and eggs of birds, such as the purple polished shell of the tinamou's egg, which intoxicated me with delight. When, riding on the plain, I discovered a patch of purple verbenas in full bloom, the creeping plants covering an area of several yards, with a moist, green sward sprinkled abundantly with the shining flower-bosses, I would throw myself from my pony with a cry of joy to lie on the turf among them and feast my sight on the brilliant colour.

It was not, I think, till my eighth year that I began to be distinctly conscious of something more than this mere childish delight in nature. It may have been there all the time from infancy – I don't know; but when I began to know it consciously it was as if some hand had surreptitiously dropped something into the honeyed cup which gave it at times a new flavour. It gave me little thrills, often purely pleasurable, at other times startling, and there were occasions when it became so poignant as to frighten me. The sight of a magnificent sunset was sometimes almost more than I could endure and made me wish to hide myself away. But when the feeling was roused by the sight of a small and beautiful or singular object, such as a flower, its sole effect was to intensify the object's loveliness. There were many flowers which produced this effect in but a slight degree, and as I grew up and the animistic sense lost its intensity, these too lost their magic and were almost like other flowers which had never had it. . .

The feeling, however, was evoked more powerfully by trees than by even the most supernatural of my flowers; it varied in power according to time and place and the appearance of the tree or trees, and always affected me most on moonlight nights. Frequently, after I had first begun to experience it consciously, I would go out of my way to meet, and I used to steal out of the house alone when the moon was at its full to stand, silent and motionless, near some group of large trees, gazing at the dusky green foliage silvered by the beams; and at such times the sense of mystery would grow until a sensation of delight would change to fear, and the fear increase until it was no longer to be borne, and I would hastily escape to recover the sense of reality and safety indoors, where there was light and company.

W. H. Hudson, *Far Away and Long Ago*

### Born for this moment

During the two years just before and after I was twenty I had two experiences which led to religious conversion. The first occurred when I was waiting at a bus stop on a wet afternoon. It was opposite the Odeon cinema, outside the station, and I was surrounded by people, shops, cars. A friend was with me. All of a sudden, for no apparent reason, everything looked different. Everything I could see shone, vibrated, throbbed with joy and with meaning. I knew that it had done this all along, and would go on doing it, but that usually I couldn't see it. It was all over in a minute or two. I climbed on the bus, saying nothing to my friend – it seemed impossible to explain – and sat stunned with astonishment and happiness.

The second experience occurred some months later. I left my office at lunch-time, stopped at a small Greek café in Fleet Street to buy some rolls and fruit, and walked up Chancery Lane. It was an August day, quite warm but cloudy, with the sun glaringly, painfully bright, behind the clouds. I had a strong sense that something was about to happen. I sat on a seat in the garden of Lincoln's Inn waiting for whatever it was to occur. The sun behind the clouds grew brighter and brighter, the clouds assumed a shape which fascinated me, and between one moment and the next, although no word had been uttered, I felt myself spoken to. I was aware of being regarded by love, of being wholly accepted, accused, forgiven, all at once. The joy of it was the greatest I had ever known in my life. I felt I had been born for this moment and had marked time till it occurred.

Monica Furlong, *Travelling In*

### My search was at an end

As I travelled up the line next morning I looked from side to side
for the crosses. There were none there, not even on those buildings that I could recognise from the previous night; but there were
lightning-conductors on high grey towers and television aerials on
suburban homes which, for one night at least, had enscribed the
cross of God magnificently on the night sky of London.

That morning something happened. I was sitting in the gloom of
St Etheldreda's in the backmost seat as usual, when a late-teenage
girl came in, drably dressed and blessed with no good looks. I took
her to be a little Irish servant girl. But as she passed me I saw the
expression on her face. She, too, was worried. Like me, she clearly
had something big on her mind. She went purposefully down the
aisle to the front, then round to the left, to a kneeling stool on
which she knelt before Our Lady, after having lit a candle and put
some coins in a box.

Through such light as managed to creep through the blacked-
out windows and by the flame of the candle, I could see her busy
with a string of beads, her hands moving, her head nodding every
now and then. This was Catholic practice, of which I knew nothing. This was the world of the Ages with a Faith. This was the
world I had been groping for. Was it superstition? Was it the
world of mumbo-jumbo? Two opposing answers came simul-
taneously to my question.

As she passed me again on her way out I looked at her face.
Whatever had been troubling her had gone. Just like that. And
I had been carrying my load around with me for months and years.

When I was sure no one was about I went, almost hang-dog
fashion, down the aisle as she had done. Down to the front, round
to the left, put some coins in the box, lit a candle, knelt on the
stool – and tried to pray to Our Lady. Might as well be hanged for
a sheep as a lamb, the two voices told me together. If you're going
to be superstitious and pray to someone who isn't there you might
just as well go one step further in your superstition and pray to an
image and have done with it.

How did one pray to Our Lady? I did not know. Did you pray
*to* her or *through* her, using her as an intermediary? Did you gaze
at the figure to see the reality behind it or was it to that figure alone
that you addressed your words? Again I did not know.

I tried to remember some prayer to her from medieval literature or something from the poems of Chesterton or Belloc. My mind was empty. The candle spluttered and flickered, growing shorter and shorter but no words came.

At last I heard myself mumbling something which seemed appropriate enough when it began but which petered out, becoming miserably inappropriate. But it did not matter. I knew my search was at an end. I had not talked to nothing.

Outside the church I tried to remember the words I had said and almost laughed as I recalled them. They were those of a dance tune of the nineteen-twenties, a gramophone record of which I had bought in my adolescence:
'O sweet and lovely lady be good
O lady be good to me.'

Douglas Hyde, *I Believed*

### The wave which cannot halt

In Lawrence's novel, *The Rainbow*, the shepherd Tom Brangwen, spending long nights with his sheep during the lambing season, wonders whether he should get married or not:

During the long February nights with the ewes in labour, looking out from the shelter into the flashing stars, he knew that he did not belong to himself. He must admit that he was only fragmentary, something incomplete and subject. There were the stars in the dark heaven travelling, the whole passing by on some eternal voyage. So he sat small and submissive to the greater ordering.

What this 'greater ordering' meant in the daily life of the farming family to which he belonged comes out in a paragraph at the beginning of the book:

The Brangwens came and went without fear of necessity, working hard because of the life that was in them, not for want of money. Neither were they thriftless. They were aware of the last halfpenny, and instinct made them not waste the peeling of their apple, for it would help to feed the cattle. But heaven and earth was teeming around them, and how should this cease? They felt the rush of the sap in spring, they knew the wave which cannot halt, but every year throws forward the seed to begetting, and, falling back, leaves the young-born on the earth. They knew the

intercourse between heaven and earth, sunshine drawn into the
breast and bowels, the rain sucked up in the daytime, nakedness
that comes under the wind in autumn, showing the birds' nests no
longer worth hiding. Their life and inter-relations were such;
feeling the pulse and body of the soil, that opened to their furrow
for the grain, and became smooth and supple after their ploughing,
and clung to their feet with a weight that pulled like desire, lying
hard and unresponsive when the crops were to be shorn away.
The young corn waved and was silken, and the lustre slid along
the limbs of the men who saw it. They took the udder of the
cows, the cows yielded milk and pulse against the hands of the
men, the pulse of the blood of the teats of the cows beat into the
pulse of the hands of the men. They mounted their horses, and
held life between the grip of their knees, they harnessed their
horses at the wagon, and, with hand on the bridle-rings, drew the
heaving of the horses after their will.

> D. H. Lawrence, *The Rainbow* (1915)

### What more do I need?

Refugees were fleeing from one district, and outside the city one
of the lady missionaries found an old man sitting on the roadside
with his long pole on which he carried his roll of bedding, his rice
pot, and a singing bird in a cage. She asked if she could help him.
He had come seventy miles, and still had another seventy to go.
He said he did not wish money as he had been robbed three times.
'Come into the city,' she said, 'and we will give you food.' He said
that he would stay where he was, because he wanted to be on the
road before the city gate was opened. And then he said: 'If I am
tired, I have my bed; if I am hungry, I have my pot; if I am sad,
I have my bird to sing to me; and I am a Christian and have God
in my heart. What more do I need?'

> Hensley Henson, *Retrospect of an Unimportant Life*

### Talking to God

Particularly in a single cell,
but even in the sections
the religious sense asserts itself,

perhaps a childhood habit of nightly prayers,
the accessibility of Bibles,
or awareness of the proximity of death:

and, of course, it is a currency –
pietistic expressions can purchase favours
and it is a way of suggesting reformation
(which can procure promotion);

and the resort of the weak
is to invoke divine revenge
against a rampaging injustice;
but in the grey silence of the empty afternoon
it is not uncommon
to find oneself talking to God.

Dennis Brutus, *Letters to Martha*

### The living stream

Religion, this feeling of contact with a Greater Power beyond the self, seems to be some fundamental feature in the natural history of man. As one travels through the English countryside, taking the lesser by-ways rather than the great, one cannot, if one goes slowly and is prepared to stop, but be struck by the beauty of the old parish churches and be made to marvel that such glories could be built by such small groups of people, just as one marvels at the great medieval cathedrals in towns, which at the time of their building, must have had only moderate populations. If one goes inside such an old country church one cannot help feeling that here is something fashioned with real love and reverence; elements of superstition there may well be, but in spite of this, surely here is something created not just by an ignorant craving for magic, but something of profound depth. A naturalist coming from another planet, if his space-ship had the ability to drift across the countryside like a balloon, could not but be struck by the prominence of these buildings in each small community. Among the little groups of houses their spires and towers stand up like the sporangia of some organism and he might well be excused for first thinking them to have the importance of some such reproductive process. Indeed they had an equal importance in the past when devotion to God was as real to the population as was that of sexuality. They hardly have the same significance today and some, alas, stand forsaken like fossil skeletons of the past; this, however, may only be a temporary phase due to the accelerated growth of a physical science, whose findings are difficult to reconcile with many of the old doctrinal dogmas. I say temporary because I believe the dogmas on both sides may be revised as theology becomes more natural and science's mechanistic interpretation of life is shown not to be the whole truth.

Religion indeed seems to be some fundamental feature in Man's make-up; something which can be as powerful as any other urge. Few can doubt that the wars of religion or of rival ideologies are more bitter than those fought for just economic ends; and we must not forget that those on the two sides of a conflict may well, through the lack of a generally accepted scientific theology, be propelled by different ideas of God that they both, in their preju-dice, passionately feel to be right. It would not surprise me if the roots of religion went much deeper down into biological history than is generally conceded, and that it *is* part of the very nature of the living stream.

Sir Alister Hardy, *The Living Stream*

## Outside and beyond themselves

No man or woman begins to live a full life until they realise they live in the presence of something greater, outside and beyond themselves. Self-consciousness truly means that you are standing over against that other than yourself and you cannot be living in truth. Wonder is at the base of true living, and wonder leads to worship and after that the great other than self; it is yet kin to you, you are one with it. Then you begin to live more completely and realise the kinship between you and Nature, that out of Nature you came and are part and parcel with it, this brings nearer faith, which is self-conscious life (opposed to birds, trees, etc.), reaching out to perfection.

G. A. Studdert Kennedy, *The New Man in Christ*

### Where God is

It is worth remembering what St Augustine says. He looked every-where for God, and at last came to find him in himself. It is im-portant, especially for someone who is worried, to realise this truth, and to know that he or she need not go to heaven to speak with God the father, or to enjoy his presence. And there is no need for anyone to speak out loud – for however quietly we may speak, God is so near that he will hear us. There is no need either to take flight to look for God, because we can always settle our-selves in peace and quiet, and see God there, within ourselves.

freely adapted from St Teresa of Avila, *The Way of Perfection*

### 'I look on nature'

I look on nature less with critic's eyes
Than with that feeling every scene supplies,
Feeling of reverence that warms and clings
Around the heart while viewing pleasant things;
And heath and pastures, hedgerow-stunted trees,
Are more than Alps with all its hills to me;
The bramble for a bower, the old mole-hill
For seat, delights me, wander where I will;
I feel a presence of delight and fear,
Of love and majesty far off and near;
Go where I will, its absence cannot be,
And solitude and God are one to me;
A presence that one's gloomiest cares caress
And fills up every place to guard and bless.

John Clare

### Tryst

She fixed me with her spinster eye –
Inquisitiveness arch and sly,
And said: 'Where have you been to-day –
That lonely walk? But I daresay
There's someone nice to meet up there . . .'
Beneath her coy expectant stare
I thought of that fern-shadowed lane;

The scent of hedgerows after rain;
Red rowan berries; the autumn note,
Plaintive and sweet, of robin's throat;
Dew-netted cobwebs; beech-leaves old,
Fluttering earthward, copper and gold;
White clouds wind-driven o'er the wood;
September peace, beatitude:
Beauty divine of sky and sod.

'Someone I meet there? Only God.'

> Teresa Hooley, *Selected Poems*

# Religion 2

### Thou art there

O Lord, thou hast searched me, and known me.
Thou knowest my downsitting and mine uprising,
Thou understandest my thought afar off.
Thou compassest my path and my lying down,
And art acquainted with all my ways.
For there is not a word in my tongue,
But lo, O Lord, thou knowest it altogether.
Thou hast beset me behind and before,
And laid thine hand upon me.
Such knowledge is too wonderful for me;
It is high, I cannot attain unto it.
Whither shall I go from thy spirit?
Or whither shall I flee from thy presence?
If I ascend up into heaven, thou art there.
If I take the wings of the morning,
And dwell in the uttermost parts of the sea,
Even there shall my hand lead me,
And thy right hand shall hold me.
If I say, 'Surely the darkness shall cover me.'
Even the night shall be light about me;

Yea, the darkness hideth not from thee,
But the night shineth as the day:
The darkness and the light are both alike to thee.
For thou hast possessed my reins;
Thou hast covered me in my mother's womb.
I will praise thee; for I am fearfully and wonderfully made:
Marvellous are thy works;
And that my soul knoweth right well.
My substance was not hid from thee,
When I was made in secret,
And curiously wrought in the lowest parts of the earth.
Thine eyes did see my substance, yet being unperfect;
And in thy book all my members were written,
Which in continuance were fashioned,
When as yet there was none of them.
How precious also are thy thoughts unto me, O God!
How great is the sum of them!

Psalm 139

## Where God is found

We apprehend Him in the alternate voids and fulnesses of a cathedral; in the space that separates the salient features of a picture; in the living geometry of a flower, a seashell, an animal; in the pauses and intervals between the notes of music, in their difference and sonority; and, finally, on the plane of conduct, in the love and gentleness, the confidence and humility, which give beauty to the relationships between human beings.

Aldous Huxley, *Ends and Means*

### Just as faithfully

A teamster* sought the Rabbi's advice as to whether he should give up his occupation because it interfered with regular attendance at the synagogue.

'Do you carry poor travellers free of charge?' asked the Rabbi.

'Yes,' answered the teamster.

'Then you serve the Lord in your occupation just as faithfully as you would by frequenting the synagogue.'

L. I. Newman (trans. and ed.), *The Hasidic Anthology*

*A teamster was a man who earned his living hauling goods with a team of horses or oxen; the closest present-day analogy is a long-distance lorry driver.

### The religion of the heart

The nature of religion is so far from consisting in forms of worship, or rites and ceremonies, that it does not properly consist in any outward actions. A man may both abstain from outward evil, and do good, and still have no religion. Two persons may do the same outward work; feeding the hungry, or clothing the naked; and one of these may be truly religious, and the other have no religion at all; for the one may act from the love of God, and the other from the love of praise. Although true religion naturally leads to every good word and work, yet the real nature thereof lies deeper still, even in 'the hidden man of the heart'.

Adapted from John Wesley, Sermon VII

### Doubts resolved

Not many years ago when I was an atheist, if anyone had asked me, 'Why do you not believe in God?' my reply would have run something like this: 'Look at the universe we live in. By far the greater part of it consists of empty space, completely dark and unimaginably cold. The bodies which move in this space are so few and so small in comparison with the space itself that even if every one of them known to be crowded as full as it could hold with perfectly happy creatures, it would still be difficult to believe that life and happiness were more than a by-product to the power that made the universe. . . History is largely a record of crime, war, disease, and terror, with just sufficient happiness interposed to give them, while it lasts, an agonised apprehension of losing it, and when it is lost, the poignant misery of remembering. Every now and then they improve their condition a little and what we call a civilization appears. But all civilizations pass away and, even while they remain, inflict peculiar sufferings of their own probably sufficient to outweigh what alleviations they may have brought to the normal pains of man . . . If you ask me to believe that this is the work of a benevolent and omnipotent spirit, I reply that all the evidence points in the opposite direction. Either there is no spirit behind the universe, or else a spirit indifferent to good and evil, or else an evil spirit.'

There was one question which I never dreamed of raising. I never noticed that the very strength and facility of the pessimists' case at once poses a problem. If the universe is so bad, or even half so bad, how on earth did human beings ever come to attribute it to the activity of a wise and good Creator?

C. S. Lewis, *The Problem of Pain*

### More than himself

Human beings in the midst of these possibilities for better and for worse which promise and menace, and for which they are responsible, need confidence, they need a boost. If this does not come from religious faith, it can come only from the available natural and human resources. Such resources are not themselves a vision that can create confidence, but they are resources which have inspired such visions in the past, and they have power to do so now. For the human being is more than himself and he has more than the present which he grasps. He may become deeply aware of the interpenetration of phases in his own life and in that of mankind. There is no present moment that is not charged with the past and pledged to the future. Within this imaginative grasp and this mortal span, I am the author of my own experience. That experience may be but a sorry or trivial tale of what happens to me. Or I may take it in hand and create an experience that is worth sharing, not for its moral but for itself. Such a creation requires an art of living which is the better part of civilization and, for the most part, is still to be learned, although its rudiments are familiar.

Humanism is an aspiration to breed this confidence rooted in available resources and an attainable art, and thus to reduce the pointlessness of individual lives which exclaim against the pointlessness of it all. The answer to the objection is necessarily a practical one, and must be judged accordingly.

H. J. Blackham, in *Objections to Humanism*

### 50,000 organ blowers

If a war should break out, not just in Europe, but if Europe went to war with Asia, and Africa, America and Australia found themselves compelled to join in, then in and for itself, by itself, this does not concern God in the least; but it would concern him that a poor man should sigh to him, for thus it pleases his majesty, and this would affect him subjectively.

But now suppose that all the emperors and kings of Europe should issue an edict, commanding all the thousands of ordained hired servants (I mean the priests and the parsons) to implore the aid of heaven *officially*. And suppose that an immense united religious service were organized, with 100,000 musicians and 50,000 organ blowers, and a million ordained hired servants to implore the aid of heaven *officially*. This would not concern the divine majesty in the least. But if a poor man walking along the street sighs in his inmost heart to God, that concerns him, it concerns him indescribably, infinitely, for thus it pleases his majesty, and this would affect him subjectively . . .

What an infinite distance it is from God when an emperor, by means of an edict composed by a minister of state, commands 10,000 ordained hired servants to bawl officially to God, what an infinite distance in comparison with a poor man who sighs in his inmost heart to God . . .

Soren Kierkegaard, *The Last Years*, translated by Ronald Gregor Smith

### The voice of God

The livid lightnings flashed in the clouds:
The leaden thunders crashed.
A worshipper raised his arm.
'Hearken! hearken! The voice of God!'

'Not so,' said a man.
'The voice of God whispers in the heart
So softly
That the soul pauses,
Making no noise,
And strives for these melodies,
Distant, sighing, like faintest breath,
And all the being is still to hear.'

Stephen Crane

## Letters from God

Why should I wish to see God better than this day?
I see something of God each hour of the twenty-four, and each
     moment then,
In the faces of men and women I see God, and in my own face in
     the glass,
I find letters from God dropped in the street, and every one is
     signed by God's name,
And I have them where they are, for I know that wheresoe'er I go
Others will punctually come for ever and ever.

Walt Whitman, from 'Song of Myself'

## Strength greater than my own

I do know that trying to be open to things that are good, and
beautiful, and true, wherever they are to be found, brings to me a
strength that is greater than my own. This is fortified by seeking
out and finding reassurance from 'good deeds in a naughty world',
which encourages the belief that goodness, courage, generosity
and heroism are possible. This remains true even when such virtues
are partially disclosed. There have been many lives like those of
St Francis, Gandhi and Schweitzer, which have shown how great
is the human potential for heroic living.

George H. Gorman, Introducing Quakers

### Preaching all the time

A boy once joined the Franciscan Order longing to become a friar preacher. He was put to work in the kitchen for the first months and got more and more restive and impatient to get on with learning to preach. Finally Francis himself drew him by the arm one day and asked him if he would like to go into the village with him to preach. The boy's heart was full as they set out. They stopped on the way to see a man whose son needed work in the town, then to call on an old woman who was sick and lonely, and to visit with a peasant at work in the fields. In the town, they saw a merchant about a post for the son, they begged some food for the brothers at home, they talked with some people in the market place, and then Francis turned to the boy and proposed that they return to the friary. 'But when are we going to preach?' asked the boy in an anguish of concern. Francis slipped his arm about him and said, 'Why, my brother, we've been preaching all the time.'

> Douglas Steere, from the Swarthmore Lecture, 'Where Words Come From'

---

# Religion 3

---

### The negative confession

The sentences below are taken from the Egyptian *Book of the Dead*, and were supposed to be spoken by the dead on entering the hall of the goddesses of Truth:

I have not wronged my kinsfolk.
I have not caused my name to appear for honours.
I have not domineered over slaves.
I have not defrauded the poor man of his goods.
I have not caused harm to be done to the slave by his master.
I have caused no man to suffer.
I have allowed no man to go hungry.
I have made no man weep.
I have slain no man.

I have not given the order for any man to be slain.
I have not cheated in measuring of grain.
I have not filched land or added thereto.
I have not encroached upon the fields of others.
I have not added to the weight of the balance.
I have not cheated with the pointer of the scales.
I have not taken away the milk from the mouths of the babes.
I have not driven away the beasts from their pastures.
I have not netted the geese of the preserves of the gods.
I have not caught fish with bait of their bodies.
I have not obstructed water when it should run.
I have not cut a cutting in a canal of running water.
I have not extinguished a flame when it ought to burn.

Translation by E. A. Wallis Budge

from **The great hymn to Shamash**

Shamash was originally a Sumerian god, but was adopted by the conquering Babylonians. Surviving because it was written on clay tablets, and 'among the longest and most beautiful of the hymns that have come down to us in cuneiform, this ranks as one of the best products of Mesopotamian religious writing' (M. Eliade).

The feeble man calls to you from the hollow of his mouth,
The humble, the weak, the afflicted, the poor,
She whose son is captive constantly and unceasingly confronts you.
He whose family is remote, whose city is distant,
The shepherd amid the terror of the steppe confronts you,
The herdsman in warfare, the keeper of sheep among enemies.
Shamash, there confronts you the caravan, those journeying in
    fear,
The travelling merchant, the agent who is carrying capital.
Shamash, there confronts you the fisherman with his net,
The hunter, the bowman who drives the game,
With his bird net the fowler confronts you.
The prowling thief, the enemy of Shamash,
The marauder along the tracks of the steppe confronts you.
The roving dead, the vagrant soul.
They confront you, Shamash, and you hear all.

Translation by W. G. Lambert, *Babylonian Wisdom Literature*

### Involved in the conflict of his time

In his feeling I see [Christ] supremely as a man of compassion. That is, he entered into every aspect and event of human life, knowing it in its truth and reality, sharing all that human beings experienced, not only perceiving what women and men felt, but feeling with them. With those who needed tenderness he was tender, but his love was not always gentle. He would not spare people the truth, even when it had to hurt. He could love the rich young man and yet say to him that he could not inherit eternal life if he did not give up his riches. He flayed the oppressors of the poor with the most biting invective that has ever been used. His love could be gentle, but it could also be stern and austere, intensely demanding.

I see him deeply involved in the conflict of his time, not standing aside or offering principles from on high, but deeply involved, right *in* the conflict, followed round by contentious groups, supported or attacked, applauded or derided, loved or feared. He was a man of passion, not only in his suffering, but throughout his life and ministry.

Kenneth C. Barnes, *The Creative Imagination*

### The God-like in men

When Christ wished to teach us what God is like he pointed to the God-like in men. Even in the worst sinner he could discover the hidden good and appeal to it, knowing that the good and not the evil is the essential man. He tells us that it is when a sinner 'comes to himself' that he 'arises and goes to his Father': the man's true self is that within him which responds to God.

G. H. C. MacGregor, *The New Testament Basis of Pacifism*

### Christ's action

Christ never did so great a work, but there
His human nature did, in part, appear:
Or ne'er so mean a piece, but men might see
Therein some beams of His divinity:
So that, in all He did, there did combine
His human nature, and His part divine.

Robert Herrick

### This fellow eats with sinners

Another time, the tax-gatherers and other bad characters were all crowding in to listen to him; and the Pharisees and the doctors of the law began grumbling among themselves; 'This fellow,' they said, 'welcomes sinners and eats with them.' He answered them with this parable: 'If one of you has a hundred sheep and loses one of them, does he not leave the ninety-nine in the open pasture and go after the missing one until he has found it? How delighted he is then! He lifts it on to his shoulders, and home he goes to call his friends and neighbours together. "Rejoice with me!" he cries. "I have found my lost sheep." In the same way, I tell you, there will be greater joy in heaven over one sinner who repents than over ninety-nine righteous people who do not need to repent.'

St Luke 15:1-7

### Buddha and the dancing-girl

In the rainy season Buddha and his disciples lived at Vaishali in a beautiful mango grove belonging to a lovely dancing-girl whose name was Amrapali.

Amrapali had heard of Buddha and she wished to see him and listen to him. One day she set out in her carriage for the mango grove but when she arrived she was met by a monk, who knowing her to be a courtesan, refused to take her to the Lord. Feeling humiliated and insulted, Amrapali was turning back. Just then another monk came and said: 'Take her to the Lord Buddha, brother, for all are welcomed by him. The Lord Buddha makes no distinction between the rich, the poor, the low-caste or the high-caste, the good or the bad.'

So the monks led Amrapali to the Buddha and the beautiful dancing-girl stood spellbound in the presence. Her pride in her own beauty, which had humbled many kings and princes, disappeared and she flung herself at the feet of the Master and worshipped him.

> Buddha then told his monks how in a previous incarnation Amrapali had been a pheasant and had been burnt to death in trying to put out a forest fire.

Before taking her leave of Buddha that evening Amrapali invited him to her home next day and asked him to honour her by taking his meal there. He agreed, and she left the mango grove rejoicing at her good fortune.

On her way back she met some princes who were going to meet Buddha and she told them that the Buddha had agreed to eat a meal at her place. They were annoyed and jealous. They said: 'How is it that the Holy One has consented to eat at the home of such a woman? Surely she is lying to us.'

They went with speed to the grove and requested Lord Buddha to eat with them the next day; but the Buddha replied: 'I have already accepted the invitation of Amrapali.'

The next day the Lord went to Amrapali's house and ate the food that the dancing-girl had prepared with love and adoration. After eating, Buddha gave Amrapali further advice and she asked if he would accept the house she lived in as a gift to the order of monks. And Buddha said 'Yes'. For he saw the generosity and goodness of the heart that gave it.

> Adapted from Shakuntala Masani, *Gautama, the Story of Lord Buddha*

### You eat with a low-caste carpenter

Nanak, the founder of the Sikh religion, was born in Pakistan in 1495. As a young man he set out to instruct and save the world, taking with him a drummer called Mardana, whose job it was to play on a rebeck or three-stringed fiddle, while Nanak sang his hymns to the people. Once he put up at the house of a poor, low-caste carpenter, Lalo by name; and this made the high-class Hindus very angry. They said, 'This man is lowering the esteem of his father's faith by dining with a low-caste Hindu and keeping the constant company of a Muslim drummer.' One of them, Malik, had arranged a feast in honour of his ancestors and invited Nanak to attend. But Nanak refused to go. At last Malik, who was an official of the local Pathan army commander, asked his servants to bring Nanak to his presence by force. Nanak went; and when he was asked, 'You come not to eat with me, and yet you eat with a low-caste carpenter? What kind of man are you?'

Nanak replied, 'In your bread is the blood of the poor, while the bread of Lalo, who earns by the sweat of his brow, is sweet like milk.'

> Based on Gopal Singh, *The Religion of the Sikhs*

### Humanity rich and deep

Jesus' 'lack of moral principles'. He sat at meal with publicans and sinners, he consorted with harlots. Did he do this to obtain their votes? Or did he think that, perhaps he could convert them by such 'appeasement'? Or was his humanity rich and deep enough to make contact, even in them, with that in human nature which is common to all men, indestructible, and upon which the future has to be built?

Dag Hammarskjöld, *Markings*

### My scheme for converting father

I don't think I had any clear conception what a mission is. Yet I had a vague idea that God had chosen me to be the instrument of my father's salvation, so that he might not be sent to hell when he died.

I recollect, to this day, the spot on which I commenced my long-projected undertaking. It was on a path which skirted, on the farther side, the lawn in front of our house and led to the garden. I could point out the very tree we were passing when – with some misgivings, now that it was to be put to the test – I sounded my father by first asking him what he thought about Jesus Christ. His reply was to the effect that I would do well to heed his teachings, especially those relating to charity and to our loving one another.

This was well enough, as far as it went; but it did not at all satisfy me. So, with some trepidation, I put the question direct, whether my father disbelieved that Christ was the Son of God?

He looked a little surprised and did not answer immediately. 'Why do you ask that question, my son?' he said at last.

'Because I am sure – ' I began eagerly.

'That he *is* God's Son?' asked my father, smiling.

'Yes, I am.'

'Did you ever hear of the Mahometans?' said my father, while I had paused to collect my proofs.

I replied that I had heard of such a people who lived somewhere far off.

'Do you know what their religion is?'

'No.'

'They believe that Christ is not the Son of God, but that another person, called Mahomet, was God's chosen prophet.'

'Do they not believe the Bible?' asked I, somewhat aghast.

'No. Mahomet wrote a book called the Koran; and Mahometans believe it to be the word of God. That book tells them that God sent Mahomet to preach the gospel to them, and to save their souls.'

Wonders crowded fast upon me. A rival Bible and a rival Saviour! Could it be? I asked, 'Are you *quite* sure this is true, papa?'

'Yes, my dear, I am quite sure.'

'But I suppose there are very few Mahometans; not near, *near* so many of them as of Christians.'

'Do you call Catholics Christians, Robert?'

'O no, papa. The Pope is Antichrist.'

My father smiled. 'Then by Christians you mean Protestants?'

'Yes.'

'Well, there are many more Mahometans than Protestants in the world; about a hundred and forty million Mahometans, and less than a hundred million Protestants.'

'I thought almost everybody believed in Christ, as mama does.'

'There are probably twelve hundred millions of people in the world. So out of every twelve persons only one is a Protestant. Are you *quite* sure that the one is right and the eleven wrong?'

And so ended this notable scheme of mine for my father's conversion.

R. D. Owen, *Threading My Way* (1874)

### Honour other religions

This is one of the Rock Edicts of the Buddhist Emperor of India, Asoka, whose reign is described on p. 158.

We should not praise up our own religion at the expense of other beliefs; instead we should always try to treat other religious bodies with respect. In this way we advance our own faith and help other religions as well. People who act otherwise do harm both to their own and to other people's religions. If a person praises his own religion and runs down others, he thinks he is doing good to his own faith, but he is not. So we should watch how we speak, and we should come to learn about and respect the teaching of other religions.

Rock Edict XII

### An old lady in Scotland

An old lady in Scotland thought all other Christians were wrong, and so started a church of her own. One day, a caller, who was interested in her point of view, said, 'Do you really believe, as people say you believe, that nobody will go to heaven except you and your coachman?' To which the old lady replied, 'Well, I'm not so sure about John.'

Anonymous

### For poor and rich alike

An Egyptian inscription 4000 years old put these words into the mouth of God:

I have created the four winds, so that every man may breathe as freely as his brother; the great waters so that there may be abundance for poor and rich alike. I have created all men in the same image. And I have forbidden that they should commit iniquity, but their hearts have undone what my word required.

Quoted in Simone Weil, *Waiting on God*

### We are the sweet selected few

We are the sweet selected few,
The rest of you be damned;
There's room enough in hell for you,
We won't have heaven crammed.

Anonymous eighteenth-century jingle, from *The Methodist Bedside Book*

### The journey

The religious man is the one who believes that life is about making some kind of journey; the non-religious man is the one who believes that there is no journey to take. The literature of the inward journey abounds with warnings about how easy it is to lose the way, how narrow is the entrance and how difficult the path.

What is the journey and where does it take us? What all the accounts, whatever their origin, have in common is a sense of the terrors to be encountered *en route*.

Monica Furlong, *Travelling In*

### 'Blessed be the day'

Blessed be the day that I began
  A pilgrim for to be:
And blessed also be that man
  That thereto moved me.

'Tis true, 'twas long ere I began
  To seek to live for ever;
But now I run as fast as I can;
  'Tis better late than never.

Some of the ditch shy are, yet can
  Lie tumbling in the mire;
Some, though they shun the frying pan,
  Do leap into the fire.

What danger is the pilgrim in,
  How many are his foes!
How many ways there are to sin
  No living mortal knows.

The Lord is only my support
  And he that doth me feed;
How can I then want anything
  Whereof I stand in need?

Our tears to joy, our fears to faith,
  Are turned as we see,
That our beginning, as one saith,
  Shows what our end will be.

John Bunyan

# Protest

Social and economic advances have been achieved under the stimulus of those who were not content with things as they found them. The advances have been made with least cost in human unhappiness when the rich and powerful as well as the poor and oppressed felt that change was necessary, and either met the pro-testers half-way or themselves initiated reforms; this has often been the case in England, and accounts for the comparative absence of civil strife in our history. Every age, our own as much as any, needs a clear-sighted look at things as they are and the way they are going. A few years ago for example the Campaign for Nuclear Disarmament organised protest marches to Alder-maston. They seemed to achieve nothing, and some of those who took part appeared rather muddle-headed. But it is now known that the marches at least prompted those in power to look at their policies. The protests affected 'scientific opinion about nuclear policies in the upper grades of Whitehall . . . they certainly made it possible for serious discussion within Whitehall' (*The Times*, 8 September 1971).

*Further reading*: Exodus 5:1-9; Daniel 6; St Mark 11:15-19; Acts 5 (17-33), 16 (16-39) and 26 (13-31); Bertolt Brecht, 'Song of the Patch and the Overcoat', in *Compact Poets*; D. H. Lawrence, 'Don'ts'; Ezra Pound, 'Commission'; P. B. Shelley, 'Song to the Men of England'; *Poems of Protest* (Studio Vista); F. du Plessis Gray, *Divine Disobedience*; Mary Palmer, *Writing and Action*.

### We must find the answer

There is a mass confusion in the minds of my generation in trying to find a solution for ourselves and the world around us.

We see the world as a huge rumble as it swiftly goes by with wars, poverty, prejudice, and the lack of understanding among people and nations.

Then we stop and think: there must be a better way and we have to find it.

We see the huge rat race of arguing people trying to beat their fellow man out. All of this builds up, causing unrest between nations and in the home. My generation is being used almost like a machine. We are to learn set standards, strive for better education so we can follow in our elders' footsteps. But why? If we are to be a generation of repetition, the situation will be worse. But how shall we change? We need a great deal of love for everyone, we need a universal understanding among people, we need to think of ourselves and to express our feelings, but that is not all. I have yet to discover what else we need, nor have I practised these things as fully as I should. Because when I try I'm sneered at by my elders and those who do not hear, or look at it with a closed mind. Computers take the place of minds; electronics are taking over, only confusing things more.

I admit we should follow some basic rules but first you should look at who is making the rules.

Sometimes I walk down a deserted beach listening to the waves and birds and I hear them forever calling and forever crying and sometimes we feel that way but everyone goes on with his own little routine, afraid to stop and listen for fear of cracking their nutshell.

The answer is out there somewhere. We need to search for it.

Shannon Dickson, 15 (Texas)

### The loan sharks

The story of the money changers (Mark 11:15-19)

One time Jesus decides he is going to go up to the church. Back in them days they had kind of a weirdo way of doing things in churches. They used to stick sheep or oxen or pigeons. And on account of people had to come a long ways sometimes it was easier to buy one of them there things and then take it into church and stick it. They called it a sacrifice. They was some guys like loan sharks, gyp artists who set up stores near the church and started sellin' sheep and ox and pigeons and double charging people' cause they knew they couldn't get 'em any place else. Then they was some other kind of people. They called 'em money changers. On account of people had to come from other places and their money was no good where they were. Then it got all the more mixed up because the church had its own money. So the people had to take the regular money and turn it in and get the church money back 'fore they could put it in the basket. And the guys that used to change the money like the loan sharks charged you an awful lot for doin' it. And the Revs. in the church got cut in on it too.

Well, this day Jesus comes and he sees what's goin' on and it don't look like a church at all but it looks more like a vegetable market with stuff all over the sidewalk and most people was interested in sellin' stuff rather than goin' to church. Well this gets Jesus really teed off and he got ahold of a whip. Then he takes the whip and he yells, 'All right, you bunch of jerks, get outta here.' Then he tipped over the tables and he yells, 'You're makin' my Father's house like a store.' Well, these guys gets real scared and they see that Jesus really means it and that he's groovin' up and down in front of them so they don't do nothin' 'bout it. So then one guy says, 'Hey man, what right have you got to do these things?' Then Jesus tells 'em, 'You kill me and in three days I'll be right back here again.' But they didn't understand this. Well, anyway, he shook people up so that they really began to believe that he was right when he said he was the Son of God. Then the people began to pay attention to 'im and follow 'im and even some of the Revs.

> Version by young American delinquents. recorded by Carl Burke, in *God is Beautiful, Man*

## A protest in the sixth year of Ch'ien Fu (A.D. 879)

The hills and rivers of the lowland country
    You have made your battle-ground.
How do you suppose the people who live there
    Will procure firewood and hay?

Do not let me hear you talking together
    About titles and promotions;
For a single general's reputation
    Is made out of ten thousand corpses.

> Ts'ao Sung (about 870-920), translated by Arthur Waley

## We are called slaves

John Ball, a priest from York, lived in Colchester about the year 1360. He had no settled parish but wandered the countryside of Essex, preaching in churches and churchyards and at market crosses. He was always in trouble with the bishops and higher clergy for his attacks on their luxurious living and disregard for the condition of the poor. He was imprisoned three times. One of his sermons has survived:

My good friends, matters will not go well in England till all things be made common; when there shall be neither serfs nor lords; when the lords shall be no more masters than ourselves. How ill they behave to us! For what reason do they thus hold us in bondage? Are we not all descended from the same parents, Adam and Eve? And what can they show, or what reason can they give, why they should be more masters than ourselves? They are clothed in velvet and rich stuffs, ornamented with ermine and other furs, while we are forced to wear poor clothing. They have wine, spices, and fine bread, while we have only rye, and the refuse of the straw; and when we drink, it must be water. They have handsome houses and manors, while we must brave the wind and rain in our labours in the field; and it is by our labours that they have wherewith to support their pomp. We are called slaves, and if we do not perform our service we are beaten, and we have no sovereign to whom we can complain or be willing to hear us.

Let us go to the King and remonstrate with him; he is young and from him we may obtain a favourable answer, and if not, we must ourselves seek to amend our condition.

John Ball became the mouthpiece of the discontent among the peasants against the feudal system which bound serfs to the land and to servitude to the lords of the manor. In 1381 they began to revolt against this serfdom and against the increased taxation their rulers needed for wars abroad. In June the peasants from Essex marched to London, everywhere storming the manor houses and destroying the scrolls on which their labour services were recorded. In Kent they broke into Maidstone gaol and released John Ball. He joined them in their march to London, and on Blackheath preached a rousing sermon announcing that the time had come for rooting up the tares that cumbered the land; the tares were the oppressive rulers. The peasants gained control of the City of London, permitted no looting, and forced Richard II to grant their demands.

But their victory was short-lived. Their military leader, Wat Tyler, also from Colchester, was assassinated by Sir William Walworth, Lord Mayor of London; and then King Richard came forward, deceiving the people, promising them their demands, and persuading them to return home – where they met his soldiers who massacred them. John Ball was captured at St Albans, and executed on July 15th.

From a pamphlet by Jack Putterill

## Only our poor brothers

The passage below comes from a pamphlet, *Our Seamen*, that Samuel Plimsoll distributed at the Trades Union Congress of 1873. In 1876 the passing of the Merchant Shipping Act stopped the sending of overladen and unseaworthy vessels to sea in order that they might be lost and the insurance money claimed. Here he describes how on a visit to a northern port he had heard of the sending to sea of a deeply laden vessel, which everyone expected to be lost.

Two workmen said to each other, 'that they would not go to sea in that ship if the owner gave them the ship'. And another workman said 'he'd rather go to prison than go in that ship'; and lastly two of the wives of the sailors at least begged the owner 'not to send the vessel to sea so deep'.

She was sent. The men were some of them threatened, and one at least had a promise of 10s. extra per month wages to induce him to go. As she steamed away, the police boat left her; the police had been on board to overawe the men into going. As the police boat left her side, two of the men, deciding at the last moment that they would rather be taken to prison, hailed the police, and begged to be taken by them. The police said 'they could not interfere', and the ship sailed. My friend was in great anxiety, and told me that if it came on to blow, the ship *could not* live.

It did blow a good half gale all the day after, Sunday – the ship sailed on Friday. I was looking seaward from the promontory on which the ruins of T – – – – Castle stands, with a heavy heart. The wind was not above force 7 – nothing to hurt a well-found and properly loaded vessel. I had often been out in much worse weather, but then this vessel was not properly loaded (and her owner stood to gain over £2,000 clear if she went down, by overinsurance), and I knew that there were many others almost as unfit as she was to encounter rough weather – ships so rotten, that if they struck they would go to pieces at once; ships so overloaded, that every sea would make a clean sweep over them, sending tons and tons of water into her hold every time, until the end came.

On Monday we heard of a ship in distress having been seen; rockets had been sent up by her; it was feared she was lost. On Tuesday, a nameboard of a boat was picked up, and this was all that was ever heard of her . . .

Working men, is it nothing to you that your fellow-workmen, fathers of families, men to whom life is as dear as it is to yourselves, men who have committed no fault, should thus shamefully be neglected? – should thus be drowned by the dozen and the score to make a few bad men richer? – and that their needless deaths should not even elicit an inquiry into the cause of it? I hate to appeal to class feelings or prejudices, but class jealousy can only be allayed by justice, not by ignoring murderous wrong; and I ask, seriously and sadly, can anyone doubt, but that if these brave men had been pigs or sheep, the Legislature had long since been compelled by powerful advocates to stop such losses? Pigs and sheep are property, and property is well represented in Parliament; but these – why they are only our poor brothers, and no one speaks for them.

Samuel Plimsoll, *Our Seamen*

### Priests in prison

Daniel and Philip Berrigan were Catholic priests who believed in a radical form of Christianity that brought them into conflict with American militarism. They will be remembered for having seized and burnt some 'draft' records of men liable for conscription in the Vietnam war in 1968 – for which they were imprisoned. This is part of their statement:

Today, May 17th, we enter Local Board No 33 . . . to seize Selective Service records and burn them with napalm manufactured by ourselves from a recipe in the Special Forces Handbook, published by the U.S. Government. We, American citizens, have worked with the poor in the ghetto and abroad. We destroy these draft records not only because they exploit our young men, but because they represent misplaced power concentrated in the ruling class of America . . . We confront the Catholic Church, other Christian bodies and the synagogues of America with their silence and cowardice in the face of our country's crimes. We are convinced that the religious bureaucracy in this country is racist, is an accomplice in war and is hostile to the poor . . . Now this injustice must be faced, and this we intend to do, with whatever strength of mind, body and grace that God will give us. May God have mercy on our nation.

### Young people driven to frenzy

Marx said prophetically . . . that now for the first time in history the human race had the technical means to cure many of its age-old ills such as hunger and homelessness and poverty. We today are in an even more remarkable situation. We are not only coming into possession of the means to cure the ills, we are in the position of not being able to avoid quite literally seeing them. On television we see the sufferings of the world, we see how other lives go to waste. As our latterday prophets keep telling us, technology is making the world into a village, bringing us closer to each other and generating immense new powers: while at the same time, we see that we are still even now patently unable to set things to rights, unable to stop famine in India or war in Africa. I think this is fundamentally the situation which drives young people into a kind of frenzy.

Iris Murdoch, in an essay, 'Existentialists and Mystics'

### The dangers of violence

To carry through a social reform which . . . will create so much opposition as to necessitate the use of violence is criminally rash. For the chances are that any reform which requires violence for its imposition will not only fail to produce the good results anticipated, but will actually make matters worse than they were before. Violence . . . can produce only the effects of violence . . . where violence has been used for a long period, a habit of violence is formed and it becomes exceedingly difficult for the perpetrators of violence to reverse their policy. Moreover, the results of violence are far-reaching beyond the wildest dreams of the often well-intentioned people who resort to it.

Aldous Huxley, *Ends and Means*

## Beware moral hardening

How they fill us with embarrassment, our fellow-Christians who are always getting worked up over things we take calmly! 'It's a scandal' they say; 'some protest must be made about it'; and we have so long grown accustomed to the scandal – some public defiance of Christian feeling, some weakness of attitude in high places; 'What good do protests do?' we ask. 'Does anybody really mind about resolutions passed at meetings, about letters to the paper?' Let us admit that we are sometimes in the right; to be always up in arms over trifles is to lessen the rarity-value of your protests; the modern public has grown distrustful of 'pressure-groups'. And the habit of constantly airing your grievances is a danger to your peace of mind.

And yet, how we despise in others the cynicism of the flabbiness which simply 'can't be bothered' in a world so fertile of abuses! At least let us beware, as age creeps on, of a certain moral hardening which familiarity with the world is apt to breed in us. Let us not despise altogether the weakness in which God's strength is made perfect.

Ronald Knox, *Lightning Meditations*

## 'Much madness is divinest sense'

Much madness is divinest sense
To a discerning eye;
Much sense the starkest madness.
'Tis the majority
In this, as all, prevails.
Assent, and you are sane;
Demur – you're straightway dangerous,
And handled with a chain.

Emily Dickinson

## Gandhi

M. K. Gandhi was born in India of devout Hindu parents, and was brought up to believe in the value of prayer, a vegetarian diet, and fasting. He was sent to England at the age of eighteen to get a legal training; this was in the 1880s, and the difficulty then of getting proper vegetarian food added to the misery of loneliness. Soon after his return to India he went to South Africa to represent an Indian firm in a legal case, and at once came up against apartheid, being forcibly ejected from a first-class carriage on a railway journey. Thus he found himself involved in organising Indians to secure their voting and other rights, and stayed twenty years in South Africa instead of the one he had expected. Here he gave up drinking cows' milk because of the cruelties inflicted on cows, and here he was nearly murdered by a mob of whites on returning from a holiday in India. After the South African war he led the resistance of Indians against finger-printing and registration orders, and was imprisoned for two months in Johannesburg. In this campaign he first preached and practised non-violence, which came to be known as 'satyagraha', and met with a measure of success after some trickery by J. C. Smuts, the South African soldier and politician.

When he returned to India, he saw that his country needed to get rid of the British and rule itself, but he also saw that he must after twenty years' absence get to know his own country and for a start to take action against the vicious caste system, which caused millions of human beings to be regarded as worse than animals. In 1916 he founded a small community, which was to be a model to the rest of India of self-help and self-respect; its members 'spun and wove their own cloth, and from this time onwards Gandhi wore only his home-made shawl, 'dhoti' and sandals. It is recorded that years later when he attended the 1931 round table conference in London on the future of India he 'was asked if he felt undressed before King George Vth, and made the immortal remark "The King wore enough for both of us" '.

When Ronald Duncan visited Gandhi in 1938 he found that as part of his effort for the betterment of Indian villages Gandhi had withdrawn to the neighbourhood of a most backward village in an unfertile district – a filthy village of improvised hovels, with apathetic inhabitants in hopeless debt. They had sunk so far that they would relieve themselves anywhere, even near their only well; and one day Gandhi scavenged the excreta and buried it himself. The villagers began to follow his example; and in Ronald Duncan's words, 'Gandhi's act of selfless . . . service had achieved in a moment what coercion or teaching could not have done in a century.'

By 1920 his course was firmly set – to get rid of the British raj by non-co-operation and non-violence. A series of arrests and imprisonments, sometimes without trial and often accompanied by fasting on Gandhi's part, helped rather than hindered his ultimate success. For in 1945 the British government agreed to independence for India, and two years later the British officially left. Violence broke out between Muslim and Hindu, especially in East Bengal, as soon as British control was removed, and Gandhi set out on tours of panic-stricken areas to spread the ideas of goodwill and co-operation. India was independent, but torn by religious strife. Gandhi started a fast as part of his effort to bring peace, and ended it after five days; but the rejoicing was cut short – for on the 30 January 1948 he was shot dead by a Hindu fanatic. Thus ended the life of a man who took on and got the better of a powerful nation, without any weapon but his own moral force.

Editor

# Work

In most ages men and women have had to work for a living. Till recently there has not been much time over for leisure pursuits, for once food and shelter were won such religion and art as came to people were geared up with their occupations; the museums today collect as treasures many of the things that in the past were produced for everyday use. It is only where power has replaced muscle that an economy of abundance obtains; and with power came factories and specialising, to create new problems.

The extracts below fall into three groups. First we have what has become the conventional view of work: however dull, it is seen as good in itself, if directed to right ends. This is beautifully expressed by George Herbert; going further, George Eliot points to the value of faithful but hidden lives.

The next section, starting with Kahlil Gibran, reminds us that the achievements of those who have come to be regarded as great are usually built on the toil of 'millions of unregarded men'.

In the third section the dilemma that faces all concerned with education is implied – that is, if our pupils are going into soul-destroying occupations, are we to educate them for their jobs or against their jobs? The short opening poem says, 'Nothing is worth the making if it does not make the man' and the Buddhist quotation adds the point that one should not follow a socially harmful occupation. Unfortunately much of industry is concerned with making goods that fill no real need but are sold in response to a demand created by advertising. Moreover, the mass-production methods required make no demand on the mind, muscle or skill of the worker, but reduce him to an automaton. There is no 'good day's work to be done', so it is in leisure that life must be lived.

*Further reading*: Ecclesiastes 3 : 10-13; Ecclesiasticus 38 : 24-35; Psalms 90 (16, 17) and 128 (1, 2); D. H. Lawrence, 'Morning Work', 'We are transmitters', 'The Combative Spirit', 'Dark Satanic mills' and other poems; Carl Sandburg, 'Child of the Romans', in *Harvest Poems*; Walt Whitman, 'A Song for Occupations'; W. H. Auden, *A Certain World*, pp. 405-6; Fred Inglis, *The Imagery of Power*; D. L. Sayers, *Unpopular Opinions*, pp. 125-6.

### Preparation

A disciple of Rabbi Schmelke's begged his master to teach him how to prepare his soul for the service of God. The master told him to go to Rabbi Abraham, who at that time was still an innkeeper. The disciple did as he was bidden and lived in the inn for several weeks without observing any vestige of holiness in the innkeeper who from morning prayer till night devoted himself to his business. Finally he asked him what he did all day. 'My most important occupation,' said Rabbi Abraham, 'is to clean the dishes properly, so that not the slightest trace of food is left, and to clean and dry the pots and pans, so that they do not rust.' When the disciple returned home and reported to Rabbi Schmelke what he had seen and heard, the rabbi said to him: 'Now you know the answer to what you asked me.'

Martin Buber (trans.), *Tales of the Hasidim*

### The farmer and his sons

A farmer, being on the point of death, wished to ensure from his sons the same care and attention to his farm that he himself had given it. He called them to his bedside, and said, 'My sons, there is a great treasure hid in one of my vineyards.' After his death the sons took their spades and mattocks, and carefully dug over every

bit of their land. They found no treasure, but the vines repaid their
labour by an extraordinary and superabundant crop.

Aesop's *Fables*

### The elixir

Teach me, my God and King,
  In all things thee to see,
And what I do in any thing,
  To do it as for thee:

Not rudely, as a beast,
  To run into an action;
But still to make thee prepossessed,
  And give it his perfection.

A man that looks on glass,
  On it may stay his eye;
Or if he pleaseth, through it pass,
  And then the heaven espy.

All may of thee partake:
  Nothing can be so mean,
Which will his tincture 'for thy sake'
  Will not grow bright and clean.

A servant with this clause
  Makes drudgery divine:
Who sweeps a room, as for thy laws,
  Make that and th' action fine.

This is the famous stone
  That turneth all to gold:
For that which God doth touch and own
  Cannot for less be told.

George Herbert

### The Lord walks among the pots and pans

It is very important for us to realize that God does not lead us all
by the same road . . . Remember that there must be someone to
cook the meals, and count yourselves happy in being able to

serve like Martha. Reflect that true humility consists to a great extent in being ready for what the Lord desires to do with you.

Remember that the Lord walks among the pots and pans and that He will help you in the inward tasks and in the outward too.

> St Teresa, *The Way of Perfection and the Foundations*, translated by E. Allison Peers

### Who lived faithfully

The growing good of the world is partly dependent on unhistoric acts; and that things are not so ill with you and me as they might have been, is half owing to the number who lived faithfully a hidden life, and rest in unvisited tombs.

> George Eliot, closing words of *Middlemarch*

### Man-making

We all are blind until we see
  That, in the human plan,
Nothing is worth the making, if
  It does not make the man.

Why build these cities glorious
  If man unbuilded goes?
In vain we build the world, unless
  The builder also grows.

> Edwin Markham

### Agriculture

Roam where they will, men must at last stand behind the plough for their food; in spite of every hardship, therefore, husbandry is the chiefest industry.

They alone live who live by tilling the ground; all others but follow in their train and eat only the bread of dependence.

Manuring profits more than the ploughing; and when the land is weeded, guarding it profits more than irrigation.

The fair one called Earth laughs to herself when she sees the sluggard cry, saying: Alas, I have nothing to eat!

> Tiru-Valluvar, about 100 B.C.

### Right livelihood

Right livelihood means that one should abstain from making one's living through a profession that brings harm to others, such as trading in arms and lethal weapons, intoxicating drinks, poisons, killing animals, cheating, etc., and should live by a profession which is honourable, blameless and innocent of harm to others. One can clearly see here that Buddhism is strongly opposed to any kind of war, when it lays down that trade in arms and lethal weapons is an evil and unjust means of livelihood.

W. Rahula, *What the Buddha Taught*

## Guidance from Christianity

Perhaps if the Churches had had the courage to lay their emphasis where Christ laid it, we might not have come to this present frame of mind in which it is assumed that the value of all work, and the value of all people, is to be assessed in terms of economics. We might not so readily take for granted that the production of anything (no matter how useless or dangerous) is justified so long as it issues in increased profits and wages; that so long as a man is well paid, it does not matter where his work is worth-while in itself or good for his soul: that so long as a business deal keeps on the windy side of the law, we need not bother about its ruinous consequences to society or to the individual. Or at any rate, now that we have seen the chaos of bloodshed which follows upon economic chaos, we might at least be able to listen with more confidence to the voice of an untainted and undivided Christendom.

Dorothy L. Sayers, *Unpopular Opinions*

## Living in our leisure

There is no prospect that machine work will ever make anything like the demand on character from the ordinary worker that the old crafts used to make and some skilled work in some callings makes today; the craftsman who knows what beauty is because his own hands bring it into being, the farmer whose work trains him in observation and sympathy, the small trader with his wide range of contacts with people, the sailor, the nurse, the teacher, all get more from their work as well as giving more to it than the modern factory worker ever can . . . If the factory worker is ever in his life to meet the experiences that call upon his purposiveness, his creative capacity, his sense of perfection, and to be conscious of carrying significant responsibility in society, it must be in his leisure.

This involves a profound re-thinking of the balance of life. We have been accustomed to think that the challenge that develops character is met in work; that work is the adventure in which you find yourself, for the sake of which you have to grow, in which you find the chief interest of life and its paramount duties. This is the Puritan conception of work; it is not true of all periods of history. [Civilisation, in the sense of spiritual achievement, has largely been the creation of human leisure; music, art, philosophy, science, have owed much to men who had time to spare from breadwinning. Working class leisure has already made its not insignificant contributions: peasant communities have developed folk dance, embroidery, wood-carving and ballad; town-dwellers have their chapels, trade unions, and brass bands. ]

Today we think of leisure as the margin of life that may rightly be spared for relaxation or enjoyment after a good day's work. But for thousands of people there will never be a good day's work to be done, there will only be a lever to be pulled (or the like) for eight or nine or ten hours. If work in the sense of breadwinning means machine minding, work that is the making of a man must be done in leisure from breadwinning. Leisure must become the most truly strenuous part of life, a tonic rather than a sedative.

Constance Reaveley and John Winnington, *Democracy and Industry*

### Work for each and all

I raise a voice . . .
To exalt the present and the real,
To teach the average man the glory of his daily work and trade,
To sing in songs how exercise and chemical life are never to be
    baffled,
To manual work for each and all, to plough, hoe, dig,
To plant and tend the tree, the berry, vegetables, flowers,
For every man to see to it that he really do something, for every
    woman too;

To use the hammer and the saw, (rip, or cross-cut)
To cultivate a turn for carpentering, plastering, painting,
To work as tailor, tailoress, nurse, hostler, porter,
To invent a little, something ingenious, to aid the washing,
    cooking, cleaning,
And hold it no disgrace to take a hand at them themselves.

Walt Whitman, from 'Song of the Exposition'

### Builders of bridges

In Antioch where the river Assi goes to meet the sea, a bridge was
built to bring one half of the city nearer to the other half. It was
built of large stones carried down from among the hills, on the
backs of the mules of Antioch.

When the bridge was finished, upon a pillar thereof was engraven in Greek and in Aramaic, 'This bridge was builded by
King Antiochus II.'

And all the people walked across the good bridge over the
goodly river Assi.

And upon an evening, a youth, deemed by some a little mad,
descended to the pillar where the words were engraven, and he
covered the graving with charcoal, and above it he wrote, 'The
stones of this bridge were brought down from the hills by the
mules. In passing to and fro over it you are riding upon the backs
of the mules of Antioch, builders of this bridge.'

And when the people read what the youth had written, some of
them laughed and some marvelled. And some said, 'Ah yes, we
know who has done this. Is he not a little mad?'

But one mule said, laughing, to another mule, 'Do you not
remember that we did carry those stones? And yet until now it has
been said that the bridge was builded by King Antiochus.'

Kahlil Gibran, *The Wanderer*

### A worker reads history

Who built the seven gates of Thebes?
The books are filled with names of kings.
Was it kings who hauled the craggy blocks of stone?
And Babylon, so many times destroyed,

Who built the city up each time? In which of Lima's houses,
That city glittering with gold, lived those who built it?
In the evening when the Chinese wall was finished
Where did the masons go? Imperial Rome
Is full of arcs of triumph. Who reared them up? Over whom
Did the Caesars triumph? Byzantium lives in song,
Were all her dwellings palaces? And even in Atlantis of the legend
The night the sea rushed in,
The drowning men still bellowed for their slaves.

Young Alexander conquered India.
He alone?
Caesar beat the Gauls.
Was there not even a cook in his army?
Philip of Spain wept as his fleet
Was sunk and destroyed. Were there no other tears?
Frederick the Great triumphed in the Seven Years War. Who
Triumphed with him?

Each page a victory,
At whose expense the victory ball?
Every ten years a great man,
Who paid the piper?

So many particulars.
So many questions.

> Bertolt Brecht, translated by H. R. Hays, in *Compact Poets*:
> *Brecht*

### Creating plenty for others

In a manner I am a Communist. Their ideal, bating some things, is
nobler than that professed by any secular statesman I know of . . .
Besides it is just – I do not mean the means of getting to it are. But
it is a dreadful thing for the greatest and most necessary part of a
very rich nation to live a hard life without dignity, knowledge,
comforts, delight, or hopes in the midst of plenty – which plenty
they make. They profess that they do not care what they wreck or
burn, the old civilisation and order must be destroyed. This a
dreadful look out but what has the old civilisation done for them?
As it at present stands in England it is in great measure itself

founded on wrecking. But they got none of the spoils, they came in for nothing but harm from it then and thereafter. England has grown hugely wealthy but this wealth has not reached the working classes; I expect it has made their condition worse. Besides this iniquitous order the old civilisation embodies another order mostly old and what is new in direct entail from the old, the old religion, learning, law, art, etc and all the history that is preserved in standing monuments. But as the working classes have not been educated they know next to nothing of all this and cannot be expected to care if they destroy it.

Gerard Manley Hopkins, from a letter

### Extol the unregarded men

Extol the unregarded men;
Always the millions of unrewarded men,
the simple ones,
crafty with weapons, ploughs, and tools,
providers for, and protectors of nations,

Thor strokes in Panama, Simplon, Assouan;
multiples of finger-tips and hammer-taps;
Wrath of Jehovah; Hitler's, Joshua's, Haig's,
manoeuvring feet of questing myrmidons:
always the millions of unrewarded men.

Ur was theirs, as Paris and Pittsburgh are,
angular templed Thebes, Rome road-radiant,
that marted Babylon, this bartering London:
Calloused palms on thighs, the doers appraised
the manifest Truth in the made thing,
downed tools to oblivion:

god in the plumb column, the masonry firm,
the accurate ministration of engines;
god spurned in themselves.
Always, alas, the millions of unregarded men?

W. Stewart Rainbird

# Quality not Quantity

Among university and college students there is a good deal of scepticism about the affluent society, in which people are judged by their money and possessions; a contribution (the first poem in the section) from the pop world is representative. But at school the colour supplement life inevitably – with all the skill and resources its money can command – brings most powerful pressures to bear; and the idea that happiness does not necessarily depend on paid-for things may not be readily accepted. An oblique approach therefore will be more helpful than a head-on attack on the only world which many young people know. Some of Carl Sandburg's poems are much to the point – the brief one called 'Happiness', for example, in which he asks professors and famous executives to tell him what is happiness, gets nothing out of them, and then by a river

> I saw a crowd of Hungarians under the trees with their women and children and a keg of beer and an accordion.

*Further reading*: Ecclesiastes 3:1-8; St John 10:10; John Clare, 'The Woodcutter's Night Song'; W. H. Davies, 'What is this life'; Thomas Hardy, 'A Private Man on Public Men'; D. H. Lawrence, many poems; Carl Sandburg, 'Happiness', in *Harvest Poems*; Edward Thomas, 'For These'; L. van der Post, parts of the first chapter of *The Lost World of the Kalahari*; D. Thompson (ed.), *Discrimination and Popular Culture*.

### How to be happy

There are various ways of being happy, and every man has the capacity to make his life what it needs to be for him to have a reasonable amount of peace in it. Why then do we persecute ourselves with illusory demands, never content until we feel we have conformed to some standard of happiness that is not good for us only, but for *everyone*? Why can we not be content with the secret gifts of the happiness that God offers us, without consulting the rest of the world? Why do we insist, rather, on a happiness that is approved by the magazines and TV? Perhaps because we do not believe in a happiness that is given to us for nothing. We do not think we can be happy with a happiness that has no price tag on it.

If we are fools enough to remain at the mercy of the people who want to sell us happiness, it will be impossible for us ever to be content with anything. How would they profit if we became content? We would no longer need their new product.

The last thing the salesman wants is for the buyer to become content. You are of no use in our affluent society unless you are always just about to grasp what you never have.

Thomas Merton, *Conjectures of a Guilty Bystander*

### Notes to the hurrying man

All day I sit here doing nothing but
watching how at daybreak
birds fly out and return no fatter
when it's over. Yet hurrying about this room
you would have me do something similar;
would have me make myself a place
in that sad traffic you call a world.
    Don't hurry me into it; offer
no excuses, no apologies.
Until their brains snap open
I have no love for those who rush
about its mad business;
put their children on a starting line and push
into Christ knows what madness.

    You will not listen.
'Work at life!' you scream,
and working I see you rushing everywhere,
so fast most times you ignore
two quarters of your half a world.
    If all slow things are useless
and take no active part in nor justify your ignorance
that's fine; but why bother screaming after me?
Afraid perhaps to come to where I've stopped
in case you find
into some slow and glowing countryside
    yourself escaping.
Screams measure and keep up the distance between us:
    Be quieter –
I really do need to escape;

take the route you might take
if ever this hurrying is over.

Brian Patten

### It is not growing like a tree

It is not growing like a tree
  In bulk, doth make man better be;
Or standing long an oak, three hundred year,
To fall a log at last, dry, bald, and sear:
  A lily of a day
  Is fairer far in May,
  Although it fall and die that night;
  It was the plant and flower of light.
In small proportions we just beauties see:
And in short measures life may perfect be.

Ben Jonson

### People matter

We must concern ourselves with getting not the most out of
people, but the best. We must rethink our plans for industry and
housing with an eye to the kind of life and atmosphere people
would find in them rather than to planning efficiency. We must
care about people being happy in their job rather than adjusted or
conditioned to it; we must think of machines as just extensions of
men, rather than their owners. Now there's plenty of evidence that
this is what man as a whole is demanding. He may do it noisily, in
marches or protest, or quietly, by turning his back on it, as the
Flower People do. He can run away into the private world of drugs,
or he can live at secondhand through mass communications. . .

We have reached an extraordinary degree of mastery over
things at the very moment when we are least able to get on terms
with human beings – 'You can control,' said an Indian, 'half a
million horsepower, but you can't keep your temper.'

What we must do is to recognise that people and our relationships with them matter more than our ability to handle things. It
is really more important, for instance to be on terms of understanding with one's children than to maintain one's car at the peak

of condition; it is more important to respect people's right to be themselves than it is to manipulate them into being something different.

Stephen Hopkinson, in *More from Ten to Eight on Radio Four*

## Bread and liberty

For the few hours of life allotted me,
Give me, great God, but bread and liberty.
I'll beg no more; if more thou art pleased to give,
I'll thankfully that over-plus receive:
If beyond this no more be freely sent,
I'll thank for this, and go away content.

Abraham Cowley

## Four things make us happy here

Health is the first good lent to men;
A gentle disposition then:
Next, to be rich by no by-ways;
Lastly, with friends to enjoy our days.

Robert Herrick

## The best medicines

Joy and Temperance and Repose
Slam the door on the doctor's nose.

Friedrich von Logau

## The lioness

There was an argument among the beasts of the field, as to which of the animals deserved the most credit for producing the greatest number of whelps at a birth. They rushed clamorously into the presence of the lioness, and demanded of her that she should settle the dispute. 'And you,' they said, 'how many sons have you at a birth?' The lioness laughed at them, and said: 'Why, I have only one; but that one is altogether a thorough-bred lion.'

The value is in the worth, not in the number.

Aesop's *Fables*

### Response to life

At its highest level . . . happiness is the ecstasy which mystics have inadequately described. At more humdrum levels it is human love, the delights and beauties of our dear earth, its colours and shapes and sounds; the enchantment of understanding and laughing, and all other exercise of such faculties as we possess; the marvel of the meaning of everything, fitfully glimpsed, inadequately expounded, but ever-present.

Such is happiness; not compressible into a pill; not translatable into a sensation; lost to whoever would grasp it to himself alone; not to be gorged out of a trough, or torn out of another's body, or paid into a bank, or driven along an autoroute, or fired in gun-salutes, or discovered in the stratosphere. Existing, intangible, in every true response to life, and absent in every false one; pro-pounded through the centuries in every noteworthy word and deed and thought; expressed in art and literature and music; in vast cathedrals and tiny melodies; in everything that is harmonious, and in the unending heroism of imperfect men reaching after perfection.

Malcolm Muggeridge, *Muggeridge through the Microphone*

### Why in such a hurry?

Amy Johnson (1904-41) was the first woman to fly solo from Eng-land to Australia, when she made a record flight to India. In her book on Miss Johnson, Constance Babington-Smith tells this apocryphal story. When news of the record flight reached Tibet it was told 'with admiration verging on awe' by an Englishman to the Dalai Lama; and he having considered the news gravely then asked, 'Why was the honourable lady in such a hurry?'

### from The Sermon on the Mount

How blest are those who know that they are poor;
  the kingdom of Heaven is theirs.
How blest are the sorrowful;
  They shall find consolation.
How blest are those of a gentle spirit;
  they shall have the earth for their possession.

How blest are those who hunger and thirst to see right prevail;
    they shall be satisfied.
How blest are they who show mercy;
    mercy shall be shown to them.
How blest are those whose hearts are pure;
    they shall see God.
How blest are the peacemakers;
    God shall call them his sons.
How blest are those who have suffered persecution for the cause
    of right;
    the kingdom of Heaven is theirs.
You are salt to the world . . . You are light for all the world.
Pass no judgement, and you will not be judged.
First take the plank out of your own eye, and then you will see
    clearly to take the speck out of your brother's.
Ask, and you will receive; seek, and you will find.
Consider how the lilies grow in the fields; they do not work, they
    do not spin; and yet, I tell you, even Solomon in all his
    splendour was not attired like one of these.

        St Matthew 5 (3-10, 13, 14), 6 (28, 29) and 7 (1-4, 7)

### Perverted saints

Football is the most popular religion in England today; but it will
not save us in either body or soul. We need a bigger game and
higher stakes. Gambling, like all vices, is the perversion of a virtue;
and the sportsmen of the lower level who hang about our street
corners buying up the sporting editions, are perverted saints, bet-
ting their pitiful poverty upon petty issues, for the sake of passing
excitement – instead of staking all the wealth and the glory of life
to attain a great and lasting achievement . . .

    The root of the sin of gambling is the perversion of the instinct
of adventure and enterprise, an instinct which is one of our most
priceless possessions. Upon that instinct real progress does, and
must always, depend, and to find an outlet for it on a mean and
trivial level is individually and socially disastrous. All sin is perverted instinct, and there is no sin which is more pregnant with
moral ruin than this.

        G. A. Studdert Kennedy, *The Wicket Gate*, in *The Best of Stud-
        dert Kennedy*

### The madman's will

In a work-house ward that was cold and bare,
  The doctor sat on a creaking chair,
By the side of a dying madman's bed.
  'He can't last much longer,' the doctor said.
But nobody cares if a pauper lives,
  And nobody cares when a pauper's dead.
The old man sighed, the doctor rose,
  And bent his head o'er the ricketty bed,
To catch the weak words one by one –
  To smile – as the dying madman said:
'Beneath my pillow when I am gone –
  Search – hidden there you will find it still!'
'Find what, old madman?' the doctor asked,
  And the old man said, as he died, 'My WILL.'
How they all laughed at the splendid jest –
  A pauper madman to leave a will.
And they straightened him out for his final rest,
  In the lonely graveyard over the hill,
And the doctor searched for the paper and found
  The red-taped parchment – untied it with zest,
While the others laughingly gathered round
  To hear the cream of the madman's jest.
Then the doctor with mocking solemnity said,
  'Silence, my friends,' and the will he read.
'I leave to the children the green fields,
  The fresh country lanes for their play,
The stories of fairies and dragons,
  The sweet smell of heather and hay.
I leave to young maidens romantic
  The dreaming which all maidens do,
And the wish that some day in the future
  Their happiest dreams will come true.
To youth I leave all youth's ambition,
  Desire, love, impetuous hate.
And to youth with years I leave wisdom,
  And the hope that it comes not too late.
I leave to old people sweet memories,
  And smiles that endure to the last,

With never a fear for the future,
   And not a regret for the past.
I die without earthly possessions,
   Without the last word of a friend,
To you all I leave good cheer and friendship
   That lasts through all time to the end.
I leave to the wide world my blessing
   In the hope that the long years will find
That my wishes shall grow like a flower
   And bring God's good peace to mankind.'
The ward doctor laid down the parchment,
   His smile had gone, turned into pain.
The faces around laughed no longer,
   But grew grave with regret that was vain.
'No wonder that he looks so happy,
   While we who derided are sad,
For the things he has left are the best things in life –
   I wonder if he *was* mad?'

      Music-hall monologue of 1925

# IV

# The Christian year

# Harvest, All Saints and All Souls

## HARVEST

Most religions have held some form of thanksgiving when the harvest was successfully gathered in. Such celebrations were part of the Jewish religious practices from very early days, going back to the time when God announced the cycle of the seasons after Noah had offered thanks for the subsiding of the Flood:

### Noah's thanksgiving

Then Noah built an altar to the Lord. He took ritually clean beasts and birds of every kind, and offered whole-offerings on the altar. When the Lord smelt the soothing odour, he said within himself, 'Never again will I curse the ground because of man, however evil his inclinations may be from his youth upwards. I will never again kill every living creature, as I have just done.
While the earth lasts
seedtime and harvest, cold and heat,
summer and winter, day and night
shall never cease.'

Genesis 8 : 20-2

Moses as religious leader of the Israelites started two great religious feasts of thanksgiving: the Feast of the Spring Harvest (also called the Feast of Weeks, or Pentecost) and the Feast of the Autumn Harvest, or Feast of Tabernacles. In one of the early books of the Bible, later much loved and quoted by Christ, we read about these harvest festivals:

### The feast of Tabernacles

Seven weeks shall be counted: start counting the seven weeks from the time when the sickle is put to the standing corn; then you shall keep the pilgrim-feast of Weeks to the Lord your God and offer a free-will offering in proportion to the blessing that the Lord your God has given you. You shall rejoice before the Lord your God, with your sons and daughters, your male and female slaves, the

Levites who live in your settlements, and the aliens, orphans and widows among you.

You shall keep the pilgrim-feast of Tabernacles for seven days, when you bring in the produce from your threshing-floor and wine-press. You shall rejoice in your feast, with your sons and daughters, your male and female slaves, the Levites, aliens, orphans, and widows who live in your settlements. For seven days you shall keep this feast to the Lord your God in the place which he will choose, when the Lord your God gives you his blessing in all your harvest and in all your work; you shall keep the feast with joy.

Deuteronomy 16:9-11, 13-15

In England and other countries of Europe there were a number of customs connected with the gathering of the season's last sheaf of corn. For example, a handful from the last or the best sheaf was quickly twisted into a little figure that looked like a human being, and taken in procession to the farm with the final load. In the early days of the English church the corn doll would be fixed above the chancel arch, and there was bell-ringing and blessings on the corn and bread. Thus, as so often, the Christian faith made good use of an ancient pagan ceremony, but the connection was broken at the time of the Reformation, 400 years ago. When in the sixteenth century Thomas Tusser wrote his handbook for farmers in verse he told them that at harvest time they were to supply plenty of cheering drink to their workers and to see that all who had helped with the harvesting were properly rewarded without cheating; and he added that God was to be thanked:

### 'Let them be merry'

In harvest-time, harvest-folk, servants and all,
should make, all together, good cheer in the hall;
And fill out the black bowl of blythe to their song,
and let them be merry all harvest-time long.

Once ended thy harvest, let none be beguiled,
please such as did help thee, man, woman, and child;
Thus doing, with alway, such help as they can,
thou winnest the praise of the labouring man.

Now look up to Godward, let tongue never cease,
in thanking of him, for his mighty increase:

Accept my good will for a proof go and try;
the better thou thrivest, the gladder am I.

*Five Hundred Good Points of Husbandry*

About a hundred years later (1640) Robert Herrick, vicar of Dean
Prior in Devon, wrote a cheerful poem on the Harvest Home and
the decorated waggon that took the last load home. He described
the splendid feast of beef and beer and pies that was provided, and
urged the workers to drink to their master, their implements and
their girls, and further to provide for the oxen which then did so
much of the work on a farm; but parson though he was he made
no mention of giving thanks to God. The ancient pagan ceremonies
continued, without the blessing of the church; and George Eliot
tells how Adam Bede going home one evening sensed that the
Harvest Home was really a sacred occasion and experienced the
religious feelings that it called forth:

### Harvest Home

As Adam was going homeward, on Wednesday evening, in the six
o'clock sunlight, he saw in the distance the last load of barley
winding its way towards the yard-gate of the Hall Farm, and
heard the chant of 'Harvest Home!' rising and sinking like a wave.
Fainter and fainter, and more musical through the growing distance, the falling dying sound still reached him, as he neared the
Willow Brook. The low westering sun shone right on the shoulders
of the old Binton Hills, turning the unconscious sheep into bright
spots of light; shone on the windows of the cottage too, and made
them a-flame with a glory beyond that of amber or amethyst. It
was enough to make Adam feel that he was in a great temple, and
that the distant chant was a sacred song.

'It's wonderful,' he thought, 'how that sound goes to one's heart
almost like a funeral bell, for all it tells one of the joyfullest time
o' the year, and the time when men are mostly the thankfullest. I
suppose it's a bit hard to us to think anything's over and gone in
our lives; and there's a parting at the root of all our joys . . .'

*Adam Bede*, Ch. 53

Such farming customs died out about a century and a half before
our time. As they came to an end the churches began to hold
harvest festivals of their own, as they do today. However, we

have little contact with farming and we do not see much of the harvesting, so for most of us there is less of an impetus to celebrate. Moreover, we depend much less on home-produced food, since we live on successful harvests all over the world and all round the calendar. For some nations, including us, modern farming has minimised the risk of starvation through poor harvests though it is a very different story in the undeveloped countries. If we, in the civilised nations, ever have to face the risk of starvation it will be our own fault for failing to tackle the problems of population, the pollution of our environment, and distribution of the wealth of the world. If we do hold any form of thanksgiving for our good fortune it will be right to remember those who die of starvation or suffer from life-long under-feeding; and to think what we can do about it.

## On the brink of famine

This newspaper report describes conditions in the Upper Volta – a 'friendly, proud, little-known country in West Africa' – which is not likely to be having a harvest festival for some time to come.

Their lives are dominated by the need and quest for water. Most people in Britain, accustomed to being able to turn a tap on and off scores of times a day, could never appreciate the value of a drop of clean water in this dry, burnt-out place. Women, carrying their babies in slings on their backs, will set off from their circle of huts with a clay pot balanced on their heads and with quiet dignity and no apparent complaint, walk miles from their homes to the nearest well: sometimes they do this two or three times a day. Like the men, they have their labours frequently mocked by unforeseen calamities. Today I had a woman pointed out to me who recently trudged, baby on her back, 12 miles for a bowl of water. She then turned and walked back. A mile from home a goat suddenly ran out from the scrub and so startled her that she dropped the bowl. Rather than face the family she set off back the twelve miles to the well . . .

Of all the help the farmers of Upper Volta need to realise even the limited potential of this arid, near-desert, they most of all need water. Rain they cannot cause or control, but when it comes it must be kept, and where possible kept clean. Unfortunately, their inadequately constructed wells tumble in if the rain is heavy and months spent each year constructing them is lost. So a major need here is a massive well-building programme. Concreted wells will save the time of the men so that they can do more in the fields; will reduce the hardship of the women and enable them to do more on the farm and also devote more time to their children; and above all will substantially reduce disease, since many of the children are riddled with disease because the family is forced to drink, wash, clean clothes and water animals with what they can cart on their collective heads from a dirty waterhole or outsize puddle.

*Thursday*

Today, while bouncing over the unbelievably bad roads in the desert to the North, I found two Americans, about 22 years old, concreting at the foot of a well forty yards deep. They were sunburnt, shiny with sweat, and surrounded by ten highly excited Africans for they had just struck water. By the way they celebrated it could have been oil. This is part of a Peace Corps operation that, with some Oxfam help, has built 750 wells in the Upper Volta. You can't help but be impressed by the enthusiasm and energy of these volunteers who have come from affluent American homes to live isolated and deprived lives for two years or more.

Des Wilson, in *The Observer*

**Prayer for Michaelmas**

Good Saint Michael, if we must
Leave our bodies here to dust,
Grant our souls a heaven where we
Still your Michaelmas may see.
Do not make me quire and sing
With radiant angels in a ring,
Nor idly tread a pearl-paved street
With my new unearthly feet;
Do not shut me in a heaven
Golden bright from morn to even,
Where no shadows and no showers
Dim the tedious, shining hours.
Grant that there be autumn still,
Smoke-blue dusk, brown crisp and chill,
And let the furrowed plough-land bare

Curve strongly to the windswept air;
Make the leafy beechwoods burn
Russet, yellow, bronze by turn,
And set the hedgerow and the briar
Thick with berries red as fire.
Let me search and gather up
Acorns green, with knobbed cup,
And prickly chestnuts, plumping down
To show a glossy kernel brown.
Splendid cities like me ill,
And for song I have no skill;
Then let me, in an autumn wood,
Sweep, and pick up sticks for God.

Viola Garvin

### 'Pleasure it is'

Pleasure it is
To hear, I wis,
   The birdes sing.
The deer in the dale,
The sheep in the vale,
   The corn springing.

God's purveyance
For sustenance
   It is for man.
Then we always
To give him praise,
   And thank him then.

William Cornish (d. 1523)

## ALL SAINTS AND ALL SOULS

As Hardy reminds us in 'Unkept Good Fridays' there have been many unknown men and women who suffered for their faith; and their successors are suffering at this moment. The early Christian church first commemorated its unknown martyrs in A.D. 615 and later, in A.D. 844, decided that the date of observance should always be 1 November. Once again the church showed its practical sense and understanding of deep human needs by making use of old customs: this time it Christianised the ancient pagan festival of fire, which was kept by the lighting of bonfires to the dying god. And more recent Halloween customs – the pretending to be ghosts, the hollowing out of a turnip to receive a lighted candle – are a survival of the time when it was believed that demons and evil spirits roamed about on 1 November to welcome the darkness that was intensified with shorter days. The attentions of these beings could be averted by offerings of food, or by pretending to be one of them and thus escaping their notice.

The original English name for All Saints' Day was All Hallows (All Holies) which has given us the popular name Halloween for 31 October. Both the old and the modern names are appropriate for the day on which are remembered all the saints who do not have a special day. It is accompanied by All Souls' Day (2 November), which is an occasion of prayer for the souls of the departed.

We quote to begin with part of George Herbert's 'To all Angels and Saints':

### To all angels and saints

Oh glorious spirits, who after all your bands
See the smooth face of God without a frown
      Or strict commands;
Where everyone is king, and hath his crown,
If not upon his head, yet in his hands:

Thou art the holy mine, whence came the gold,
The great restorative for all decay
      in young and old;
Thou art the cabinet where the jewel lay:
Chiefly to thee would I my soul unfold . . .

    George Herbert

### We need saints

Our is an age of violence and disbelief. But in spite of that or perhaps because of it, the earth's interest in virtuous accomplishment is stronger now than it has been at any time since the Age of Reason began ousting religion from its seat of authority. God may be dead insofar as theological concepts no longer direct political and economic affairs. But His heroes still interest the race. They are quoted by columnists, cited by historians, their names taken not always in vain by novelists, biographers, and agnostic tractarians. Thomas More was not long ago the protagonist of a noble play, a notable film; as was Becket twice in a decade. Joan of Arc never fails the playwright. Not long ago in the sober *New York Times* an editorial recommended that in our dealings with nature we try, for the sake of conservation, to become more like Francis of Assisi who considered all living creatures his brothers.

In times of crisis we need saints; and we often breed them, too. They appeared by hundreds in the first centuries of Christianity when Europe was struggling out of nearly universal darkness into what then passed for the light of civilisation. They flourished during the Reformation on both sides of the conflict. Wherever and whenever an evil has existed, from slave-trading to the miseries of famine and war, saints have sprung up to mitigate those evils. They may well be arising among us now, preparing to lead us out of the onrushing night which so threateningly descends. As a matter of fact, I think I number two or three among my acquaintances . . .

One of them spends himself among impoverished Negroes of the South, one wears himself out in Northern slums, the third (completely without personal possessions) by some sleight of hand and heart feeds and lodges hundreds of Bowery derelicts each week.

Phyllis McGinley, *Saint-Watching*

### Memories

Secular remembrance, as well as Church custom, causes us to think especially of our dead each November. As we tidy away the fallen leaves, we are to recall the memories of those friendships which the year has cost us, and by the exchange of prayer represent to ourselves the absent.

Ronald Knox, *Lightning Meditations*

### A home in the minds of men

The bravest are surely those who have the clearest vision of what is before them, glory and danger alike, and yet notwithstanding go out to meet it . . .

They gave their bodies to the commonwealth and received, each for his own memory, praise that will never die, and with it the grandest of all sepulchres, not that in which their mortal bones are laid, but a home in the minds of men, where their glory remains fresh to stir to speech or action as the occasion comes by. For the whole earth is the sepulchre of famous men; and their story is not graven only on stone over their native earth, but lives on far away, without visible symbol, woven into the stuff of other men's lives.

Thucydides, part of Pericles' Funeral Oration

### To rest in Christ is to live

All Souls' Day: Some seem to want to make All Souls' Day a feast of death, with much rattling of bones and many skulls. The cult of cemeteries not as places where bodies sleep in peace awaiting the Resurrection, but where they lie and rot, eaten by worms. In this cult of death more than anywhere else there is danger of the universal vulgarity and stupidity of middle-class culture corrupting the Christian spirit. Money has a lot to do with this. The disposal of dead bodies is a lucrative and scandalous business – scandalous in the way sorrow is exploited and insulted with small, unctuous, frightful, utterly useless, and expensive toys. The paint, the cushions, the things that light up, the things that play music.

But our dead rest in Christ. The cemetery is the symbol of Christ. To rest in Christ is to live (hence cypresses, green even in winter, are not supposed to suggest melancholy thoughts . . . just the opposite!).

Thomas Merton, *Conjectures of a Guilty Bystander*

# Advent

Advent used to be known as 'The Lent of St Martin' because it was a time for reflection upon judgement and the last days. It now offers the opportunity to start thinking about what the coming of Christ meant originally, and about what it means nowadays – when 'the depth of the human capacity for destructive evil is an aspect of reality which a twentieth-century man is unlikely to take lightly' (from an Advent order of service at St John's College, Cambridge). As well as being a season for feeding the hope of deliverance from evil, Advent is the time for the physical preparations for a modern Christmas.

Advent has been observed since the sixth century as a reminder to men that they must make themselves fit for Christ's arrival. It is also the occasion for singing the first carols. Some of them, including the best, are so old that they go back to the time when a carol was a dance in a ring, accompanied by a song, but quite unconnected with the church. An example is one, more than 600 years old and known to Chaucer, that has kept its dance tune:

Gabriel to Mary came,
A gentle message bare he;
Deep in awe the Maiden bowed
To hear him say 'Hail, Mary.'
There, heaven and earth received his call,
'Hail, hail thou queen of virgins all;
　　Thou, yet undefiled,
　　Shalt bear a child
　　Of sovereign grace,
To comfort all mankind;
Thou shalt bear him, Lord and God of all,
To save our human race.'

The complete translation from the medieval Latin, with the tune, is No. 1 in the *Penguin Book of Christmas Carols*.

Christmas is a time when many people follow the pagan Roman custom of having an annual spell of eating, drinking and riotous living generally; they called it the Saturnalia. Among all this certain truths about Christ's advent come to be neglected; for example, that he came to disturb people; to shake their complacency; to upset comfortable ideas, and to knock some sense into the heads of political and religious leaders. Such points as these are well brought out by modern writers, some of whom are quoted below.

*Further reading*: St Luke 1:26ff.; W. H. Auden, 'Advent' section of *For the Time Being*, in *Collected Longer Poems*; the Chester Nativity Play, in *The Chester Mystery Plays*, ed. M. P. Hussey; Philip Collins, *English Christmas*; the Coventry Nativity Play in *Three Medieval Plays*, ed. John Allen; Walter de la Mare, 'Before Dawn'; Thomas Hardy, 'The Oxen', and Chapter 3 of *Under the Greenwood Tree*; F. X. Weiser, *The Christmas Book*; and Laurence Whistler, *The English Festivals*, pp. 25, 26.

### I will not forget

Wherewithal shall a young man cleanse his way; even by ruling himself after thy word.
With my whole heart have I sought thee: O let me not go wrong out of thy commandments.
Thy words have I hid within my heart: that I should not sin against thee.
Blessed art thou O Lord: O teach me thy statutes.
With my lips have I been telling of all the judgements of thy mouth.
I have had as great delight in the way of thy testimonies, as in all manner of riches.
I will talk of thy commandments and have respect unto thy ways;
My delight shall be in thy statutes, and I will not forget thy word.

Psalm 119:9-16

### The customs of advent

Advent is the time of preparation for Christmas, in the secular as in the religious sense; the time in which presents are bought and made, good food and drink laid in, carols sung, a Christmas tree prepared, holly and mistletoe looked for, churches and houses decorated. Many of these customs are very old – so old that the entire recorded part of human history has occurred since they came into being, no one knows where or when. At Midwinter, when the hours of daylight were fewest, the warmth of the sun weakest, and life itself seemingly at a standstill, our ancestors, the archaic peoples of Europe and Western Asia, kept festivals by lighting bonfires and decorating their buildings with evergreens. They did so, according to the anthropologist, out of a savage belief that the dying sun could be enheartened by imitative fire, and the life of the buried seed assured by the ritual use of branches, evergreen branches that were lively even in the dead season; and these practices and others like them have been called acts of imitative magic.

Laurence Whistler, *The English Festivals*

### A week to Christmas

A week to Christmas, cards of snow and holly,
    Gimcracks in the shops,
Wishes and memories wrapped in tissue paper,
    Trinkets, gadgets and lollipops
And as if through coloured glasses
    We remember our childhood's thrill
Waking in the morning to the rustling of paper,
    The eiderdown heaped in a hill
Of wogs and dogs and bears and bricks and apples
    And the feeling that Christmas Day
Was a coral island in time where we land and eat our lotus
    But where we can never stay.
There was a star in the East, the magi in their turbans
    Brought their luxury toys
In homage to a child born to capsize their values
    And wreck their equipoise.

A smell of hay like peace in the dark stable –
    Not peace however but a sword
To cut the Gordian knot of logical self-interest,
    The fool-proof golden cord;
For Christ walked in where no philosopher treads
    But armed with more than folly,
Making the smooth place rough and knocking the heads
    Of Church and State together.
In honour of whom we have taken over the pagan
    Saturnalia for our annual treat
Letting the belly have its say, ignoring
    The spirit while we eat.
And Conscience still goes crying through the desert
    With sackcloth round his loins:
A week to Christmas – hark the herald angels
    Beg for copper coins.

Louis MacNeice, *Collected Poems*

### Preparations

Yet if His Majesty, our sovereign lord,
Should of his own accord
Friendly himself invite,
And say 'I'll be your guest tomorrow night,'
How we should stir ourselves, call and command
All hands to work! 'Let no man idle stand!

'Set me fine Spanish tables in the hall;
See they be fitted all;
Let there be room to eat
And order taken that there want no meat.
See every sconce and candlestick made bright,
That without tapers they may give a light.

'Look to the presence: are the carpets spread,
The dazie* o'er the head,
The cushions in the chairs,
And all the candles lighted on the stairs?
Perfume the chambers, and in any case
Let each man give attendance in his place!'

Thus, if a king were coming, would we do;
And 'twere good reason too;
For 'tis a duteous thing
To show all honour to an earthly king,
And after all our travail and our cost,
So he be pleased, to think no labour lost.

But at the coming of the King of Heaven
All's set at six and seven;
We wallow in our sin,
Christ cannot find a chamber in the inn.
We entertain Him always like a stranger,
And, as at first, still lodge Him in the manger.

Anonymous, sixteenth century

*dazie*: canopy

### No room in the inn

When Caesar Augustus had raised a taxation,
He assessed all the people that dwelt in the nation;
The Jews at that time being under Rome's sway
Appeared in the city their tribute to pay:
Then Joseph and Mary, who from David did spring,
Went up to the city of David their king,
And, there being entered, cold welcome they find –
From the rich to the poor they are mostly unkind.

They sought entertainment, but none could they find,
Great numbers of strangers had fillèd the inn;
They knockèd and callèd all this at the door,
But found not a friend where in kind they had store;
Their kindred accounted they come were too soon;
'Too late,' said the innkeeper, 'here is no room.'
Amongst strangers and kinsfolk cold welcome they find –
From the rich to the poor they are mostly unkind.

Good Joseph was troubled, but most for his dear,
For her blessèd burden whose time now drew near;
His heart with true sorrow was sorely afflicted
That his virgin spouse was so rudely neglected.
He could get no house-room who houses did frame,
But Joseph and Mary must go as they came.
For little is the favour the poor man can find –
From the rich to the poor they are mostly unkind.

Whilst the great and the wealthy do frolic in hall,
Possess all the ground-rooms and chambers and all,
Poor Joseph and Mary are thrust in a stable
In Bethlehem city, ground inhospitáble,
And with their mean lodging contented they be;
For the minds of the just with their fortunes agree;
They bear all affronts with their meekness of mind,
And be not offended though the rich be unkind.

O Bethlehem, Bethlehem, welcome this stranger
That was born in a stable and laid in a manger;
For he is a Physician to heal all our smarts –
Come welcome, sweet Jesus, and lodge in our hearts.

Traditional

### Upon Christ His birth

Strange news! a city full? will none give way
To lodge a guest that comes not every day?
No inn, nor tavern void? yet I descry
One empty place alone, where we may lie:

In too much fulness is some want: but where?
Men's empty hearts: let's ask for lodging there.
But if they not admit us, then we'll say
Their hearts, as well as inn's, are made of clay.

Sir John Suckling

# Christmas

One problem is to rescue the truths of Christmas from the commercial jungle, without preaching and without thwarting the true festal impulse. The first passage approaches obliquely, but with interest and simple lucidity, its conclusion that Christ brought light into darkness. The choice of something written more than a generation ago is deliberate, because events have made it even more relevant to us than it was to its first readers. There has been so much evil and cruelty abroad since Kennedy wrote that now the practice of Christianity is needed as much as it ever has been. If cuts are needed, the beginning of the second paragraph should go first. After this introduction there follow a number of extracts which show what the season has meant to Christians at various times, ending with modern examples that may be the best way to bring out the significance of Christmas today.

At this season of carols it is worth looking at the words of some of them as well as singing them. Medieval Christianity used the cheerful dance-in-a-ring with chorus to tell the story of Christmas and the legends that grew up around it in a form intelligible and enjoyable to everyone. They did this well, and their vitality endures; they were the popular songs of their period. A very simple version of the Nativity for example is found in No. 91 in the *Oxford Book of Carols*; in the form of a dialogue for four speakers, it can be sung or read or performed as a play by quite young children; it is also printed in some English text-books. Another one for young children is No. 88 in the same collection.

Legends are recounted in such carols as No. 54 ('King Herod and the Cock'), No. 56 ('The Holy Well' – and cf. a folk song 'The Bitter Withy', in which Mary chastises her son), and No. 56 ('The Cherry Tree Carol'); the Massacre of the Innocents is the subject of the Coventry Carol, No. 22, or No. 16 in the *Penguin Book of Christmas Carols*. In some of them there are traces of the ancient pagan wish to keep life going in the winter by such aids and reminders as evergreen decorations, as in the 'Wassail Song' (No. 15, *Oxford Book*; No. 26, *Penguin Book*) and 'The Holly and Ivy' (No. 38, *Oxford Book*; No. 42, *Penguin Book*).

The image of Christ coming as light in darkness, and still more so that of Christ as spring after winter, are common in English writers; Robert Herrick for instance wrote his carol to be sung with music by Henry Lawes before Charles I. For hundreds of years the observance of Christmas was a matter of decorating, eating, drinking and showing general goodwill, but without presents or cards or trees, except perhaps a few gifts for any children in the family; some of the traditional goings-on are described by George Wither. But in 1647 the Puritans abolished Christmas for some years, and in John Evelyn's Diary for 25 December 1657 there is a vivid page telling how troops interrupted the Christmas service he was attending, and arrested everyone present.

For John Clare (see 'December' in the anthology mentioned below) early last century, and for Dickens later, Christmas was still the season for decorations, feasting and singing. Dickens wrote much about Christmas, and his *A Christmas Carol* is still compelling. The chief character is Scrooge, an old miser who despises Christmas. His mind is changed by a series of dreams, in one of which he sees his underpaid clerk, Bob Cratchit, keeping Christmas with his family. The account of their Christmas dinner (about a third of the way through Stave 4, from 'Such a bustle ensued . . .' to Bob's proposing the toast) reads aloud very well; so does the description of another Christmas dinner in Chapter 4 of *Great Expectations*. Country people who still kept up old customs appear in Hardy's *Under the Greenwood Tree* (Ch. 4), and there are two good stories about village choirs in pp. 267-74 of his *Life's Little Ironies*.

*Further reading*: St Luke 2:2-20; L. Ferlinghetti, 'Christ climbed down', in *A Coney Island of the Mind* and in anthologies; Thomas Hardy, 'The Oxen'; James Kirkup, 'Riddles for Christmas', in *White Shadows, Black Shadows*; Alfred Tennyson, 'Ring out, wild bells'; Philip Collins, *English Christmas*; Aldous Huxley, 'New Fashioned Christmas', in *The Olive Tree*; Laurence Whistler, *The English Festivals*.

### Roots in the depths of the past

The fourth Glacial Age reached its bitterest climax about fifty thousand years ago, and that it was amidst the snows of that long universal winter of the world that the first man-like beings lived upon our planet, and looked with frightened eyes upon the huge, ungainly mammoth whose monstrous bones are left to tell the tale. When I have been reading of those far-off times, and as I ponder over the record of the rocks trying to picture to myself what it must have been like to live in those days when the wintry death of the great ice age crept southward over the earth, when the arctic musk and the reindeer herds roamed round Oxford Street and Piccadilly, the years when there was no spring, I have often laid down my book and asked myself, with a kind of awe and wonder in my inmost soul, 'What if there had been no spring? What if the ice had never broken, and the white snow never ceased to fall?'

'Absurd,' you say. Perhaps all questions as to what might have been are absurd. The past is past and our only concern with it is to use it as a foundation for the future. And yet to think upon what might have been may help us to appreciate what is. To picture to ourselves that endless winter may help us to see with clearer eyes the splendour of God's spring. The connection between Christmas and the end of the great world winter is perhaps closer than anyone ignorant of history would suppose. Why is December 25th kept as Christmas Day? Why does it come in the very depth of winter? We do not really know the exact date of Christ's birth. December 25th was not fixed as the Birthday Festival of Christ until three hundred years after He died. It was then settled, not because December 25th was known to be the true date of His Birth, but because it was the day of the heathen midwinter festival. Traces of that heathen festival are still with us. The burning of the Yule log goes back to days long, long before Christ, and so do Christmas trees. Behind the ancient winter festival there lay the dread that in the depth of some bleak winter the sun might really die, bleeding out its life in the flames of one last awful sunset across the western sky. The primitive dread that made the ancients pile the Yule logs up to warm the sun lest it die in winter's grip was a racial memory of the long world winter their fathers had endured.

The more we know of the human mind the more reason we have for believing that the roots of our common customs strike down into the depths of an unconsciously remembered past. The instinct that made the early Christians keep the Festival of Christ's Birth upon midwinter day was the result of very vivid experience. They felt that the coming of Christ into the world had been like the return of the sun, the winter of the world's soul was over and the spring had come. The contrast between the darkness before Him and the Light which He brought was to them a startling and glaring contrast because the memory of the darkness was still fresh, and the remains of it were still with them. It is less glaring to us because Christ has been at work for many years, and the memory of the darkness has faded into the dim background of our minds. We cannot easily recall it. It is only by using the written and recorded memory of history that we can make the darkness real to ourselves. The only word which would serve to convey any idea of the darkness from which the early Christians felt that Christ had saved them would be 'devilry.' There has existed in the world a depth of sinister, callous, cold-blooded, cruel wickedness which we rarely meet with today, but it was common and powerful in the ancient world. If you want to get back into that atmosphere you must study the history of superstition and remember that the ancient world was sunk in superstition. It is terrible reading. Truth is stronger than fiction, and the mind reels and is shocked by these records of the foul, filthy, cruel things men have believed, and the ghastly deeds that have been done because of those beliefs.

G. A. Studdert Kennedy, *The New Man in Christ*

### Christmas husbandly fare, 1571

Good husband and housewife, now chiefly be glad
things handsome to have, as they ought to be had.
They both do provide, against Christmas do come,
to welcome their neighbours, good cheer to have some.

Good bread and good drink, a good fire in the hall,
brawn, pudding, and souse,* and good mustard withall.
Beef, mutton, and pork, and good pies of the best,
pig, veal, goose, and capon, and turkey well dressed,

Cheese, apples, and nuts, and good carols to hear,
as then in the country is counted good cheer.

What cost to good husband is any of this?
– good household provision only it is:
Of other the like, I do leave out a many,
that costeth the husband never a penny.

> Thomas Tusser (see Harvest section)

> *souse*: pickled pork

## A Christmas carol

So now is come our joyful feast,
    Let every man be jolly;
Each room with ivy leaves is dressed,
    And every post with holly.
        Though some churls at our mirth repine,
        Round your foreheads garlands twine,
        Drown sorrow in a cup of wine,
    And let us all be merry.

Now all our neighbours' chimneys smoke,
    And Christmas blocks are burning;
Their ovens they with baked meats choke,
    And all their spits are turning.
        Without the door let sorrow lie,
        And if for cold it hap to die,
        We'll bury it in a Christmas pie;
    And evermore be merry.

Good farmers in the country nurse
    The poor, that else were undone:
Some landlords spend their money worse,
    On lust and pride at London.
        There the roysters they do play,
        Drab and dice their land away,
        Which may be ours another day;
    And therefore let's be merry.

The client now his suit forbears,
    The prisoner's heart is e=sed;

The debtor drinks away his cares,
   And for the time is pleaséd.
      Though others' purses be more fat,
      Why should we pine or grieve at that;
      Hang sorrow, care will kill a cat,
   And therefore let's be merry . . .

   George Wither


## A Christmas carol

Dark and dull night, fly hence away,
And give the honour to this day,
That sees December turned to May.

If we may ask the reason, say
The why and wherefore all things here
Seem like the Spring-time of the year?

Why does the chilling Winter's morn
Smile, like a field beset with corn?
Or smell, like to a mead new-shorn,
Thus, on the sudden? Come and see
The cause, why things thus fragrant be:
'Tis He is born, whose quickening Birth
Gives life and lustre, public mirth,
To heaven, and the under-earth.

   Robert Herrick


## The Bethlehem star

Moonless darkness stands between.
Past, the Past, no more be seen!
But the Bethlehem star may lead me
To the sight of Him Who freed me
From the self that I have been.
Make me pure, Lord: Thou art holy;
Make me meek, Lord: Thou wert lowly;
Now beginning, and alway:
Now begin, on Christmas day.

   Gerard Manley Hopkins

## The safety of the world

I saw a stable, low and very bare,
A little Child in a manger,
The oxen knew Him, had Him in their care.
To men He was a stranger.
The safety of the world was lying there
And the world's danger.

Mary Coleridge


## Christmas in war-time

I heard the bells on Christmas day
Their old familiar carols play,
  And wild and sweet
  The words repeat
Of peace on earth, good-will to men!

And thought how, as the day had come,
The belfries of all Christendom
  Had rolled along
  The unbroken song
Of peace on earth, good-will to men!

Then from each black accursed mouth
The cannon thundered in the South,
  And with the sound
  The carols drowned
Of peace on earth, good-will to men!

It was as if an earthquake rent
The hearthstones of a continent,
  And made forlorn
  The households born
Of peace on earth, good-will to men!

And in despair I bowed my head;
'There is no peace on earth,' I said;
  'For hate is strong
  And mocks the song
Of peace on earth, good-will to men!'

Then pealed the bells more loud and deep:
'God is not dead; nor doth he sleep!
   The wrong shall fail,
   The right prevail,
With peace on earth, good-will to men!'

      H. W. Longfellow

### Instead of a carol

No, not for us the plastic and the foil
Of decorations in symmetric coil
Decked out with vulgar art across the street
And shown to children for a festive treat.
Nor sordid artificial christmas tree
With squalid tinsel where the leaves should be.
Nor disenchanting santa in the store
With beery double in the shop next door.

Instead for us the exiled son of man,
New born in outhouse lying in the cold,
Though not for us one special holy boy
But everyone unwanted and unloved,
The lonely and the helpless and the poor,
The little hungry child in every land.

      Tom Earley

### A small dry voice

And I remember that we went singing carols once, a night or two
before Christmas Eve, when there wasn't the shaving of a moon to
light the secret, white-flying streets. At the end of a long road was
a drive that led to a large house, and we stumbled up the darkness
of the drive that night, each one of us afraid, each one holding a
stone in his hand in case, and all of us too brave to say a word. The
wind made through the drive-trees noises as of old and unpleasant
and maybe web-footed men wheezing in caves. We reached the
black bulk of the house.

   'What shall we give them?' Dan whispered.

   ' "Hark the Herald"? "Christmas comes but once a year"?'

   'No,' Jack said: 'We'll sing "Good King Wenceslas." I'll count
three.'

One, two, three, and we began to sing, our voices high and seemingly distant in the snow-felted darkness round the house that was occupied by nobody we knew. We stood close together, near the dark door.

Good King Wenceslas looked out
On the Feast of Stephen.

And then a small, dry voice, like the voice of someone who has not spoken for a long time, suddenly joined our singing: a small, dry voice from the other side of the door: a small, dry voice through the keyhole. And when we stopped running we were outside *our* house; the front room was lovely and bright; the gramophone was playing; we saw the red and white balloons hanging from the gas-bracket; uncles and aunts sat by the fire: I thought I smelt our supper being fried in the kitchen. Everything was good again, and Christmas shone through all the familiar town.

'Perhaps it was a ghost,' Jim said.

'Perhaps it was trolls,' Dan said, who was always reading.

'Let's go in and see if there's any jelly left,' Jack said. And we did that.

Dylan Thomas, *Quite Early One Morning*

### A sense of mystery and rousedness

Gradually there gathered the feeling of expectation. Christmas was coming. In the shed, at nights, a secret candle was burning, a sound of veiled voices was heard. The boys were learning the old mystery play of St George and Beelzebub. Twice a week, by lamplight, there was choir practice in the church, for the learning of old carols Brangwen wanted to hear. The girls went to these practices. Everywhere was a sense of mystery and rousedness. Everybody was preparing for something.

The time came near, the girls were decorating the church, with cold fingers binding holly and fir and yew about the pillars, till a new spirit was in the church, the stone broke out into dark, rich leaf, the arches put forth their buds, and cold flowers rose to blossom in the dim, mystic atmosphere. Ursula must weave mistletoe over the door, and over the screen, and hang a silver dove from a sprig of yew, till dusk came down, and the church was a grove.

In the cow-shed the boys were blacking their faces for a dress-rehearsal; the turkey hung dead, with opened, speckled wings, in the dairy. The time was come to make pies, in readiness.

The expectation grew more tense. The star was risen into the sky, the songs, the carols were ready to hail it. The star was the sign in the sky. Earth too should give a sign. As evening drew on, hearts beat fast with anticipation, hands were full of ready gifts. There were the tremulously expectant words of the church service, the night was past and the morning was come, the gifts were given and received, joy and peace made a flapping of wings in each heart, there was a great burst of carols, the Peace of the World had dawned, strife had passed away, every hand was linked in hand, every heart was singing.

It was bitter, though, that Christmas day, as it drew on to evening, and night became a sort of bank holiday, flat and stale. The morning was so wonderful, but in the afternoon and evening the ecstasy perished like a nipped thing, like a bud in false spring. Alas, that Christmas was only a domestic feast, a feast of sweetmeats and toys! Why did not the grown-ups also change their everyday hearts, and give way to ecstasy? Where was the ecstasy?

How passionately the Brangwens craved for it, the ecstasy. The father was troubled, dark-faced and disconsolate, on Christmas night, because the passion was not there, because the day was become as every day, and hearts were not aflame. Upon the mother was a kind of absentness, as ever, as if she were exiled for all her life. Where was the fiery heart of joy, now the coming was fulfilled; where was the star, the Magi's transport, the thrill of new being that shook the earth?

Still it was there, even it were faint and inadequate. The cycle of creation still wheeled in the Church year. After Christmas, the ecstasy slowly sank and changed. Sunday followed Sunday, trailing a fine movement, a finely developed transformation over the heart of the family. The heart that was big with joy, that had seen the star and had followed to the inner walls of the Nativity, that there had swooned in the great light, must now feel the light slowly withdrawing, a shadow falling, darkening. The chill crept in, silence came over the earth, and then all was darkness. The veil of the temple was rent, each heart gave up the ghost, and sank dead . . .

So the children lived the year of Christianity, the epic of the soul of mankind. Year by year the inner, unknown drama went on in them, their hearts were born and came to fulness, suffered on the cross, gave up the ghost, and rose again to unnumbered days, untired, having at least this rhythm of eternity in a ragged, inconsequential life.

D. H. Lawrence, *The Rainbow* (1915)

### The soup run

It is difficult to see the spirit of Christmas in London this week through the commercial good will, the ~~Gadarene~~ stampede of shoppers, the office parties and the other flashy wrappings. But it survives.

| Very early tomorrow morning Joe Burlison and Bernard North of the Salvation Army will drive through the empty streets on a journey that St Nicholas would approve of, carrying secondhand underwear and socks in paper bags to give to the derelicts and dossers shipwrecked without shelter. Twice a week in the middle of the night, after their regular work as youth leaders, they distribute free bread and soup. They give clothes only to a particular man whose needs they know, because they have found that to hand out a pile of old clothes can lead to fighting and selling of the clothes.

Their first call is underneath the arches at Charing Cross Underground station, where rows of solitaries sleep on the pavement, wrapped in newspapers and seclusion, their heads and feet in cardboard boxes, their backs turned on the world. They walk through Embankment Gardens, telling the men lying on the benches that the soup has arrived. They do not disturb those who are sleeping because it is hard enough for a man to fall asleep on a bench in the open once in a night, without being woken up and having to start all over again. On cold nights they blow ~~on the balls~~ of their thumbs and hold them on the eyes of their customers to thaw the frost and allow them to see. They have found two men dead of cold already this year.

The last call is Spitalfields market, known with reason by ~~deni-zens~~ inhabitants of this ghost world as 'the graveyard'. Men stand and sit around a bonfire of cardboard boxes and garbage that burns all night. Swarms of sparks fly upwards as sure as man is born to trouble, lighting up shadowy figures sitting in the heaps of rubbish and drinking from dirty bottles and eating from dirty tins. Many are too lethargic to collect soup or even to move out of the way of the sparks. The Salvation Army does not consider that it does any good to carry soup to a man who will not make the effort to fetch it. The dossers in Spitalfields are the hardest in London to communicate with, the most disturbed and the farthest away from the ordinary world. When the soup run started just over a year ago they seldom accepted the soup or made any noise except a grunt. Today many drink soup and some of them are beginning to talk to the men who bring it. In all there were about two hundred customers for soup last night. Since an estimated 5,000 people sleep rough around the streets of London every night, the operation reaches only a few of those lonely people in need of food and human contact. But it is more relevant to what happened at Christmas than most of the ways in which London celebrates this week.

> Philip Howard, 'Where Real Spirit of Goodwill Survives', in *The Times* 22 December 1971

> Christ brought a message of peace to all ranks of society and to people of all nations. In many ages he came as spring after winter; today he is often seen as a disturber of accepted values, teaching men how to achieve their truest humanity. Recent writers especially show us a Christ who despises the fripperies of a trade-exploited festival and invites us to care for the unwanted and unloved,
> The lonely and the helpless and the poor.

# Saint Stephen and Epiphany

## ST STEPHEN

Who was the Stephen on whose festival Wenceslas looked out? In many European countries in the past you would have been told that he was the patron saint of horses, and that on his day horses were ridden round the church and blessed, while the housewives baked bread in the shape of a horse-shoe. There is nothing at all in his life to account for the connection; it probably arose from the fact that 26 December, the day on which he is commemorated, came at the beginning of the Twelve Days of Christmas, which in the middle ages were a time of rest for domestic animals.

All we know of him is recorded in the Acts of the Apostles, where we learn that he was the first Christian martyr. There had been complaints in the growing Christian community in Jerusalem that some poor widows were being unfairly treated when food was distributed; so Stephen and six other respected men were appointed to handle this charity, in order that the apostles themselves might have more time for prayer and preaching. Stephen, however, was himself a most vigorous preacher, much disliked by the Jewish ecclesiastical establishment because they could not get the better of him, and perhaps because his face appeared to them like the face of an angel. They were especially stung by his denunciation of their treatment of Christ, so they produced bogus charges, concocted evidence against him, and rigged a trial before their Council. Here he counter-attacked bitterly, as the Acts tell us:

### St Stephen martyred

'How stubborn you are, heathen still at heart and deaf to the truth! You always fight against the Holy Spirit. Like fathers, like sons. Was there ever a prophet whom your fathers did not persecute? They killed those who foretold the coming of the Righteous One; and now you have betrayed him and murdered him, you who received the Law as God's angels gave it to you, and yet have not kept it.'

This touched them on the raw and they ground their teeth with fury. But Stephen, filled with the Holy Spirit, and gazing intently up to heaven, saw the glory of God, and Jesus standing at God's right hand. 'Look,' he said, 'there is a rift in the sky; I can see the Son of Man standing at God's right hand!' At this they gave a great shout and stopped their ears. Then they made one rush at him and, flinging him out of the city, set about stoning him. The witnesses laid their coats at the feet of a young man named Saul. So they stoned Stephen, and as they did so, he called out, 'Lord Jesus, receive my spirit.' Then he fell on his knees and cried aloud, 'Lord, do not hold this sin against them', and with that he died. And Saul was among those who approved of his murder.

Acts 7:51-60

It may have been Stephen's example of calm and courage that

started Saul's conversion, recorded in Acts 9:1-19. There is a carol about him; No. 26 in the *Oxford Book of Carols.*

## EPIPHANY

St Matthew is our only source for the visit of the Magi – and he does not record their number, their names or their origin. But the observation of Epiphany on 6 January is one of the oldest Christian holy days; the number of the visitors was probably settled by the number of their gifts; and since the year 735 the givers have been known as Casper (incense), Melchior (gold) and Baltasar (myrrh). They came from the three parts of the world then known: Europe, Asia and Africa – with Casper always being portrayed as a black man. Many legends have grown up round these figures, who as travellers and thus patrons of voyagers and pilgrims became supplements to St Christopher.

Their gifts remind us of three aspects of Christ. Gold was a royal gift and colour, and thus Christ was recognised as a king. Incense has been used in places of worship from ancient times, for example as a symbol of prayer rising up to God; and so the frankincense was a tribute to Christ as the Son of God. (The spice used in Christmas cooking may be a half-memory of this offering.) Myrrh, an aromatic gum used in medicine and for embalming, foreshadowed Christ's sufferings and death. The fact that the wise men – the astrologers – came from outside Judaea was the first piece of evidence that Christ was to be king not only of the Jews but of all mankind.

Epiphany marks the end of the twelve days of Christmas, and when holy days were observed more than they are nowadays it was an occasion for carrying out special ceremonies and baking special cakes. Today, however, Twelfth Night is not much more than a reminder to take down the Christmas decorations. To poets the mysterious three 'kings' have always been an attractive subject: T. S. Eliot's 'Journey of the Magi' reads well aloud; W. H. Auden also brings out the human weakness of the magi in their search for guidance on how to be truly human.

*Further reading*: St Matthew 22:1-12; 'The Golden Carol' (*c.* 1460) in *Oxford Book of Carols*, No. 173; Charles Causley, 'Ballad of the Bread Man', in *Underneath the Water* and in anthologies; W. H. Auden, 'For the Time Being, A Christmas Oratorio'.

### Three old sinners

The weather has been awful,
   The countryside is dreary,
Marsh, jungle, rock; and echoes mock,
   Calling our hope unlawful;
But a silly song can help along
   Yours ever and sincerely:
At least we know for certain that we are three old sinners,
That this journey is much too long, that we want our dinners,
   And miss our wives, our books, our dogs,
But have only the vaguest idea why we are what we are.
   To discover how to be human now
   Is the reason we follow this star.

      W. H. Auden, *For the Time Being*

### The three kings

Three Kings came riding from far away,
   Melchior and Caspar and Baltasar;
Three wise men out of the East were they,
And they travelled by night and they slept by day,
   For their guide was a beautiful, wonderful star.

And so the three kings rode into the West,
   Through the dusk of night, over hill and dell,
And sometimes they nodded with beard on breast,
And sometimes talked, as they paused to rest,
   With the people they met at some roadside well.

'Of the child that is born,' said Baltasar,
   'Good people, I pray you, tell us the news;
For we in the East have seen his star,
And have ridden fast, and have ridden far,
   To find and worship the King of the Jews.'

And the people answered, 'You ask in vain;
   We know of no king but Herod the Great!'
They thought the wise men were men insane,
As they spurred their horses across the plain,
   Like riders in haste, and who cannot wait.

And the three kings rode through the gate and the guard,
    Through the silent street, till their horses turned
And neighed as they entered the great inn-yard;
But the windows were closed, and the doors were barred,
    And only a light in the stable burned.

And cradled there in the scented hay,
    In the air made sweet by the breath of kine,
The little child in the manger lay,
The child, that would be king one day
    Of a kingdom not human but divine.

They laid their offerings at his feet:
    The gold was their tribute to a king,
The frankincense, with its odour sweet,
Was for the priest, the paraclete,
    The myrrh for the body's burying.

Then the kings rode out of the city gate,
    With a clatter of hoofs in proud array;
But they went not back to Herod the Great,
For they knew his malice and feared his hate,
    And returned to their homes by another way.

     H. W. Longfellow

# Lent

The three days – Sunday, Monday and Tuesday – immediately before the beginning of Lent itself were the original Shrovetide, the time for confessing sins and doing penance. Ash Wednesday, the first day of Lent, derives its name from the custom of sprinkling ash on the heads of priests and penitents as a sign of their repentance. The word Lent itself may stem from the same root as 'long', 'lengthen'; in Anglo-Saxon it meant 'spring', when the days lengthen and the forty days are observed.

The fasting days used to be strictly kept, so that the day before they started was an opportunity for indulgence before abstinence; and the pancakes are a surviving token of this. Though Lent has been observed as a period of sober preparation for Easter since the seventh century, it seems that the connection of the Lenten fast with the forty days Christ spent in the wilderness was an afterthought.

In his poem 'Lent' George Herbert urges that

> True Christians should be glad of an occasion
> To use their temperance seeking no evasion,
>     When good is seasonable

and adds that over-indulgence is unhealthy, and that though we cannot go the whole way with Christ and fast the full number of days

> Yet to go part of that religious way
>     Is better than to rest.

The petition with which he ends is important to Christians:

> Yet Lord instruct us to improve our fast
> By starving sin . . .

Another seventeenth-century poet neatly makes a similar point in the first poem of the section. In this century Ronald Knox sees Lent as a time to get things done, and David Sellick has suggested that nowadays people give up things in Lent, first to ensure that the mind is master of the body, and secondly to sacrifice something that can then be used or spent in helping others.

## To keep a true Lent

Is this a fast, to keep
    The larder lean?
        And clean
From fat of veals, and sheep?

Is it to quit the dish
    Of flesh, yet still
        To fill
The platter high with fish?

Is it to fast an hour,
    Or ragged to go,
        Or show
A down-cast look, and sour?

No: 'tis a fast, to dole
Thy sheaf of wheat,
        And meat,
Unto the hungry soul.

It is to fast from strife,
  From old debate,
    And hate;
To circumcise thy life.

To show a heart grief-rent;
  To starve thy sin,
    Not bin;
And that's to keep thy Lent.

> Robert Herrick


## Get something done

Lent ought to pass like a flash, with a sense of desperate hurry. Good Heavens! The second Sunday already, and still so little to show for it! Lent is the sacramental expression of the brief life we spend here, a life of probation, without a moment in it we can afford to waste. That is why it begins with St Paul's metaphor of an ambassador delivering an ultimatum; we have only a few 'days of grace' to make our peace with God. Ash Wednesday recalls our ignominious, earthy origins, Easter looks forward to our eternity . . .

Which is why . . . I always encourage my friends, when Lent comes round, not to do without something but to get something done. For many of us if that pile of unanswered letters on the writing-table – with all their background of disappointment, distress and inconvenience – could disappear by the time Easter comes. The manuscript we promised to read, the aunts we promised to visit – if only we could cheat ourselves into the feeling that these forty days were our last chance, how quickly they would run their course!

> Ronald Knox, *Lightning Meditations*


## In the wilderness

In the passage below the devil speaks of his plan to overcome Christ, who is fasting in solitude to prepare himself for the work he had to do. The introduction of the devil is a dramatic way of making real to us the temptations that would assail any human being who became conscious that he could exert great power. The

other temptations are recounted in the next section of the poem
(p. 633, Oxford edition) and in the fourth chapters of St Matthew
and St Luke.

Not in the lightning's flash, nor in the thunder,
Not in the tempest, nor the cloudy storm,
    Will I array my form;
But part invisible these boughs asunder,
And move and murmur, as the wind upheaves
    And whispers in the leaves.

Not as a terror and a desolation,
Not in my natural shape, inspiring fear
    And dread, will I appear;
But in soft tones of sweetness and persuasion,
A sound as of the fall of mountain streams,
    Or voices heard in dreams.

He sitteth there in silence, worn and wasted
With famine, and uplifts his hollow eyes
    To the unpitying skies;
For forty days and nights he hath not tasted
Of food or drink, his parted lips are pale,
Surely his strength must fail.

Wherefore dost thou in penitential fasting
Waste and consume the beauty of thy youth?
    Ah, if thou be in truth

The Son of the Unnamed, the Everlasting,
Command these stones beneath thy feet to be
    Changed into bread for thee!

*Christ replies*:

'Tis written: Man shall not live by bread alone,
But by each word that from God's mouth proceedeth!

                H. W. Longfellow, from *The First Passover*

### The three apprentices

Three apprentice devils, fully trained and ready for their first job, were being interviewed by their master.

'You'll find,' he told them, 'that it's easier to *lead* men into evil than to *push* them into it. You'll have to be very crafty.'

He looked the three devils over.

'Have you any ideas?' he asked.

Number one devil was arrogant.

'Oh yes, I shall tell men that there is no God,' he answered, full of confidence.

Satan looked doubtful.

'Well,' he said, 'you can try it, but most men know, even if they won't admit it, that God is real.'

Number two devil looked craftily at his master.

'I shall tell men that there is no Hell.'

Satan did not think much of this idea, either.

'You won't find that much good. You'll soon discover that most men have been there already. Man knows all about Hell.'

The third devil was quite unlike his companions. There was an easy, indulgent look about him, and Satan turned to him for his plan of campaign.

Number three devil bowed low.

'I shall tell men that God is real, that He is good and all-powerful, and I shall assure them of the reality of Hell, but I shall also tell them that there's plenty of time, that there's no need to hurry.'

Satan was delighted.

'Off you go,' he shouted, 'you'll do more damage in a day than these two'll do in a month.'

Mary Tayler, in *Stories and Prayers at Five to Ten*

# Passion Sunday to Easter Eve

Before Holy Week comes Passion Sunday, so called because on this day Christ began openly to predict his coming sufferings. Palm Sunday stands at the beginning of Holy Week, and reminds us how people spread branches in Christ's path when he entered Jerusalem – cf. St Matthew 21; St Mark 11. For Holy Week itself some relevant passages are Isaiah 53 : 1-6; St Matthew 27; and St John 18 : 33-40. The day before Good Friday is known as Maundy Thursday, on which specially minted coins are distributed to selected objects of the Crown's charity. This practice recalls the washing of the disciples' feet by Christ (St John 13), when he said to them, 'A new commandment I give unto you, that ye love one another; as I have loved you, that ye also love one another.' In the Vulgate, the official Latin Bible of the Roman Catholic Church, the word for 'commandment' is 'mandatum', from which comes our 'maundy'. The word has been in circulation since about 1300, and brings to mind the washing of the feet of the poor by princes and ecclesiastics, for it formed part of the antiphon which was sung at the service for such ceremonies.

For Good Friday the New Testament reading is again St Matthew 27. In addition to the poems printed here: Edwin Muir's 'The Killing'; Clive Sansom's *The Witnesses*; and Ernest Hemingway's ten-minute play (in the Penguin *Essential Hemingway*). The Hardy poem below seems very topical, with its conclusion that the world was not worthy to taunt the unworldly and better-than-human aspirations of the unknown martyrs.

## The donkey's owner

Snaffled my donkey, he did – good luck to him! –
Rode him astride, feet dangling, near scraping the ground.
Gave me the laugh of my life when I first see them,
Remembering yesterday – you know, how Pilate come
Bouncing the same road, only that horse of his
Big as a bloody house and the armour shining
And half Rome trotting behind. Tight-mouthed he was,
Looking he owned the world.
        Then today,
Him and my little donkey! Ha! – laugh? –
I thought I'd kill myself when he first started.

So did the rest of them. Gave him a cheer
Like he was Caesar himself, only more hearty:
Tore off some palm-twigs and followed shouting,
Whacking the donkey's behind . . . Then suddenly
We see his face.
The smile had gone, and somehow the way he sat
Was different – like he was much older – you know –
Didn't want to laugh no more.

Clive Sansom, *The Witnesses*

### The merchant's carol

As we rode down the steep hillside,
Twelve merchants with our fairing,
A shout across the hollow land
Came loud upon our hearing,
A shout, a song, a thousand strong,
A thousand lusty voices:
'Make haste,' said I, I knew not why,
'Jerusalem rejoices!'

Beneath the olives fast we rode,
And louder came the shouting:
'So great a noise must mean,' said we,
'A king, beyond all doubting,'
Spurred on, did we, this king to see,
And left the mules to follow;
And nearer, clearer rang the noise
Along the Kidron hollow.

Behold a many-coloured crowd
About the gate we found there;
But one among them all, we marked,
One man who made no sound there;
Still louder ever rose the crowd's
'Hosanna in the highest!'
'O King,' thought I, 'I know not why
In all this joy thou sighest.'

Then he looked up, he looked at me
But whether he spoke I doubted:

How could I hear so calm a speech
When all the rabble shouted?
And yet these words, it seems, I heard:
'I shall be crowned tomorrow.'
They struck my heart with sudden smart,
And filled my bones with sorrow.

We followed far, we traded not,
But long we could not find him.
The very folk that called him king
Let robbers go and bind him.
We found him then, the sport of men,
Still calm among their crying;
And well we knew his words were true –
He was most kingly dying.

Frank Kendon

## 'It was but now'

It was but now their sounding clamours sung,
'Blessed is he, that comes from the Most High',
And all the mountains with 'Hosanna' rung,
And now, 'Away with him away', they cry,
And nothing can be heard but 'Crucify!'
    It was but now the crown itself they save,*
    And golden name of King unto him gave,
And now no King but only Caesar they will have.

It was but now they gathered blooming May,
And of its arms disrobed the branching tree,
To strew with boughs and blossoms all thy way,
And now, the branchless trunk a cross for thee,
And May, dismayed, thy coronet must be:
    It was but now they were so kind to throw
    Their own best garments where thy feet should go,
And now, thyself they strip, and bleeding wounds they show.

See where the author of all life is dying.
O fearful day! He dead, what hope of living?
See where the hopes of all our lives are buying.†
O cheerful day! They bought, what fear of grieving?

252 THE CHRISTIAN YEAR

Love love for hate, and death for life is giving:
  Lo, how his arms are stretched abroad to grace thee,
  And, as they open stand, call to embrace thee.
Why stay'st thou then my soul; O fly, fly thither haste thee.

        Giles Fletcher (1586–1623)

        *save*: were keeping for themselves  †*buying*: are being bought

### His words to Christ, going to the Cross

When thou wast taken, Lord, I oft have read,
All Thy disciples Thee forsook, and fled.
Let their example not a pattern be
For me to fly, but now to follow Thee.

        Robert Herrick

### Christ on the Cross

White was his naked breast,
  and red with blood his side;
Blooded his beauteous face,
  deep were his wounds, and wide.

Stiffened were his arms,
  High spread upon the rood.
From five places in his body
  there ran out streams of blood.

        Anonymous *c*. 1300

### The legend of the crossbill

On the cross the dying Saviour
  Heavenward lifts his eyelids calm,
Feels, but scarcely feels, a trembling
  In his pierced and bleeding palm.

And by all the world forsaken,
  Sees he how with zealous care
At the ruthless nail of iron
  A little bird is striving there.

Stained with blood and never tiring,

With its beak it doth not cease,
From the cross 'twould free the Saviour,
  Its creator's son release.

And the Saviour speaks in mildness:
  'Blest be thou of all the good!
Bear, as token of this moment,
  Marks of blood and holy rood!'

And that bird is called the crossbill;
  Covered all with blood so clear.
In the groves of pine it singeth
  Songs, like legends, strange to hear.

          H. W. Longfellow, from the German of Julius Mosen


### The musician

A memory of Kreisler once:
At some recital in this same city,
The seats all taken, I found myself pushed
On to the stage with a few others,
So near that I could see the toil
Of his face muscles, a pulse like a moth
Fluttering under the fine skin,
And the indelible veins of his smooth brow.

I could see, too, the twitching of the fingers,
Caught temporarily in art's neurosis,
As we sat there or warmly applauded
This player who so beautifully suffered
For each of us upon his instrument.

So it must have been on Calvary
In the fiercer light of the thorns' halo:
The men standing by and that one figure,
The hands bleeding, the mind bruised but calm,
Making such music as lives still.
And no one daring to interrupt
Because it was himself that he played
And closer than all of them the God listened.

          R. S. Thomas, *Tares*

## Unkept Good Fridays

There are many more Good Fridays
  Than this, if we but knew
The names, and could relate them,
  Of men whom rulers slew
For their goodwill, and date them
As runs the twelvemonth through.

These nameless Christs' Good Fridays,
  Whose virtues wrought their end,
Bore days of bonds and burning,
  With no man to their friend,
Of mockeries, and spurning;
  Yet they are all unpenned.

When they had their Good Fridays
  Of bloody sweat and strain
Oblivion hides. We quote not
  Their dying words of pain,
Their sepulchres we note not,
  Unwitting where they have lain.

No annual Good Fridays
  Gained they from cross and cord,
From being sawn asunder,
  Disfigured and abhorred,
Smitten and trampled under:
  Such dates no hands have scored.

Let be. Let lack Good Fridays
  These Christs of unwrit names;
The world was not even worthy
  To taunt their hopes and aims,
As little of earth, earthy,
  As his mankind proclaims.

Thomas Hardy, Collected Poems

### Easter Even

There is nothing more that they can do
  For all their rage and boast;
Caiaphas with his blaspheming crew,
  Herod with his host,

Pontius Pilate in his Judgement-hall
  Judging their Judge and his,
Or he who led them all and passed them all,
  Arch-Judas with his kiss.

The sepulchre made sure with ponderous stone,
  Seal that same stone, O priest;
It may be thou shalt block the holy One
  From rising in the east.

God Almighty, He can break a seal
  And roll away a stone,
Can grind the proud in dust who would not kneel,
  And crush the mighty one . . .

There is nothing more that they can do
  For all their passionate care,
Those who sit in dust, the blessed few,
  And weep and rend their hair:

Peter, Thomas, Mary Magdalene,
  The Virgin unreproved,
Joseph, with Nicodemus, foremost men,
  And John the well-beloved,

Lay Him in the garden-rock to rest;
  Rest you the Sabbath length:
The Sun that went down crimson in the west
  Shall rise renewed in strength.

God Almighty shall give joy for pain,
  Shall comfort him who grieves:
Lo! He with joy shall doubtless come again,
  And with Him bring His sheaves.

     Christina Rossetti

**Easter Eve**

At length the worst is o'er, and Thou art laid
    Deep in Thy darksome bed;
All still and cold beneath yon dreary stone
    Thy sacred form is gone;
Around those lips where power and mercy hung,
    The dews of death have clung;
The dull earth o'er Thee, and Thy foes around,
Thou sleep'st a silent corse, in funeral fetters
    wound.

John Keble, *The Christian Year*

# Easter

Easter Day is the most important of the Christian festivals, and like some others among them it has an older and wider than Christian significance. First, it is grafted on an old pagan root: the 'death' and burial and re-emergence of the seed on which human life came to depend. The myths of several civilisations are built on the need to encourage and celebrate the continuance of the vegetable cycle and the fertility of animals – from such elaborations as the Greek story of the dead and risen Adonis to our native John Barleycorn.

Secondly, the events commemorated by Easter took place at the time of a Jewish festival, the Passover. This was, and is, a period of eight days, in March-April, which reminds Jewish believers to give thanks for the deliverance of the Israelites from Egypt about 1400 B.C.

The Christian festival is the main occasion of rejoicing for the life and resurrection of Christ. The name comes from the Anglo-Saxon 'Eastre', the pagan festival at the spring equinox in honour of the Teutonic goddess of dawn, which coincided more or less with the Passover; it was adopted as a translation of 'pasche', the original word for the Passover. To the early Christians especially the Resurrection was the core of their faith.

For most of Christian history Easter has been supreme among festivals because it celebrated the resurrection of the Christ who came to earth to redeem man from guilt and sin. The medieval

'The angel Gabriel to the Virgin Mary' is an expression of this belief. In the middle ages too the clergy began to organise dramatic versions of the story of Holy Week and Easter. They acted the Resurrection in church, with a sepulchre beside the altar, and the women looking for him:

> '*Quem quaeritis*?' recited the clergy on one side of the choir taking the part of the Angel at the Tomb after the resurrection, 'Whom do you seek?' Those opposite responded in the words of the three Maries, and were finally told, '*Surrexit, non est hic*; he has risen, he is not here.' In this scene, the *Quem Quaeritis*, is the seed of all Western theatre.

Maurice Hussey, introduction to *The Chester Mystery Plays*

Later, performances became more elaborate and were given outside churches, with the trade guilds supplying actors and properties according to their resources as the scope of the plays developed; the Plasterers would enact the Creation, the Fishmongers the Flood, the Blacksmiths the Harrowing of Hell, and so on. A passage from one of the Chester plays on the Resurrection and Ascension is printed below; after his ascension Christ speaks with an angel.

*Further reading*: St Matthew 28; St Luke 24; St John 20; poems on Easter by George Herbert (p. 35, World's Classics edition), Gerard Manley Hopkins and John Betjeman (in *Poems in the Porch*); an Easter tune is No. 117 in the *Cambridge Hymnal*, to which Sydney Carter's 'Lord of the Dance' (Galliard Ltd) will fit if modern words are required; Laurence Whistler, *The English Festivals*; F. Morison, *Who Moved the Stone?*

### John Barleycorn

There were three kings came from the West
　　Their fortunes for to try;
And they have taken a solemn oath
　　John Barleycorn should die.

They ploughed, they sowed, they harrowed him in,
　　Throwed clods upon his head;
And they have taken a solemn oath
　　John Barleycorn is dead.

So there he lay for a full fortnight
　　Till the dew on him did fall:
Then Barleycorn sprang up again
　　And that surprised them all.

There he remained till midsummer
  And looked both pale and wan;
Till Barleycorn he got a beard
  And so became a man.

Then they sent men with scythes so sharp
  To cut him off at knee;
And then poor John Barleycorn,
  They served him barbarously.

O Barleycorn is the choicest grain
  That e'er was sown on land;
It will do more than any grain,
  By the turning of your hand.

> Traditional

### The good news

In the earliest days of Christianity an 'apostle' was first and foremost a man who claimed to be an eye-witness of the Resurrection. Only a few days after the Crucifixion when two candidates were nominated for the vacancy created by the treachery of Judas, their qualification was that they had known Jesus personally both before and after His death and could offer first-hand evidence of the Resurrection in addressing the outer world (Acts 1 : 22) . . .

The Resurrection is the central theme in every Christian sermon reported in the Acts. The Resurrection, and its consequences, were the 'gospel' or good news which the Christians brought : what we call the 'gospels', the narratives of Our Lord's life and death, were composed later for the benefit of those who had already accepted the *Gospel*. They were in no sense the basis of Christianity : they were written for those already converted. The miracle of the Resurrection, and the theology of that miracle, comes first : the biography comes later as a comment on it . . .

When modern writers talk of the Resurrection they usually mean one particular moment – the discovery of the Empty Tomb and the appearance of Jesus a few yards away from it. The story of that moment is what Christian apologists now chiefly try to support and sceptics chiefly to impugn. But this almost exclusive concentration on the first five minutes or so of the Resurrection would have astonished the earliest Christian teachers. In claiming to have

seen the Resurrection they were not necessarily claiming to have
seen *that*. Some of them had, some of them had not. It had no more
importance than any of the other appearances of the risen Jesus –
apart from the poetic and dramatic importance which the beginnings of things must always have. What they were claiming was
that they had all, at one time or another, met Jesus during the six
or seven weeks that followed His death. Sometimes they seem to
have been alone when they did so, but on one occasion twelve of
them saw Him together, and on another occasion about five hundred of them. St Paul says that the majority of the five hundred
were still alive when he wrote the *First Letter to the Corinthians*,
i.e. in about 55 A.D.

> C. S. Lewis, *Miracles*

### The Angel Gabriel to the Virgin Mary

Fillèd full of charity,
Thou matchless maiden-mother,
Pray for us to him that He
For thy love above all other,
Away our sin and guilt should take,
And clean of every stain us make
And heaven's bliss, when our time is to die,
Would give us for thy sake;
With grace to serve him by
Till He us to him take. Amen.

> Fourteenth century, modernised by Gerard Manley Hopkins

### Redeemer

*Christ*:  I that speak righteousness
Have brought man out of distress;
For Buyer I am called and was
Of àll mankind through grace.
My people that were from Me reft
Through sin and through the devil's craft
To heaven I bring and not one left
All that in Hell there was.

*Angel*:  Why is thy body now so red?
Thy body is bloody and thy head?
Thy clothes are those which fit the dead
And stained as with red wine.

*Christ*:  These drops now, with good intent,
To my Father I will present
That good men that to earth be lent
Shall know certainly,
How graciously that I them bought
And for good works that they wrought
The everlasting bliss they have sought
I proved the good worthy.
For this cause, believe you Me,
The drops I shed on the rood tree
All fresh shall reserved be
Ever till the last day.

Chester play, adapted by Maurice Hussey, from *The Chester Mystery Plays*

### He keeps on showing us new things

If my mind can't quite take certain things – such as the physical Resurrection – does it matter, so long as it doesn't get in the way of belief in Christ as master and saviour and helper, to be sought and served? I know it mattered to the early church, and was perhaps the only way in which they could be convinced – but should one try to force or persuade one's mind to it, if one feels one doesn't need it?

You say 'We cannot be expected to do more than yield to God the minds which we actually possess,' so I suppose God takes them and does what he can with them. And of course in time they might develop new powers of faith; as you say, it depends on what happens to make connections. He keeps on showing us new things, new light on the past, new roads for the future, and one hopes for new powers . . .

It seems almost better . . . that God should have sent his Incarnation on earth in form fully human, with human birth and death. I would almost *rather* think He was born like us and died like us, and that it was his spirit only that lived after death, taking the form His friends would recognise. But of course this is no argument at all, and I don't try to make up my mind about it. I don't feel either way that it could make any difference to what I value more and more – the relationship that one tries to keep. But I will keep my mind open about it, and try and think it out. I felt, at the Easter mass, that here was Christ risen and with us, and I didn't care how.

Rose Macaulay, *Letters to a Friend, 1950–52*

## The Risen Lord

In the countries of the Mediterranean, Easter has always been the greatest of the holy days, the gladdest and holiest, not Christmas, the birth of the Child. Easter, Christ Risen, the Risen Lord, this, to the old faith, is still the first day in the year. The Easter festivities are the most joyful, the Easter processions the finest, the Easter ceremonies the most splendid. In Sicily the women take into church the saucers of growing corn, the green blades rising tender and slim like green light, in little pools, filling round the altar. It is Adonis. It is the re-born year. It is Christ Risen. It is the Risen Lord. And in the warm south still a great joy floods the hearts of the people on Easter Sunday. They feel it, they feel it everywhere. The Lord is risen. The Lord of the rising wheat and the plum blossoms is warm and kind upon earth again, after having been done to death by the evil and the jealous ones . . .

This is the image of the young: the Risen Lord. The teaching is over, the crucifixion is over, the sacrifice is made, the salvation is accomplished. Now comes the true life, man living his full life on earth, as flowers live their full life, without rhyme or reason except the magnificence of coming forth into fulness . . .

If Jesus rose a full man in the flesh, He rose to do His share in the world's work, something he really liked doing. And if He remembered His first life, it would neither be teaching nor preaching, but probably carpentering again, with joy, among the shavings. If Jesus rose a full man in the flesh, He rose to continue His fight with the hard-boiled conventionalists like Roman judges and Jewish priests and money-makers of every sort. But this time, it would no longer be the fight of self-sacrifice that would end in crucifixion.

This time it would be a freed man fighting to shelter the rose of life from being trampled on by the pigs. This time, if Satan attempted temptation in the wilderness, the Risen Lord would answer: Satan, your silly temptations no longer tempt me. Luckily, I have died to that sort of self-importance and self-conceit. But let me tell you something, old man! Your name's Satan, isn't it? And your name is Mammon? You are the selfish hog that's got hold of all the world, aren't you? Well, look here, my boy, I'm going to take it all from you, so don't worry. The world and the power and the riches thereof, I'm going to take them all from you, Satan or Mammon or whatever your name is. Because you don't know how to use them. The earth is the Lord's, and the fulness thereof, and it's going to be. Men have risen from the dead and learned not to be so greedy and self-important. We left most of that behind in the late tomb. Men have risen beyond you, Mammon, they are your risen lords. And so, you hook-nosed, glistening-eyed, ugly, money-smelling anachronism, you've got to get out. Men have not died and risen again for nothing . . .

D. H. Lawrence, *Phoenix* II

**Easter Sunday**

Christ has risen, our true sun in the darkness of
the night . . .
And the bees fly here and there, rejoicing in their
work,
Noisily collecting honey from the flowers, white and
red.
Birds of many kinds make soft the air with singing,
And nightly now the nightingale pours out her lovely
notes.
Now churches too are filled with the sound of
chanting,
As the people sing their Alleluias, Alleluias
hundredfold.

Adapted from Sedulius Scotus, about 860

### Easter wings

Lord, who createdst man in wealth and store,
　　Though foolishly he lost the same,
　　　　Decaying more and more,
　　　　　　Till he became
　　　　　　　Most poor:
　　　　　　　With Thee
　　　　　　O let me rise
　　　　As larks, harmoniously,
　　And sing this day Thy victories:
Then shall the Fall further the flight in me.

My tender age in sorrow did begin:
　　And still with sicknesses and shame
　　　　Thou didst so punish sin,
　　　　　　That I became
　　　　　　　Most thin.
　　　　　　　With Thee
　　　　　　Let me combine,
　　　　And feel this day thy victory,
　　For if I imp* my wing on thine
Affliction shall advance the flight in me.

George Herbert

*_imp_: strengthen

### 'Get you packing'

Death and darkness, get you packing!
Nothing now to man is lacking,
All your triumphs now are ended,
And what Adam marr'd is mended.

Graves are beds now for the weary,
Death a nap, to wake more merry;
Youth now, full of pious duty,
Seeks in thee for perfect beauty.

Then unto him who thus hath thrown
Ev'n to contempt thy kingdom down,
　And by his blood did us advance

Unto his own inheritance,
To him be glory, power, praise,
From this, unto the last of days.

Henry Vaughan

### The morning comes

The morning comes, the night decays, the watchmen leave their
    stations;
The grave is burst, the spices shed, the linen wrapped up;
The bones of death, the covering clay, the sinews shrunk and
    dried
Reviving shake, inspiring move, breathing, awakening,
Spring like redeemed captives when their bonds and bars are
    burst.
Let the slave grinding at the mill run out into the field,
Let him look up into the heavens and laugh in the bright air;
Let the inchained soul, shut up in darkness and in sighing,
Whose face has never seen a smile in thirty weary years,
Rise and look out; his chains are loose, his dungeon doors
    are open;
And let his wife and children return from the oppressor's scourge.

William Blake, from 'America'

### Freedom to live

In writing about Jesus we must not distort the fact that he was a
man, born of human parents. He undoubtedly made a tremendous
impact on many people, some of whom found relief from physical
illness as the result of their trust in him. In their desire to em-
phasise his supreme value to them, some of his followers in later
years described his life and activities in miraculous terms. Whether
we accept this explanation is not important; what matters is the
greatness of his personality and his spiritual insight. Because his
teaching and way of life ran counter to the convictions and practices of the religious leaders of his time, they, with the consent of
the populace, engineered his trial and execution. Men do not like
goodness if it challenges their moral failure, or loyalty to truth
that calls for a revolutionary change of mind. They killed Jesus
because they were afraid of him.

As in his life, so in his approach to death Jesus never faltered in his trust in love, and forgave those who rejected him. By this creative attitude Jesus radically changed a most heinous act of human wickedness into an event that has released love and forgiveness into a dark world. For ever after men know that such love can overcome evil, and in this knowledge found freedom to live.

Many Friends are sceptical about the New Testament accounts of the physical resurrection of Jesus, although for some this is a crucial element in their faith. Most would agree that the essential meaning behind the story of the first Easter is that death could not destroy all that was of real value in the earthly life of Jesus. The love experienced by his disciples could not be taken from them by his death, because they recognised that it was of an infinite and eternal quality. In fact, it was only after his death that they came to understand and to appreciate fully the deep meaning of his life and to be set free by it.

George H. Gorman, *Introducing Quakers*

### Easter

No human eye was by
To witness Christ arise,
But I, this morning heard
The Resurrection of the Word.

It sprang through night, opaque,
A note so pure and clear,
I felt my spirit wake –
It flooded everywhere.

I know that it has been;
There is a vision new.
I see the universe
Divinely bathed in dew.

Sister Mary Agnes, *Daffodils in Ice*

# Whitsun

The event commemorated at this season is described in the Acts of the Apostles, a book which was probably written by St Luke and is our chief source of knowledge about early Christianity. Except in English-speaking countries the festival is known as Pentecost, because the Holy Spirit descended on the apostles at the time of the Jewish festival of that name, when large numbers of pilgrims assembled at Jerusalem. Our name comes from the Anglo-Saxon 'Hwfta Sunnandaeg' – White Sunday – because in Saxon days it was a time for baptising, and large numbers of newly baptised people put on white garments.

Ever since St Luke reported that at Christ's baptism the Holy Spirit descended on him like a dove, a dove has been the symbol of the Spirit; and the kind of power given by the Holy Spirit is forcefully explained by St Paul in his first letter to the Christians at Corinth. To his followers Christ was a person, and when his work on earth was finished he left behind with them his Spirit to guide and strengthen them. Whitsunday commemorates not only the descent of the Holy Spirit upon the apostles and disciples but also 'the fruits and effects of that event: the completion of the work of redemption, the fullness of grace for the Church and her children, and the gift of faith for all nations' (*The Holyday Book*).

## They began to talk in other tongues

While the day of Pentecost was running its course [the apostles] were all together in one place, when suddenly there came from the sky a noise like that of a strong driving wind, which filled the whole house where they were sitting. And there appeared to them tongues like flames of fire, dispersed among them and resting on each one. And they were all filled with the Holy Spirit and began to talk in other tongues, as the Spirit gave them power of utterance.

Acts 2:1-4

## Dove devices

In medieval times the figure of a dove was widely used to enact in a dramatic way the descent of the Holy Spirit on Pentecost Sunday. When the priest had arrived at the sequence, he sang the first words in a loud and solemn voice: *Veni Sancte Spiritus* (Come, Holy Ghost). Immediately there arose in the church a sound 'as of a violent wind blowing' (Acts 2:2). This noise was produced in some countries, like France, by the blowing of trumpets; in others by the choir boys, who hissed, hummed, pressed windbags, and rattled the benches. All eyes turned towards the ceiling of the church where from an opening called the 'Holy Ghost Hole' there appeared a disc the size of a cartwheel, which slowly descended in horizontal position, swinging in ever-widening circles. Upon a blue background, broken by bundles of golden rays, it bore on its underside the figure of a white dove.

Meanwhile the choir sang the sequence. At its conclusion the dove came to rest, hanging suspended in the middle of the church. There followed a 'rain' of flowers indicating the gifts of the Holy Spirit, and of water symbolising baptism. In some towns of central Europe people even went so far as to drop pieces of burning wick or straw from the Holy Ghost Hole, to represent the flaming tongues of Pentecost. This practice, however, was eventually stopped because it tended to put the people on fire externally, instead of internally as the Holy Spirit had done at Jerusalem. In the thirteenth century in many cathedrals of France real white pigeons were released during the singing of the sequence and flew around in the church while roses were dropped from the Holy Ghost Hole.

Francis X. Weiser, *The Holyday Book*

### Gifts of the Spirit

About gifts of the Spirit, there are some things of which I do not wish you to remain ignorant.

There are varieties of gifts, but the same Spirit. There are varieties of service, but the same Lord. There are many forms of work, but all of them, in all men, are the work of the same God. In each of us the Spirit is manifested in one particular way, for some useful purpose. One man, through the Spirit, has the gift of wise speech, while another, by the power of the same Spirit, can put the deepest knowledge into words. Another, by the same Spirit, is granted faith; another, by the one Spirit, gifts of healing, and another miraculous powers; another has the gift of prophecy, and another ability to distinguish true spirits from false; yet another has the gift of ecstatic utterance of different kinds, and another the ability to interpret it. But all these gifts are the work of one and the same Spirit, distributing them separately to each individual at will.

St Paul, I Corinthians 12:1, 4-11

### The seven gifts

And there shall come forth a rod out of the stem of Jesse, and a Branch shall grow out of his roots; and the spirit of the Lord shall rest upon him, the spirit of wisdom and understanding, the spirit of counsel and might, the spirit of knowledge and of the fear of the Lord; and shall make him of quick understanding in the fear of the Lord; and he shall not judge after the sight of his eyes . . .

Isaiah 11:1-3

### The twelve disciples

The twelve disciples didn't know what next they ought to do.
They had seen their risen lord ascend, go in triumph from their
    view.
They met to pray and break the bread, they had no other plan;
But then the Holy Spirit came, and he filled them to a man.

They burst into the crowded street to tell the passers-by,
But excitement made them all confused, and the crowd thought
    they were high.
'The pubs aren't open,' Peter said, 'We haven't had a drop.
If we're drunk, we're only drunk with joy, but our joy will never
    stop.
'Our Master is alive,' he said, 'Although we know He died,
Death had no hold on Jesus Christ – that's the man you crucified.'

The crowd were filled with fear and shame. 'What shall we
    do?' they cried.
'Repent and be converted now, repent and be baptized.'

On that same day three thousand men responded to the call,
And the Holy Spirit filled their hearts, spreading love
    and joy to all.

Handley Stevens, *Songs from Notting Hill*

### The Day of Pentecost

Try and imagine the picture of it; Jerusalem, quite a small town, with very narrow streets at that, crowded with thousands of Jewish pilgrims from all over the known world. They had come there to celebrate the Feast of Weeks, which was the Jewish harvest festival; because in that part of the world you get the wheat harvest in by Whit Sunday . . . Were they really very much interested in thanking God for the harvest having been got in in one rather unimportant district of the province of Syria? No, but it was the tradition to rally round when the great feasts came on in Jerusalem; their fathers had always done it, and they weren't going to give it up; they were devout men, and it was the thing to do . . . So they drifted about the streets, a great tide of humanity, without any vital religious inspiration to rally them . . . Was it possible that the Spirit of God would move on these sluggish waters, too?

And of course, quite suddenly, it did. Quite suddenly, here and there in the crowd, you saw the extraordinary sight of a working man from Galilee making his way to the temple, shouting out God's praises in an uncontrollable way that made you wonder whether he was drunk, though you had just cleared away breakfast. And when you got nearer, you found that it was St Peter shouting out phrases in the language of Cappadocia, or St Thomas talking fluent Parthian, or St Matthew giving you bits of his Gospel in the Berber dialect of Northern Africa. And the infection of their example spread; people took up their cries, hardly knowing what they were doing, in a babel of strange tongues; and . . . the response of the Holy Spirit went up once more in aspirations of love towards the God who had made all nations to dwell on the face of the earth.

Ronald Knox, *The Creed in Slow Motion*

# BOOK LIST

### Background

Huxley, Julian. *Religion Without Revelation*. Watts.
Kierkegaard, S. *The Last Years: Journals 1853–55*. Fontana
MacKinnon, D. M. *The Stripping of the Altars*. Fontana.
Robinson, J. A. T. *Honest to God*. Student Christian Movement Press.
Roszak, Theodore. *The Making of a Counter Culture*. Faber.

### Religion in Education

Bielby, A. R. *Education through Worship*. Student Christian Movement Press.
Dean, Joan. *Religious Education for Children*. Ward Lock Educational.
Hinnells, J. R. (ed.). *Comparative Religion in Education*. Oriel Press.
Jones, C. M. (ed.). *School Worship* (especially for a contribution by Kenneth C. Barnes). University of Leeds.
Sellick, David. *Christianity and the Teenage Thinker*. A. R. Mowbray.

### Assembly

Hobden, Sheila M. *Explorations in Worship*. Lutterworth Press.
Jones, Richard. *Worship for Today* (accounts of experiments, with critical comment). Epworth Press.
White, Peter A. *Dramatic Assemblies*. Religious Education Press.

# INDEX OF PROPER NAMES

# INDEX OF SUBJECTS